PENGUIN BOOKS

THE SECOND BILLION

★★★★★★★★★★★★★★★★★★★★★★★★★★★★★★★★★★★★★★

Penny Kane is a writer on population and development topics. She has worked in family planning and population for 15 years, in Britain and Australia, and, during six years with an international organization, travelled widely looking at programmes around the world. She wrote the *Which? Guide to Birth Control* for the Consumers' Association; it was adapted in 1984 by John Porter and published in Australia as the *Choice? Guide*.

She first visited China in 1975, to look at population issues, and has returned regularly ever since. With Delia Davin and Elisabeth Croll, she edited a book on the *Single Child Family in China*, and she has written many other books and journals on the Chinese programme, as well as lecturing in a number of universities. This book was written while she was a Visitor at the Australian National University; she has now married an Australian and lives in Canberra.

Penny Kane

★★★★★★★★★★★★★★★★★★★★★★★★★★★★★★★★

THE SECOND BILLION

★★★★★★★★★★★★★★★★★★★★★★★★★★★★★★★★

Population and Family Planning in China

PENGUIN BOOKS

★★★★★★★★★★★★★★★★★★★★★★★★★★★★★★★★★★★★

Penguin Books Australia Ltd,
487 Maroondah Highway, P.O. Box 257
Ringwood, Victoria 3134, Australia
Penguin Books Ltd,
Harmondsworth, Middlesex, England
Penguin Books,
40 West 23rd Street, New York, N.Y. 10010, U.S.A.
Penguin Books Canada Limited,
2801 John Street, Markham, Ontario, Canada L3R 1B4
Penguin Books (N.Z.) Ltd,
182-190 Wairau Road, Auckland 10, New Zealand

First published by Penguin Books Australia, 1987

Copyright © Penny Kane, 1987

All Rights Reserved. Without limiting the rights under copyright reserved
above, no part of this publication may be reproduced, stored in or introduced
into a retrieval system, or transmitted, in any form or by any means
(electronic, mechanical, photocopying, recording or otherwise), without
the prior written permission of both the copyright owner and the above
publisher of this book.

Typeset in Garamond by Leader Composition
Made and printed in Australia by Australian Print Group,
Maryborough, Vic.

Kane, Penny, 1945–
The second billion.

Bibliography.
Includes index.
ISBN 0 14 008657 9.

1. Birth control – China. 2. Family policy – China.
I. Title.

304.6'6'0951

CONTENTS

★★★

ACKNOWLEDGEMENTS

★★★

This book could not have been written without the help and support, first of all, of the Chinese. Officials and staff of the Family Planning Commission, the China Family Planning Association, the Ministry of Health and the Chinese People's Association for Friendship with Foreign Countries have been extraordinarily patient in meeting my requests for information and in arranging for me to see and talk to as many people as possible at national, provincial and local level. Many people were prepared to talk frankly, thoughtfully and often with humour, about family planning and their own experiences; they are of course not responsible for any errors of interpretation or fact.

Listing the names of those within the various organizations to whom I owe such a debt of gratitude would be almost impossible. I can only say that the gratitude is deeply felt.

I am also grateful to the International Planned Parenthood Federation which allowed me the time to write this book, and to the Department of Demography at the Australian National University, for giving me a place as a Visitor where it could be written. The Director, Jack Caldwell, and the staff of the Department have given me valuable insights and help in dealing with issues raised in the book. Dorothy Trueland, Margaret Smither and Kae Mardus looked after me and the manuscript with great kindness.

Over the years, many people have been generous with their

time and information in helping me to know more about China and its population. Chen Pi-Chao, H. Yuan Tien, Elisabeth Croll, Delia Davin, Sheila Hillier, Jonathan Mirsky, Larry Jagan, Roland Berger and Judith Banister have all been particularly generous. Again, they are not responsible for the outcome. C. K. Lam, Ching Choy and Rose Heatley have given much assistance with Chinese documents.

As always, I relied upon the support and care of Bruce Hunter and his colleagues at David Higham Associates, together this time with Rosemary Cresswell in Australia. A further source of support was Anne Gunn, without whose meticulous editing skills the book would have suffered.

But there are four people to whom above all I am indebted. Graham Leonard first made it possible for me to go to China, and has continued to encourage my interest and help me learn ever since. The late Caspar Brook gave me the time and the backing to expand my knowledge and endured my enthusiasm; I am glad that before his untimely death in 1983 he went with me to China and became an enthusiast himself. The late Peter Kane, despite great personal suffering, encouraged my visits to China and patiently endured the time spent on things Chinese over eight years. Lado Ruzicka made the wish to write this book into a practical reality, supported me throughout the writing and gave me invaluable assistance with it.

This book is for Graham and Lado, and in memory of Caspar and Peter.

INTRODUCTION
★★★

'The history of the socialist movement is not long and that of
the socialist countries even shorter. Some of the laws govern-
ing the development of socialist society are relatively clear,
but many more remain to be explored.' This cry of anguish
from the Resolution on Chinese Communist Party history
(1949-81) is both a warning to those who attempt to describe
and interpret aspects of the policies and programmes of
China, and an encouragement.

China — as is frequently remarked — has a long, complex
and remarkable history. Its development since 1949 has been
no less remarkable or complex. There is much that we still do
not know about how that development has taken place, and
many facets of that development remain unclear.

To focus on any particular ingredient may be to distort it;
even to talk of 'China' may be seriously misleading. The cities
are not the same as the countryside — but neither is Shanghai
like Beijing, and 'the countryside' itself covers 800 million
people who grow and eat different foods, have different
customs, different preoccupations and different looks. A
campaign being waged with maximum intensity in one area
may have been superseded in a second and may never have got
off the ground in a third. Thus the most meticulous report may
be valid only for the area specifically described.

The release of an increasing variety of national statistics by
the Chinese has made it possible to compare local reports

1

against an overall picture, but national totals in turn ignore the variety of this enormous country. In writing about China, one can only say with due humility that certain things appear to be in general so; and that other things appear to be somewhat more local. A book in which every statement had some such qualification would be unreadable. I can only hope that readers will bear my overall diffidence in mind.

This book is an attempt to describe Chinese population policies and family-planning programmes in the context of tradition, of other development policies and of social change. China's family-planning programme has been successful on a scale not previously seen anywhere; it has therefore attracted interest from a range of people. Those interested in fertility control, however, have often known too little of China to be able to grasp the background to the programme. Those interested in other aspects of China's development have had similar difficulties with the demographic issues. And a large number of visitors to China, or others with a casual interest, have heard in the last few years of the emphasis given by the Chinese to family planning and population matters and have wondered what it was all about.

In an attempt to meet the needs of that variety of readers, I have inevitably had to leave a lot of things out. Population policy is a broad term which covers topics like internal and external migration, policies towards special groups such as national minorities, policies on population distribution, the growth of cities, and so on. Although they are not completely ignored here, I have concentrated on population issues concerned with fertility. The space gained by excluding those other areas has been given over instead to as much illustrative material — quotations, anecdotes and examples — as I could include, in an attempt to bring to life people's attitudes to these policies.

Much of the material I have used has come direct to me from Chinese sources. I have not attributed such material except where it exists in published form; government servants in any country tend to prefer anonymity. I can only say that I am willing to share unattributed sources with any serious inquirer. Other sources for the book have been Chinese published materials from demographic papers to newspapers, together with Western reports and analyses.

Demographers and anybody else with a statistical background may well be upset by the air of spurious accuracy conferred by providing a statistic to two decimal places in the tables. Until recently, however, Chinese statistics tended to be vague: 'around 10 per cent' might mean no more than 'a small number' and there was no convention about rounding up or down. Those of us who collected the then rare population statistics therefore reported them in full wherever possible, simply to show that these were unadjusted. That convention will linger until more information is routinely available.

CHAPTER ONE

THE CHINESE FAMILY AND CHANGE

★★

The Family in Traditional China

The family is one of those concepts we all think we can recognize, but which presents real problems to anthropologists and other social scientists. The traditional Chinese family is no exception: different definitions of it, and thus descriptions of it, have been offered at different times. In the widest sense, the family was the clan. All those who carried the same family name and were descended from a common traceable ancestor were members of the same clan. Within the clan there would be families *(jia)* and households *(hu)*. The *jia* was the group of relatives who shared income and property, and were maintained out of the common funds. Often, but not invariably, they all lived together, or saw themselves as having a common home even when some of the family members actually worked and lived elsewhere. The *hu* was the household group which might include servants, slaves and concubines and their children.

For many of the peasants, of course, there was no distinction between *jia* and *hu;* the household consisted of family members alone. In looking at the traditional Chinese family and how it has adapted to new pressures, the peasant viewpoint will be followed and it will be generally assumed that the family and the household were not very different. This assumption is the easier to make because it seems that family or household size and composition changed very little over time.

During the past two thousand years, reported average household size in China varied between 4.5 and 7.1 people. The limitations of these statistics are discussed in Chapter 2, but household size remained remarkably constant over time – the earlier figures are consistent with the 4.5 to 6 members found in the studies which were done in the first half of this century. Between 1932 and 1942 ten small-scale censuses were carried out and produced average family-size figures ranging from 4.2 to 6.2 people. Data from a field survey between 1929 and 1931 suggest that nuclear families accounted for more than three-fifths of the total households, and that over three-quarters of all family members in the sample were heads, their wives, and children.

Given the tenacity with which the belief continues, in China as well as outside, that the traditional Chinese family was a large, extended one in which three, four or even the more or less mythical five generations lived together, these small families may come as a surprise. But in a society with high infant death rates and low life expectancy, it is clear that only a minority of people ever lived to see their grandchildren grow up – and that the grandchildren who did grow up tended to be few. This was particularly the case among the poor, whose conditions were least favourable for survival.

For different periods of time a family would be structured in different ways. As families were patrilocal – the daughters joined their husbands' families – when the eldest son married there would be a time during which he and his wife would be living with one or both of his parents and perhaps a sister or younger brother. Then the sister would marry and move out; before or after the father's death the brother would leave home to find a living elsewhere and the household would, in due course, become that of the elder son, his wife and children, and perhaps his ageing mother. As the children grew up, the cycle would begin all over again.

The family unit was the basis of Chinese society. 'The individual's loyalty towards the family transcended all his other social obligations . . . the family was the determining factor in the total pattern of social obligation.'[1] Confucian philosophy considered human society as a vast collection of families under the emperor. Natural order on earth depended on virtuous conduct leading to an orderly human society, in which everybody had a place under Heaven and knew it. 'Five cardinal relations' indicated the behaviour expected between prince and subject, father and son, husband and wife, elder and younger brother, and among friends. All other relationships reflected the situations prescribed in the 'five relations'.

It was no accident that three of the five concerned family relations, dealing with parents and children, husbands and wives, and siblings: they reflected the actual relationships likely to be found under a single roof.

The authority of the father was absolute, at least in theory. He officiated in the ceremonies of ancestor worship, marriage and at funerals. He held the family property, including the earnings and savings of all the family members. He could sell family members into slavery. A son or grandson who died as a result of being chastised by him 'in a lawful and customary manner' was not redressed. Nevertheless, his powers were not unlimited: he could not disinherit his sons, for example, for he was the custodian rather than the outright owner of the family property. Despite the 'reverential awe' with which he was supposed to be treated, once he became old and weak he might get no more than lip-service.

His son, on the other hand, had no rights, but only duties: to love and obey his father, support him in old age, and marry the girl his father chose for him in order to produce a son to carry on the family. Again, however, the reality was not always quite like that: while 'Chinese history and literature show that Confucian ideas were carried out in practice and that the Sage succeeded in creating a nation of obedient and devoted sons and daughters',[2] the poorer a family, the less incentive a son had to compete for parental approval. 'The old men, being poor, have little material wealth to give . . . whereas wealthy fathers can express their pleasure or displeasure in very material ways.'[3]

Despite these caveats, the following description of the upbringing of sons is probably not far from the truth:

The boy was usually treated with the utmost severity. The virtue of filial piety was drummed into him and he came to see the world of both today and yesterday as a vast hierarchy of families, each headed by a male whom it was his duty to serve – in return for which he would get material reward. The first born son and, to a lesser extent, the other sons knew that some day they would be in the same position as their father – head of the family. The son's attitude towards his father was characterised more by fear and avoidance than love and respect or even rivalry and contempt.[4]

The relationship between husbands and wives was a reflection of that between father and sons, if a little less all-embracing. The wife entered the family of her husband, had to show filial respect for her parents-in-law, and respect, obedience and faithfulness to her husband. Should her husband die, the respect and obedience were transferred to her son, who was now the head of the family.

Here too the lives of actual individual women did not always support convention. Mao Zedong noted in Hunan in 1927 that 'as to the authority of the husband, it has always been comparatively weak among the poor peasants because the poor peasant women, for financial reasons compelled to engage in more manual work than women of the wealthier classes, have obtained greater rights to speak and more power to make decisions in family matters. They also enjoy sexual freedom.'[5] And those older women who survived often became dominant mothers-in-law, terrorizing not only their daughters-in-law (as they were perfectly entitled to) but their sons as well. The importance of the mother-in-law in the family is expressed not only in traditional literature, but in the amount of effort the present Chinese government has put into educational materials designed to counter her 'feudal' influences and enlist her in the battles to reform the family. All the same, even the most strong-minded woman only exercized power in defiance of perceived roles and against 'natural order' and it is probable that life for the majority of wives was restricted and often far from happy.

Siblings, especially brothers, had the duty of obedience and respect not just to their parents but to any elder brothers. Unless and until a man left home to set up a separate household, he would contribute his earnings to the common fund (even when he was working in a different part of the country) from which would come bride price – if the family could afford one – for the marriage his father arranged and out of which, after his father died, he would get a share which he might take out of the *jia* to begin a new family.

The exact position of every family member in relation to every other was reflected in the way each was addressed: not by name, but by relationship, as 'Elder Brother' or 'Father's Second Brother's Wife'. Outside the immediate family of parents, children and siblings, deference to other relatives was in direct relation to their age and position on the family tree. Thus anybody of a superior generation – the brother of your father, for instance – was senior, regardless of his actual age, and could not be argued with.

Both generational age and personal age imposed dominance. 'Functioning through the strength of filial piety and veneration of age, the hierarchy of age served to provide a status symbol for the operation of family authority, to firmly initiate the young into the institution of family life until they reached maturity, to establish security for the old, and to impress upon the individual the dominance of the family as a corporate body.'[6] If the head of the house or other family member was too incapacitated by age, or just too weak, to enforce this hierarchy, then the rest of the clan would impose discipline. The author just quoted recalled that in his childhood 'there was still the frequent verbal threat of being taken back to the ancestral village "to be drowned in a pig's cage by the clan elders" . . .' in case of gross disobedience to the parents even though he was brought up in a city, far from the direct influence of the clan.[7]

The clan had other functions than merely to frighten small boys. Its elder and more prestigious members would sit in judgement on disputes between or within families. Its common funds would finance the ancestral temples, ancestral sacrifices and the spring and autumn feasts which followed the twice yearly sacrifices to the ancestors. Income from clan properties (which in some parts of China were considerable) financed the village school, repair of roads and even road building, irrigation schemes and military defence of the village. Clan members would be called upon for support by their poor relatives, could be asked for jobs or to use their influence on behalf of any of their kin, or could be called upon to defend or fight for others within the clan. In short, the clan provided the administrative, economic and social support, as well as very often the only security, for the basic Chinese family.

Marriage

Marriage played an important part in cementing family links. It was far too important an event to be left to the young people themselves. A matchmaker – often professional, but sometimes an amateur in the community – would identify a suitable choice of spouse and undertake many of the negotiations between the two families. Finding a suitable spouse was not always easy; law and custom dictated that a person might not marry another of the same surname, regardless of how distant the relationship was or whether the lineage was different. 'Since the number of surnames has been estimated at approximately 500, this rule had succeeded in substantially circumscribing the list of eligibles',[8] especially as a village might consist of only two or three clans. Not surprisingly, the rule was far from universally applied. Additionally, the social and economic position of the bride and groom was expected to be similar.

The bridegroom's family was expected to pay a bride price. The amount varied, of course, depending on the prosperity of the families, but a betrothal gift of some sort was an essential compensation to the bride's family for the costs of bringing up the girl. In Beijing in the 1940s a wedding cost four to five months' family income; Hebei, three to six months' income. Among the wealthier families, an equivalent sum was often returned to the bridegroom's family in the form of the wife's trousseau, household furniture and so on; among the poorer people a substantial proportion of the betrothal gift was kept by the wife's family. The cost of marrying off a son could cripple those without considerable savings, and the poorest men were unlikely to be able to marry at all.

One way around the betrothal gift was to take in a child

bride. Her family would avoid the expense of her upbringing, while her husband's family would avoid having to pay out a lump sum for her and would get the benefits of her labour as she grew. Although the legal age of marriage from the time of the Song dynasty (960–1279) was sixteen for men and fourteen for women, the betrothal of children was common. If a poor family could not find a husband for their daughter, or needed money rather than just fewer mouths to feed, the girl might be sold outright as a slave or concubine.

There was considerable local variation in the age of marriage although overall it tended to be higher in the southern provinces. One study carried out in eleven provinces between 1929 and 1931 found 62.2 per cent of men and 79.6 per cent of women in north China married before the age of nineteen, compared with 46.4 per cent of men and 67.5 per cent in the south. For the country as a whole, the study showed the percentage of men and women married at different ages as indicated in Table 1.

Table 1 Age of Marriage in Republican China (Percentage Distribution)

Years	Male	Female
Under 14	4.8%	5.4%
15-19	40.3%	66.8%
20-24	39.4%	25.4%
25-29	10.1%	2.3%
30 and over	5.4%	0.1%
TOTAL	100.0%	100.0%

Source: Croll, 1981.

Almost everybody did get married; marriage rates were high in China, as in other Asian countries, compared with Europe. Divorce, theoretically possible on the initiative of either partner, was effectively only obtainable if sought by the husband. It was extremely rare (as can be seen from Table 2) for the excellent reason that marriage was a family alliance and personal preferences were irrelevant. Additionally, once the wife had married into her husband's family, she was so dependent on it that she had everything to gain by being as obedient and accommodating as possible. If she returned to her family they were unlikely, except perhaps in a case of notorious ill-treatment, to support her against the family with whom they had chosen to ally themselves, let alone to offer her support and a place to live.

Table 2 Marital Condition of Women aged 15+ in Five Areas of Republican China

Location	Unmar-ried	Mar-ried	Wid-owed	Divo-rced	Un-known	Total
Jiang Ying	9.00	71.80	17.30	0.00	1.90	100.00
Ding Xian	7.31	75.00	17.68	0.01	–	100.00
Zheng Gong	6.01	74.51	19.30	–	0.18	100.00
Sichuan	7.40	69.50	23.00	0.10	–	100.00
Kunming Lake Region	10.04	70.78	18.72	0.09	0.36	99.99

Source: Chen Da, 1946

By convention widows were not supposed to remarry. They still belonged to their late husband's family, whose permission would be needed for remarriage. That permission, which reflected badly upon the family, was seldom given. A widow was supposed to be virtuous and dutiful and she had few chances to be anything else. As one writer pointed out, 'Merry widows were rare in traditional China and those who were seldom came to a merry end.'[9]

A marriage was recognized when the two families had completed their negotiations, the betrothal gift had been paid, and the bride had been escorted to her husband's home in a sedan-chair, with her clothes and household articles carried in procession behind. She was then presented to the household gods of her new family, who invited relatives to a marriage feast.

Her primary tasks in marriage were to produce children to carry on the family and to work for that family. Barrenness was not grounds for divorce; if a male child was not born to the couple, one could be adopted from within the clan. In carrying out her duties she was subordinate to her parents-in-law, especially her mother-in-law, as well as to her husband. The husband often did the shopping and ordered the meals, as well as directing much of the other household work, even among many peasant families. The poorest woman probably had most say in family affairs, and more freedom; she was also less likely, even in the north, to have bound feet, and was able as a result to take a more active part in work inside and outside the home. Such women gathered firewood, planted and harvested rice, raised silkworms and wove and spun. A survey of 15,316 farms carried out between 1929 and 1932 showed that 14 per cent of farmwork was undertaken by women, and 7 per cent by children. The one area in which women had a major say was in the decision about who their children should marry, especially in decisions about prospective daughters-in-law.

All in all, it is not surprising that one of the Five Classics, the *Shi jing,* or Book of Songs, should sum up the futures for a newly born boy or girl in such contrasting verses:

Sons shall be born to him:
They will be put to sleep on couches;
They will be clothed in robes;
They will have sceptres to play with;
Their cry will be loud.
They will be resplendent with red knee-covers,
The king, the princes of the land.

Daughters shall be born to him:
They will be put to sleep on the ground;
They will be clothed in wrappers;
They will have tiles to play with.
It will be theirs neither to do wrong nor to do good.
Only about the spirits and the food will they have to think,
And to cause no sorrow to their parents. [10]

The Changing Family: Republican

Towards the end of the nineteenth century, exposure to foreign ideas gave young Chinese intellectuals the chance to question traditional family attitudes and values. Simultaneously, traditional systems were being undermined by economic pressures. The import of cheap cotton goods threatened local spinning and weaving activities, increasing the need for cash in families and reducing the household contribution of women. A series of rebellions resulting from the weakness of the declining Manchu dynasty led to ravaged lands and much peasant poverty. Industry began to expand, especially on the east coast, and provided new types of occupation for migrants. Many Chinese, adventurous or desperate for a living, went abroad as indentured labour. The process of change intensified after the 1911 Revolution, and further impetus was given by the increasing influence of foreigners and outside ideas. Some of the change weakened traditional concepts of the family, as will be seen. Other aspects of change – for example, the breakdown of government and increased local instability during the period of the feuding warlords, followed by civil war and the war with Japan – may have in some ways intensified reliance on the family and the clan as the sole source of support for its members. The family might undergo alteration: that did not necessarily mean a decline in its power.

One significant area of change which impinged on the family was migration. Migration was nothing new: poverty, exacerbated by wars and natural disasters, had always caused movements of population, as had new opportunities in particular parts of the country – for example, the south. The extraordinary conditions of the first half of this century, though, and the growth of new industries (by 1919 there were some three million industrial workers) gave rise to major movements. Migration to the cities offered new opportunities, a different culture; while some workers severed their ties with a too-authoritarian family, the majority did not, and their visits home and reports to the family helped to diffuse new ideas.

Faced with a difficult father, or an arranged marriage he disliked, a young man might go to seek his fortune in the cities. During these years, however, most young men left because the land could not support them. The survey of farms in 1929–32 referred to above found that 41 per cent of them had members working at least part-time outside. A village study of a comparatively fertile area in Guangdong in the late

1940s indicated that more than a third of the income of the village came from non-agricultural activities. The sons of poor peasants were the most likely to have to hire themselves out to richer farmers, or to go in search of city jobs.

Not only the men went to work in the cities. Women became workers in the tobacco, match, electrical appliance and other industries and, above all, in textiles. By 1927, 72.3 per cent of cotton-spinners in Shanghai were female, and Shanghai actually had more women than men workers, with 58.7 per cent of the workforce female. One report noted that industry preferred to employ women, who were more docile and could be paid less. Once female labour became more common, women were employed in other work, becoming, for example, shop assistants, teachers, waitresses or unskilled labourers.

Remittances sent to the family were often a substantial proportion of the family budget. Even the lower-paid female workers might be able to contribute a considerable sum. A study in Jiangsu suggested that in the mid–1930s, women working in Wuxi factories might send back enough to pay the rent on 10 to 12 *mu* (1 *mu* = ⅙ of an acre) of land a year. These women – and indeed young men too, who in their traditional environment might have had no say in family affairs – were knowledgeable about the income and property of the family, the prices of land, rice and wheat, rates of interest and so on. The women tended to have far more say in family matters than was traditionally acceptable and when they married expected a similar decision-making role, especially if their marriage was to a peasant. One peasant wife from Wuxi who ran the family explained that her husband was not very competent and never had any ideas, whereas 'I have worked in the factory since I was very young and I know more of the world than my husband, who never left his native village.'[11]

Among the educated, the arranged marriage might never take place. The younger generation 'had begun to demand the free choice of marriage partner or the non-intervention of parents or third parties and the establishment of independent households on marriage. A variety of new marriage procedures emerged in the cities in the earlier decades of this century . . .'[12]

Even where the marriages were still arranged by the family, the age of marriage for workers was higher than for peasants. Parents with a wage-earning daughter were not anxious for her to become part of another family; factory women who were unmarried at twenty-five, twenty-seven and even twenty-eight were quite common. Once they did marry, they tended to have smaller families, and have them later, than peasants (see Chapter 3).

In some areas of China, factory opportunities were taken up largely by men, but this too had an effect on the family and the position of its women members. The city of Kunming, in Yunnan, grew by almost 40 per cent between 1938 and the end of 1941 as a result of migration caused by the war with Japan. At the same time it changed from a rural centre where farm produce was exchanged for local handicrafts, to an increasingly industrial modern city. More than 54 per cent of the males in the districts around Kunming Lake worked in the non-agricultural sector, while nearly 79 per cent of the women were in agriculture. Although Yunnan was tradition-ally a part of China in which women did work on the land, the indication from these figures is that in many cases they were now the main source of farm labour, and that their judgement and ability to run the family's farm were increasingly relied upon. Additionally, many women were forced to take over family responsibilities because their men were recruited into the armed forces.

Women were entitled to a share of the family property in their own right, under a law passed by the Nationalist government. But few beyond the emancipated factory workers even knew such a law existed, let alone attempted to put it into effect. At least, as the practice of foot-binding died out (it had been forbidden after the 1911 Revolution but took time to disappear) and as new job opportunities opened up, more women contributed directly to the family income and thus came to have a greater say in family decision-making.

The spread of education also contributed to change and is discussed in more detail elsewhere (see Chapter 5). So too are the political campaigns and those broader educational efforts directed at improving rural health or otherwise 'modernizing' peasant communities. Each had the effect of undermining the traditional belief that knowledge and authority were to be found solely in the old. As the outside world impinged ever further upon life in China an uneasy awareness grew that the family's collective wisdom and established practices might not be enough to enable its members to meet new challenges.

The Changing Family: 1949 and After

By the time the Chinese Communist Party gained power in 1949, it had acquired considerable experience in dealing with family issues in the areas of China it had controlled. This is not the place to explore the shifts in Party policy towards the family which had taken place during the 1930s and 1940s, except to note that efforts in the Jiangxi Soviet were concentrated largely on getting women to work the land, in order that their menfolk might be freed to fight, and that after the Long March attempts to improve the status of women in the family were subordinated to economic issues. Indeed, problems of 'the family' itself were set aside in an effort to concentrate on the development of collective economic strength. An analysis of the women's movement during the anti-Japanese war defined the family as the basic economic unit, but not the small (conjugal) family of capitalist society: rather the 'big family' of the village which was seen as providing the most effective use of labour power. The 'big family' was the basis of the rural economy which was supporting the resistance war, and thus the basis for action should, it was thought, be the reform and consolidation of this type of family.

By the early 1940s the war was entering a crucial stage. Japanese offensives had reduced the size of the liberated areas, where the population had gone down from 44 to 25 million, and there was a blockade of the liberated areas by the Nationalists which meant supplies of any sort were virtually unobtainable. 'The situation was critical for a regime which depended for survival on popular support.'[13] In the circumstances it was inevitable that the Party should soft-pedal on issues like land reform, or the status of women, which were bound to be deeply divisive.

However, some women in backward Shaanxi did learn to work the land, and many more went into production, particularly textile production. The additional income they brought in provided some inducement to their mothers-in-law to undertake more of the household tasks for which these working women now had little time. 'This was hard on the older women who had formerly been able to sit back a bit and supervise the household. Now they were often left both with the cooking and the children . . . in Zhehu some of them were very annoyed. When their daughters-in-law returned from work they dished up only cold food and grumbled "Everything is upside down since the Communist Party came. Mothers-in-law have become daughters-in-law." '14

As well as earning an income and having to forge new relationships with their mothers-in-law, these women, who tended to work in groups either to share tasks or overheads, discovered the benefits of more communal and less family-centred activities. Their previously 'enclosed and solitary lives' were transformed by shared tasks, shared childminding, and shared experiences. Women's Associations were set up in the liberated villages, to encourage more participation and still greater contributions to the war effort by women.

The men, too, were organized. The 'big family' as defined by the Party went beyond the traditional family and clan confines and although it did not directly conflict with them, it subordinated them to overall direction of effort by the Party cadres. Within this framework, Peasants' Associations encouraged everybody to participate, to discuss and to make decisions; not merely the elders alone, but the young and the poor.

The process was intensified after the end of the Japanese war, when the Party was able to turn its attention to land reform. The Central Committee of the Party, in a resolution on women-work in 1948, reaffirmed that 'men and women have equal rights to land. Every member of the family has democratic rights in the disposal of the property. When necessary, land deeds for women can be issued separately.'15 Mass meetings to catalogue local land, decide on its division – including the division of land confiscated from landlords – and to decide on the treatment of the landlords themselves, involved every individual in the community.

Simultaneously, land reform was striking at two fundamental aspects of traditional family life. By allocating land on an individual basis and suggesting that separate title deeds could be given to different family members – even to women – it was dealing a blow to the concept of family possessions held in common and managed entirely by the senior male. By involving the women in the process of land reform, and giving them equal property entitlement, it was offering them economic independence and the right to participate in decision making. In some areas, where most of the men were away fighting, women were the main agents of land reform.

Naturally, in most instances, the family continued to work as a family, with little visible change in its organization. Even the women who said 'when I get my share I'll separate from my husband, then he won't be able to oppress me any more' did not all leave when it came to the point.[16] The threat was enough. It was also enough to encourage the family head to consult on, rather than order, a son's work in the fields, especially when the particular field might now belong to that son. If fathers, mothers-in-law or husbands were slow to get the message, they might find the Peasants' Association or the Women's Association on their backs. In the village of Longbow, in Shaanxi, once the Women's Association had beaten up one husband who punished his wife for going to meetings, the others quickly became more permissive.

Family and clan authority was further undermined by the existence of a new focus of power. In Longbow, during the campaign to reorganise and rectify the Communist Party, local peasant members, who had hitherto kept their membership secret for security reasons, finally announced themselves with a garbled and tuneless version of the *Internationale:*

The song, despite the grave defects of rendition, made a powerful impression upon us all. It revealed in an unexpected and dramatic way the existence, hitherto only conjectured, of a strong, organized centre at the heart of village life, a centre which followed a well-established tradition – however new or strange that tradition might be – and obviously commanded great loyalty from its adherents. Certainly no coercion could have caused these stolid peasants to attempt in public a song only half learned. With this revelation any tendency that one might have to view the village as 'a pile of loose sand' could hardly help but crumble. Here stood in solid if somewhat ragged phalanx the vertebrae of the community's backbone.[17]

The Marriage Law

It is generally agreed that as an instrument of family change, the Marriage Law of 1950 was uniquely significant. That it was intended to be is clear from its first Article:

The feudal system, based on arbitrary and compulsory arrangement and the supremacy of man over woman, and in disregard for the interests of the children, is abolished. The new democratic marriage system, which is based on the free choice of partners, on monogamy, on equal rights for both sexes, and on the protection of the lawful interests of children, is put into effect.[18]

As Article 1 suggests, the purpose of the Law was a wider one than merely to regulate marriages:

To marry according to the Marriage Law required revolutionary courage in the countryside . . . The accent fell on the conclusion of marriage as an act of defiance, the introduction of class struggle into the very bosom of the family. If the Law had been called a family law, that dynamic appeal would have been lost and an important psychological factor would have been missed. The Law addressed itself to young people in the first place and called upon them to rebel . . . The 'marriage system' was something different from the family system; more important, the family was a consequence of the marriage.[19]

The free choice of partners implied that marriage was no longer to be a business of alliance between families. Even its ceremony reflected this approach, with the couple – in the 1960s – either proclaiming themselves man and wife in front of, or bowing to, the portrait of Mao Zedong. The bowing, as one anthropologist pointed out, was reminiscent of the old obeisance before the family ancestors, but now symbolised political rather than religious recognition. 'The political respects are said to symbolise the commitment of the couple, beyond their immediate households and kin groups, to the local and national communities.'[20]

For the first time, marriages were made official by the state, which in its Marriage Law said that marriages should be registered. This implied that the state had an interest in those marriages, as well as providing an opportunity for the young either to repudiate a forced marriage, or to claim state support for their wish for a free-choice arrangement. In fact, in the early days of the Revolution, this provision was far from successful in its aims. Couples wanting to escape from an arranged marriage often found local cadres siding with the traditional family and refusing to help them, while those seeking a free-choice marriage too often had their marriages denied. Extensive educational efforts had to be made by the Party in an attempt to change the views not only of families but of lower-level cadres.

Many people simply did not bother to register marriages at all. There were no sanctions against them if they did not register, and the marriage was still acceptable as legal. Marriage was publicly living together, which, given household structure, usually implied living together as members of one or other partner's family. It is probably reasonable to assume that in the early days registration was more likely when the couple wanted or needed the support of the government for the marriage, than where the couple and their families were satisfied with the arrangement.

Even in 1980, a survey of Huaide, in Jilin Province, indicated that a substantial proportion of marriages were not registered until the couple wanted to apply for permission to have a child. The public security statistics on households were still seen primarily as a check on movement in or out of the local area, and the officials collecting them were far less concerned with marriages, divorces, or, at some periods, births.

Free-choice marriages were supposed to make bride-gifts and dowries unnecessary. These were seen as part of the old 'feudal' system in which a woman was bought by the man's family, rather than being an independent, economically self-sufficient individual. In any society, however, it is difficult to define very clearly where personal savings designed to set up a home, or the gifts of family and friends to help a couple start their new lives together, cease to be prudence and generosity and become a hindrance to free choice, or a feudal remnant of a commercial transaction.

A father in northern Shaanxi in the early 1960s was blunt enough in his 'feudalism'. He had paid a great deal for his wife, and was determined to get paid for his daughter, for 'Look at the cost of a daughter!' But he was modern enough to have accepted the new system, free of bride price, for his sons, whose weddings he thus did not have to pay for.[21] At different times, notably during the anti-Confucius campaign of 1974–5, there have been major educational efforts to stop the practice, and much was made by the media of couples who married without gifts, or indeed without expensive ceremonial. There are no signs, however, that betrothal gifts are on the wane; indeed, with the increase of consumer goods available from the late 1970s, recent impressions have been of an increase in the amounts involved.

These impressions were confirmed by the results of a survey in a 'fairly typical' village in Hebei Province in 1980, which revealed that it cost an average young peasant 3000 *yuan* to marry, or perhaps up to ten times his annual cash income. Two-thirds of this went on building a home and furnishing it (his parents would have started to collect the bricks and tiles when he entered his teens) and 1000 *yuan* on the wedding feast and gifts. Some 200 *yuan* was spent on the bride's clothes, and the young man may also have had to provide a bicycle, sewing machine or wristwatch. A demanding bride might require all three and sum up her demand as 'the things that go round'.

In the cities, a three-piece suite, television set or a tape-recorder may be required, though couples making free-choice marriages tend to dispense with betrothal gifts.

Dowries provided by the woman seem to have disappeared, probably as the result of her working and thus having an evident and independent income, which means she no longer needs to boost her status in her new family with a dowry.

It was perhaps too much to hope that bride price would disappear before arranged marriage. And in spite of the brave words of the Marriage Law, the old system is far from abolished. Elisabeth Croll identified four types of marriage in China in the late 1970s (see Table 3) and concluded that the immediate models 2 and 3 were probably the most common, especially in the rural areas. Under model 2 the parents initiate the negotiations but turn to the boy and girl for agreement before concluding them. Under models 3a and 3b the young couple make the first approaches and then ask their parents for consent; the only difference between the two sub-models is that in 3b the parents, having given their blessing, play no further part in the negotiations, which are concluded by the two people directly involved.

Table 3 The Range of Conscious Models in the People's Republic of China

	Initiations of Negotiations	Consent	Conclusion of Negotiations
Old ideological model 1	Parents	–	Parents
Immediate model 2	Parents	Parties	Parents
Immediate model 3a	Parties	Parents	Parents
Immediate model 3b	Parties	Parents	Parties
New ideological model 4	Parents	Political associations	Parties

Source: Croll, 1981.

A not-dissimilar analysis was reported in a Chinese magazine in 1981. In an article describing the need for a new marriage law, it identified free-choice marriages, where the couple chose for themselves and might call in official organizations to support them, if necessary, against their parents; marriages with the help of parents or a go-between; and arranged marriages.

Marriage with the help of parents or a go-between was described as follows:

A second form of free choice in marriage, somewhat modified, allows the couple to decide on marriage with the help of the parents and a go-between. This form is more prevalent in China's rural areas, since it conforms with the economic and cultural development there. In the countryside a production unit is based on a natural village, and often people in a village have little contact with the outside world. There, because of geographical and cultural limitations, it is almost impossible to have a totally free choice in marriage. So marriage is first agreed upon and then the two young people try to develop compatability.

Though this method represents progress over the strictly arranged marriages that took place before liberation, it is still not based initially on genuine love but rather on material considerations. Introduced by a go-between, the parents of both parties first consider how many members in each family share the family income and property, how many people in each family can work, and its annual income before they ask their children's opinion. Then a meeting is arranged between the young man and woman.

If the man is satisfied with the woman, he will leave some gift (usually money); if the woman accepts it, this means that the engagement is on. In the Beijing area the gift − from 10 to 20 yuan wrapped in a handkerchief − is usually presented by the mother of the would-be groom. The wedding is held about a year later. During the ensuing time, besides visiting each other, the young man and his fiancee go shopping in town several times, he trying to satisfy her requests. Some young people like to have a picture taken to show their engagement.[22]

The article reported a survey in two counties of Anhui Province in 1979, which found that of 14,586 marriages 'in recent years', 15 per cent were free choice, 75 per cent were marriage with the help of parents or go-betweens, and 10 per cent were arranged matches. These last were described as due to political circumstances during the Cultural Revolution, or extreme poverty, as a result of which it became difficult for some families to find partners and so they had agreed to exchange daughters.

Croll argues that there is a direct correlation between household composition, the economic interdependence of its members, and the degree of parental participation in the procedures of mate selection. Household composition and the economic interdependence of its members will be examined in more detail in the latter part of this chapter; here it is sufficient to note that the goal of free-choice marriage is far from achieved, but that fully traditional marriage with the young couple as helpless pawns in a game of family alliances is probably now rare.

One reason for the change has been the strong emphasis on raising the age of marriage. This policy has been urged by the Party since the days when it ruled only in the liberated areas, not on demographic grounds but to ensure the participation of young women in the labour force, and to give them the mental and financial independence to make their own sensible marriage choices. Although primarily aimed at improving the status of women, the policy also helped to give young men a larger voice in the choice of a marriage partner: there is, after all, a difference in attitude to parental authority between a nineteen-year-old boy and a man of twenty-five.

The Marriage Law stipulated a minimum age of marriage of eighteen for women and twenty for men. In the mid–1950s it appears that most couples got married as soon as they reached the legal age, and in some years, the modal marriage age was noticeably below that legal age. By the 1960s, the norm for urban marriages at least had risen to around twenty-three years, and the mid–1970s the acceptable ages to which the policy suggested people should adhere were different for rural and urban dwellers, with a recommended age in the country of 23-25 for women and 25-28 for men. While the target ages were by no means universally adhered to, they did have a considerable impact on overall marriage ages. Compared with the target ages, the minimum age under the Law was almost forgotten: marriages were contracted in accordance with, or in defiance of, the recommended ages rather than those set by the Law.

Educational materials designed to persuade young people to delay marriage stressed that work, or studies, would be undermined by the pressures of family life, for the assumption until the 1970s was that the first child would be conceived shortly after marriage. The propaganda indicated that the family would suffer financial hardship, while the health of both mother and child would be affected. These materials imply a new way of looking at the family: one in which the young couple rather than the traditional family unit are responsible for the income on which to raise their children, and in which the individual opportunities or contribution to the economy through study or work on the part of young people outweigh the demands on the family.

The combination of raising the age of marriage and whittling away the authority of the older generation in marriage arrangements (the models 2 and 3 in Croll's analysis, and the assisted-by-parent model presented by the Chinese, both call for negotiation, at least, between parent and child) was extremely effective in altering the balance of power within the family. The effect of the Marriage Law was summed up in one bitter poem:

With freedom of marriage
Gone is the father's prestige
Now comes the Marriage Law
Mothers are no longer held in awe.[23]

Worse still, parents who had suffered the humiliation of consulting their young about the proposed marriage found that the new daughter-in-law was an independent young woman who worked for her living. Mothers who had entered the household in the old way, had suffered for years under the tyranny of their own mothers-in-law and were now looking forward to at last sitting back while their son's wife performed all the chores at their bidding, were appalled. 'From being her daughter-in-law's supervisor, the mother-in-law was often relegated to the position of her helpmate. While the girl went out to work, the older woman might look after her grandchildren and do the menial tasks once done by the younger woman. Some mothers took a permissible escape from this fate and began to work outside the home themselves . . .'[24]

Major educational campaigns, via the Women's Federation and the mass media, for example, were needed to help both sides to come to terms. As the pattern of late marriage became more common, and as more and more women were drawn into the workforce, the older women became somewhat more resigned to their fate and appreciative of the comforts which an additional income brought to the home. But a recent sociological study of a neighbourhood in Tianjin reported that conflict between mother and daughter-in-law was the most common reason for dissolution of the extended family, noting that 'The mother-in-law, mainly occupied with household chores, hopes to keep control over her big family, but the daughter-in-law, mainly occupied in social labour, hopes to organise her independent small family . . .'[25]

The daughter-in-law was not only older; she tended, as time went on, to have an education. This was not simply a matter of being able to read and write – although, in a world in which the state impinged far more closely upon families than in the past and often through written exhortations or directives, the need to rely on a son or daughter to interpret further undermined the authority of the old. Education involved new ways of doing things; new questioning of old beliefs. Child-care, for instance, was a continuing preoccupation of the Party, and women were instructed about cleanliness, diet, and so on, in ways which were often contrary to traditional lore. Efforts were made to involve the older generation in the educational process, and to explain, for example, the scientific basis of nutritional advice, but many must have been affronted by the challenge to the wisdom of experience. The young, on the other hand, learned that experience was not the only, or always the best, guide.

If the relationships between the young and the old had altered, so too did the relationship between the partners to a marriage. Five conditions for a happy marriage were spelled out in a booklet on the Marriage Law published in 1964:

1. The man and the woman must have good relations, understand, love and respect one another.
2. The relations between the woman and her in-laws must be good, especially those with the mother-in-law.
3. The labour and production of both parties must be in order; each must stimulate the other.
4. Both parties must have a positive attitude towards their work. When life is satisfactory and the family a harmonious unit, old and young will love the Party and socialism still more and contribute their labour to Party and state in a positive way.
5. Both parties must be in good health: then they will produce healthy children.[26]

The couple, as the foundation of the new family, were seen as partners in the task of raising a family, looking after their aged relatives, and contributing to the building of a socialist society. Their partnership was more important than 'love'. They had few opportunities to meet alone before their engagement, or to go out with a variety of individuals before making up their minds which to marry ('dating' in the Western sense being regarded as improper) and the choice of whom to marry was expected to be based on criteria of suitability – political, family background, education and so on – rather than upon overwhelming attraction of 'love' alone. But once married they were intended to 'understand, love and respect' one another and to have a closer relationship than would have been either necessary or desirable in the traditional marriage.

As women began increasingly to achieve education and to work outside the home, the possibilities of a real partnership – in interests, communication and contribution – increased. Even the tensions which have been generated by the new marriage system between the young and older generations may have helped to bring a couple closer together in mutual support. When the wife worked, particularly in the cities where the couple might not be living with a resident mother-in-law, her husband would probably have to take a greater part (though it was seldom an equal part) in household chores and child-care. Chinese men are frequently enthusiastic cooks, and there is no cultural taboo on men minding the baby.

Table 4 Divorces Contested in Courts — 1950–56

Year	
1950–June 1951	99 300
July 1950–Dec. 1952	Not available
1953	1 170 000
1954	710 000
1955	610 000
1956	510 000

Source: Davin, 1976.

Divorce, when a marriage did not succeed, was provided for in the Marriage Law, and in the first years after its enactment there were a very large number of divorces, as well as suicides by those who failed to obtain one. Figures for divorces in the early 1950s which were contested, and thus had to be settled in the courts, are given in Table 4.

These divorces were largely of couples who had been forced into unhappy marriages before the new Law. The logic of the Marriage Law, however, was that marriages were unlikely to go wrong once they had ceased to be feudal, and from the late 1950s onwards divorce became increasingly difficult to obtain. It had been extremely unpopular, except with those who managed to separate under it, and it appears that the Party was unwilling to continue with a policy so disapproved of once the original rationale of forced marriages had largely vanished.

Even forced marriages, later on, were not considered sufficient justification on their own for breaking up an established family. A case reported in 1979 concerned a couple, Liu and Ren, who had been married off by their parents in 1950. They apparently made no attempt in the years following to get a divorce, and had three children. However, in 1976 the family moved to the city and shortly afterwards Liu asked for a divorce. Refused by his district court, he appealed to the municipal intermediate court. The judges, along with Liu's work colleagues and several people from the family's old village, seemed to think that Liu had, on coming to the city, got tired of his peasant wife (though she too was criticized, for not being very considerate towards her mother-in-law) and refused the divorce. 'It is to be hoped', they added, 'that both the husband and wife will be considerate towards each other and do their best to improve family relations, work for unity, and contribute to the building of socialism.' The presiding judge of the municipal intermediate court was asked to comment on the judges' decision and said: 'Our constitution and Marriage Law protect the interests of women and children. The latter, in particular, guarantees the freedom to ask for divorce, but, in the interests of the parties involved, and of the children and the society as a whole, it rules against precipitate action.'[27] Individual boredom or resentment, in fact, are of less importance than the family and the state.

Under the new Marriage Law of 1981 divorce apparently became easier to obtain, as is discussed below. However, the total number of divorces has presumably remained small, for a sample fertility survey carried out in China in 1982 suggested that only 0.2 per cent of women are divorced and not remarried, while a further 2.9 per cent of women are married for a second time: the latter group presumably includes both divorced and widowed women.

The Constitution, the new Marriage Law and the Family

The original Constitution of the People's Republic of China was published in 1954. Left untouched until 1975, it was then revised and much shortened (from 106 to 30 articles); revised again in 1978 and again in 1982. Each version proclaims that the state protects the marriage, the family, and the mother and child, as well as guaranteeing equal rights for men and women. However, the 1978 Constitution felt it necessary to state that men and women should marry of their own free will – perhaps this was a pointer to continuing unease about traditional marriage, and to the introduction of a new marriage law, which was in fact published two years later, to come into effect on 1 January 1981. The 1978 Constitution also introduced, for the first time, an indication of what it saw as a duty of marriage: 'the state advocates and encourages family planning'.

The 1982 Constitution was a great deal more expansive in discussing what the family protected by the Constitution should do. It is now a constitutional duty of parents to rear and to educate their children, and it is the duty of children, once they are grown up, to support and assist their parents. It is everybody's duty (as well as right) to be educated and to work for the benefit of society; to take care of the old and not maltreat them; and to practise family planning.

The Marriage Law of 1981

The duties regarding family and family life spelled out in the 1982 Constitution were not really new; they had already been incorporated into the new Marriage Law of 1981. The differences between it and the 1950 Law were few, but significant. Some provisions of the old Law were dropped – such as those against concubines, child brides and the ban on widows remarrying – because they were no longer necessary: they referred, as one magazine article put it, to things which were now 'ancient history'.[28] That, in itself, is one measure of the changes which have taken place in the Chinese family.

The age of marriage under the new Law was put at twenty for women and twenty-two for men. Given that this was well below the minimum ages which had been recommended for the past ten years at least, it seemed to many observers surprising that it was not higher. The reason, quite simply, was that a higher age would have been unenforceable. As the same magazine article explained:

. . . such a regulation runs counter to the physiological needs of young people and can cause further problems. Studies show that because of restriction on marriage the number of instances of couples living together before marriage, illegitimate children, and abortions by unmarried mothers has increased. So has the practice of holding 'weddings' among family and friends to gain social recognition without legal sanction. A survey in Guizhou province in 1977 showed that unions without legal registration then made up 40 per cent of the total number of marriages. Thus, even tougher restrictions on marriage would be self-defeating.[29]

Indeed, one of the first results of the new Marriage Law was a dramatic increase in the numbers marrying in China in 1981; rather more than double the number who married in 1980. A large proportion of these marriages would have probably taken place anyway, but without registration. Guizhou's figures may or may not be representative for the country as a whole, but even if they are well above average that would still suggest that a quite substantial proportion of couples have been marrying in defiance of the recommended ages and did not register the marriage. Many of those who registered their marriage in 1981 may have married a year or two previously at younger than recommended ages, and were prepared to admit it now that the new Law gave them support. Yet others were marriages of those who had previously been prepared to wait until the recommended ages, but could now quote the new Law to show there was no need for them to postpone marriage.

None the less, the legal age of marriage in China is high, and few countries in the world have a higher. The actual age of marriage is also high, and rising, A national fertility sample survey, involving the questioning of 310,485 women between the ages of 15 and 67 and carried out in September 1982, produced an average age of marriage in the 1970s of 21.6 and a 1980 average of 23 years. (The 1981 average was 22.8, but this year's figures will have been distorted by the new Law).

Divorce was made somewhat easier under the new Law. The old Law said that a divorce 'may be granted' if mediation fails when only one party wants the divorce. The new Law states that if mediation fails, divorce 'should be granted'. There are as yet no figures which give a breakdown in different years before and after 1980, but it is probable that 1981 and 1982 saw an upsurge in the number, as those who had been unable previously to obtain a divorce took advantage of the new Law. My impression is that there were quite a number of people in such a position, especially among cadres whose mobility makes marriage less stable.

The inherent difficulty of being fair to both parties in a divorce has been admitted in Chinese commentaries on the new Law. On the one hand a woman who has cared for a husband and brought up a family may not wish for a divorce which enables the man to go off with a younger woman. 'Does the new marriage law open the door to men who are fickle in their love and who purposely create problems in order to get a divorce?' wrote one woman. 'It is said that men and women are equal before the law but divorce hurts the woman more.'[30] But, as the Chairwoman of the All China Women's Federation noted, if one party is really determined, refusal to grant a divorce 'only prolongs the misery on both sides and even causes lifelong tragedy. Refusal to get divorced under such a circumstance is detrimental to both husband and wife, to their children and to society . . .'[31]

How far the rights of the child have received recognition can be seen from the provisions in the Marriage Law for the children of divorced parents. In traditional China they were of course the property of the husband's family; after 1950 they more often remained with the mother, although both parties had the duty to support them. The new Law adds to that joint duty of support the general principle that the mother should have custody of a baby still being breast-fed, but that after that stage, if custody cannot be agreed upon by the couple, the court 'shall render a decision in accordance with the interests of the child'. That rights imply duties is made clear in the provision that alimony may be payable by either party, if the spouse is in difficulties.

Two of the main reasons for the revision of the Marriage Law seem to have been the desire to include family planning as a legal requirement for both men and women (see Chapter 2) and the concern of the state about the continuing difficulty of ensuring free marriage, and the abolition of betrothal gifts. 'This type of arbitrary and venal marriage', said the Women's Federation Chairwoman Kang Keqing, 'undermines the socialist legal system, infringes on citizens' democratic rights, damages the vital interests of young men and women, and affects stability and unity.'[32]

Economic and Organizational Change

After land reform, the peasants were encouraged to form groups to work the land more effectively. First came 'mutual aid teams' in which a few families helped each other with labour, and then co-operatives, in which they might pool their land as well as their equipment. These in turn gave way to advanced co-operatives with collective land ownership and, in the Great Leap Forward of 1958, to full-scale communes – divided into brigades and work teams – which controlled agriculture, industrial resources, taxes, schools, nurseries, public kitchens, old people's homes, cemeteries and indeed the whole local infrastructure.

Some form of co-operation clearly made sense. Individual landholdings after land reform were generally small and often scattered; even more important, probably, was the shortage of equipment. There simply was not enough to go round and attempts to share what there was led to neglect and recriminations, especially when the equipment was something like a donkey which nobody was fully responsible for looking after or feeding and which died as a result. Sharing labour but not land led to further disputes, because somebody's land was always going to be the last to be harvested and that somebody might suffer in consequence.

Up to a point, therefore, the peasant family was willing to learn the advantages of co-operation. They were in any case not entirely new to the idea: the clans had been able to call on their members, in the past, to carry out irrigation works or to finance the local school. And, given that connected families tended to live in groups, especially in the south, a family would often be working with relatives in a team. In the village studies by Croll in 1977, the grouping of families looked like this:

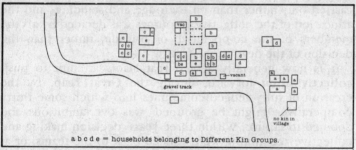

a b c d e = households belonging to Different Kin Groups.

Plan of kinship organization: Jiang Village

Even where families were not working with relatives, they were working with their nearest and probably best-known neighbours, with whom relationships were inevitably fairly close.

Two major differences from the past were that the entire group, including women and the young, rather than just the clan elders, were now involved in the decision making, and that the guidance was again coming not from the elders, but from a cadre. This latter change was not achieved overnight. It is reported that not far from the model brigade of Dazhai three villages were combined into a new brigade. Unfortunately 'the three hostile clans who had formerly each inhabited a separate village were not prepared to accept leading cadres from either of the other clans. It happened time and time again that a newly chosen brigade leader would be harrassed out of his office.'[33] It was impossible, for several years, to create an administrative infrastructure and the stalemate was only resolved when the local Party committee handed over the brigade's leadership to the then famous, though later much-criticized, Dazhai secretary Chen Yonggui.

The common ownership of land, and the introduction of a system of workpoints as remuneration, contributed to a further weakening of the power of the family head, though not necessarily of the power of the clan in a clan-dominated village now defined as a 'work team'. The choice of work to be done by each family member was now made by the team or brigade leader, rather than the family head; the contribution of each family member was calculated on work actually carried out, rather than on their age and standing; and the allocation of the collective resources was decided by all the members of the co-operative or brigade, rather than the decision of the head of the family.

It is now generally agreed that Mao's attempt to push collectivization forward, during the Great Leap, by the creation of fully-fledged communes into which some thirty co-operatives might be grouped, was over-ambitious and doomed to failure. Within three years, decision making and collective accounting were handed back to the teams, or at best to the brigades, private plots of land were returned to peasant families, and many of the initiatives for collective living, such as communal dining rooms designed to free women for productive work, were dismantled.

Nevertheless, the movement did produce its gains, especially for women. A massive propaganda campaign was launched to persuade women to join in productive work, and to persuade both men and women that women were just as capable of work as men, and just as necessary to the building of new China. Women in the countryside who had still hesitated to work, or whose traditionally-minded menfolk had discouraged them, now came out into the fields. By 1958, women constituted more than half of the total agricultural labour force. The emphasis on small-scale local industry, though often misguided in its production (for example, the backyard steelworks which produced such low quality steel as to be unusable) meant that communes began to set up small factories, often employing women, which laid the foundations for the later extremely successful decentralized local industry policies. In the cities, too, local women banded together to form enterprises, making whatever seemed to be in local demand and acquiring both an income and self-confidence, as a worker from a small medical apparatus factory in Beijing later explained:

We brought our own tools from home: hammers, pliers, a few screwdrivers, nails and so on. We had nothing else. We went to factories to salvage sheets of scrap metal and iron tubes and we set to work . . . Finally, by a process of trial and error, we succeeded in making kettles and stove-pipes by hand. These products were accepted by the State. That was our first victory. A few ordinary, unskilled housewives helping one another had actually managed, by dint of sheer energy and obstinacy, to manufacture household appliances of a high enough quality for the State to buy . . .[34]

One measure of the very success of the Great Leap in mobilizing women may be the level of fear it generated that family life was threatened. The communal dining rooms were abandoned; so too were many of the crèches, especially in the rural areas, in the wake of the collapse of the movement. Some of the women returned home, but more accepted with more or less resignation that they were going to have to combine outside work with family responsibilities. They got fewer workpoints than men, or, if they worked in a neighbourhood factory, they received none of the benefits – pensions, welfare facilities – of their menfolk in state factories. But they were working; they contributed to the family income; they contributed to the state. They had a place.

In contrast to the Great Leap Forward, the next major upheaval in Chinese policies, the Cultural Revolution of 1966–9, was pre-eminently a revolution of the young against the old, and as such infinitely more destructive of family ties or conventions. For a time, with the schools closed and free passage available on trains or other transport for those 'making the revolution', bands of young people roamed the country, immune to family influence and critical of all authority. Some found partners, and lived together, or married in defiance of the plans or wishes of their parents. Others denounced their families for reactionary tendencies or for belonging to a rival Cultural Revolutionary group. For many of them, 'it sometimes appeared as if being revolutionary was synonymous with being modern, and destroying and rejecting the old was its recurrent corollary'.[35] As they wrecked temples and beat up elderly professors many must have felt, with exhilaration, that the traditional suppression of youth was over at last.

If young people were the major activists in the Cultural Revolution, it was far too remarkable a convulsion not to have had its effect on others, too. Husbands yet again came under pressure. In the village of Liu Ling, Yunnan, despite the presence of a few militant women, meetings had previously been largely attended by men. Now the women enquired why they should not take part in the decision making.

The brigade discussed this a great deal. Then the masses decided that men, too, were under an obligation to do their share of housework. At first some of the men got up and said we simply couldn't make such decisions. To look after children, that was women's work. They were unwilling. They pointed out how children cry for their mummies at nights. They said it wasn't right, for the children's sake, for women to attend meetings while the men sat at home. It wouldn't be good for the children, they said.

Then we women put the question to the brigade: are we, or are we not, to participate in political work? Many discussions followed. We also told the men it would be good for them to learn to look after children. Finally the brigade came to a unanimous opinion: it was decided that when the women go to meetings, the men shall stay at home and look after children. In this way it wouldn't only be men who spoke at meetings and decided things.[36]

Even after order had been restored, the gains made by the young were significant. The People's Liberation Army had been brought in to assist in quelling the disruptions brought about by the Cultural Revolution and during 1967-8 it helped to set up, and then participate in, the new revolutionary committees which were installed as administrative units from the province level downwards. These committees were originally made up of Army personnel, Party cadres and representatives of the masses. Over time, however, the Party's efforts to re-establish itself and to remove the PLA led to revolutionary committees consisting of 'the old, the middle-aged and the young', designed to provide experienced cadre leadership and at the same time build a bridge between the young revolutionaries and the Party. Thus, even after the end of the fighting, the young had a visible, institutionalized presence on the organizing committees of factories and other units, and in the communes and brigades. Exactly how much real power they had and how radical the new committees were is debatable. In a visit to China in 1975, questions at each place visited elicited the information that with a single exception the pre-Cultural Revolution management was the main current revolutionary committee leadership. Nevertheless, the young had a voice and it appears improbable that the voice could have been altogether ignored.

Many families were broken up as an outcome of the Cultural Revolution. Some, especially the families of cadres and intellectuals, were split for a period of one or more years when either husband or wife or both were imprisoned or sent to the countryside for 're-education'. Their children were taken in by family or neighbours. Many more, in the cities, lost a child or children when the latter were posted to work in the countryside on an organized basis following the Cultural Revolution.

Working in the countryside was not new; the idea that city people, and particularly those who did not do manual work, needed to be reminded of the existence of the vast mass of the Chinese peasantry and of the difficulty of peasant life, was a continuing feature of the Chinese revolution. There had been a number of previous movements to send people to the countryside for shorter or longer periods, most notably at the time of the Great Leap Forward. But during the 1970s, the policy of reallocating school-leavers for life to work in the country became a major feature of urban existence.

One reason for it was to reduce the number of young people

in the cities; the urban, educated young had been the prime movers in the Cultural Revolution and nobody was anxious to risk another disturbance on that scale. Equally importantly, the cities themselves were under enormous pressure from increasing numbers, despite tight controls which prevented rural people from shifting to the towns. There were not enough jobs and not enough houses or services to cater for the increasing population. Meanwhile, there was land to be reclaimed, terraced and irrigated, the hope that educated young people could aid the peasants with their skills, and the ideological conviction that at any rate it would be good for them not merely to assist the peasants but to learn from them. An estimated 15 million such young people were relocated.

Some of them settled down in the village and married into peasant families there. Most, it seems, did not. There is, as there has always been, a gulf between the city and the country in China, and between the educated and the peasants. While many young people were willing to spend some years on the farm, and some gave dedicated service there, few were prepared to marry into a peasant family. Girls were slightly more likely to do so than boys, partly because given the traditional Chinese view of the lesser importance of women, marrying down might be somewhat less shocking in the case of a woman. Also, of course, if a girl married a peasant she at least had the peasant's home to go to. If a city boy married a peasant girl, he either had to move into her home in defiance of all convention (the Party occasionally publicized such cases as models, but they remained rare) or to set up house on his own small earnings, without the support of his own family far away in Tianjin or Shanghai, who probably disapproved of the match in any case.

The family might be arbitrarily split, but its influence remained. In 1977-78, 'the word got out that the "down to the countryside" movement was being wound down, and young people all over China began inventing excuses and clambering onto trains to get back to their homes. The Chinese New Year of 1979 gave them a specially good pretext, for it had been accepted practice to let young people visit their families at that time of the year . . . This time, a lot of young people just refused to go back.'[37]

One further campaign, in 1974-5, brought the roles of the family and of women into question. This was the campaign to criticize Confucius and Lin Biao. There have been various explanations of its real nature and purpose but in many areas of the country the criticism of Confucian values, attitudes and beliefs meant, above all, a questioning of the Confucian view of the family and of the authority given to the old, and to the men.

The campaign achieved less dramatic, immediately measurable effects than earlier ones partly because the position of women had in many ways already changed: both in cities and in the country, virtually all women worked, for instance. In addition, after the excesses of the Cultural Revolution many people were a little weary – and wary – of campaigns which brought deep-seated beliefs into question. At best, it gave women and young people additional ammunition to act against tradition, but there may have been only one area, where tradition was under attack from a variety of sources, in which the campaign strongly reinforced those attacks. That area was family size and family planning, whose impact on the family and vice versa are discussed in more detail in the rest of this book.

Following the deaths of Mao and Zhou Enlai and the fall of the Gang of Four, China's new leadership, in the last years of the 1970s, began to experiment with new economic strategies in pursuit of the Four Modernizations – the overall plan to modernize industry, agriculture, science and technology, and the army.

In an effort to increase agricultural production, free markets were introduced through which peasants could sell their products, largely from private plots. Communes were encouraged to make contracts with work teams or individual families, setting a production quota to be met and allowing a profit on the sale of everything above the quota. The amount of land which could be allocated as private plots was increased. Many of the local government functions which the communes undertook are being transferred back to a local government structure. The detailed implementation of these initiatives, and their effects on women and on fertility, are discussed elsewhere in this book. Here, the concern is with the possible implications for the family.

The purpose of these economic initiatives is to give incentives directly related to output, and to encourage families or teams to produce not only more, but a greater variety, of foods for sale. Contracts drawn up with an individual family leave it to that family to decide how they should be met; which probably means a return to greater power by the family head, for he now directs the family labour. The fact that the contract is with the family, unlike the old system of awarding individual workpoints, may mean that income is more liable to be seen as family income, rather than the individual contribution of members of the family. It has been suggested that women members of the family will be encouraged to work at family 'sideline activities' – growing vegetables on the private plot, doing handicrafts and so on – rather than going out to work in rural industry, or participating in mainstream agricultural activities. It has also been suggested that the reduction of services at brigade and commune level will mean fewer opportunities to embark on 'professional' work. Where contracts are made with a work team, it is possible that where such teams tend to follow the old clan structure, they will reinforce it by giving the team more authority and autonomy. Reducing the responsibilities of the commune may lead to less involvement by the ordinary peasant in the processes of local government, and thus to a lessening of the status of women, or the young.

On the other hand, it is possible that the growth of disposable income under the new schemes, and of goods to spend that income on, may mean that the contributions of every family member are more noted and more appreciated and that the value of a daughter, for instance, might therefore increase. It is also conceivable that the transfer of some activities to local government will provide new job opportunities less directly in the control of existing peasant structures and thus potentially more open to women, in particular.

Limitations on Change

The problems of eradicating 'arbitrary and venal marriage' give an indication of the continuing limitations to change in the traditional Chinese family. As we have seen, there has in many ways been a shift of power from the clan to the state, and from the head of the family to all family members. Women, and the young, have gained in economic independence and in decision-making potential both within the family and outside it. But if some of the policies of the Party have weakened old family ties, others have given new strength to the family.

The very large investment in health care and health education has resulted in average life expectancy more than doubling since 1949, so that most people can now expect to live well into their sixties. As a result the three or even four-generation family so beloved in Chinese tradition is for the first time something of a reality. The old, to whom deference and obedience was traditionally required, are around in ever-increasing numbers.

Table 5 Average Size of Household: Guangdong 1977

	Number of Persons	Number of Households	Average Size of Households
Jiang village	147	27	5.44
Number 11 production team	250	55	4.54
Huadong commune	63 200	13 400	4.71
Yue village	585	145	4.03
Renhe commune	73 532	15 568	4.70
Haomei village	480	110	4.40
Dali commune	68 000	15 900	4.30

Source: Croll, 1981.

Household size does not appear to have increased as the result of this demographic revolution (see Table 5). There have, however, been changes in family composition. The oldest son has always tended to establish a separate household when the second son marries, or when he himself produced his own children. The difference now is that there often is a second surviving son, as the result of better health care and nutrition; in the village in Figure 1, an average of 2.5 sons had survived for each mother over the age of forty. Thus, the old distinction between families and households, *jia* and *hu*, has become something of a reality for the peasants. The *jia* may no longer be an economic unit, but beyond a single household there will be other households containing close relatives and normally living very close to each other.

There has been no attempt to move or rearrange rural families. Rural households continue to be grouped in villages, and when the communes were formed, the villages – depending on their size – became either the brigade or the work team. 'Apart from the exchange of women in marriage, there is now little permanent movement between production brigades, teams or villages, and this very important demographic factor encourages a high level of involvement in primary groups.'[38]

Under the 1950 Marriage Law, the old rules on consanguinity were considerably relaxed, and one consequence of this was that people no longer had to look so far afield for a marriage partner. Given that it is still difficult for young people in the countryside to meet each other or conduct a courtship, it is not surprising that most Chinese peasants seem to marry somebody from within the same commune or even the same brigade.

Except for cadres, and certain workers with special skills, most people in China are born, live and die in the same area – in the same commune or town. Migration is strictly controlled, and has been since the late 1950s (see Chapter 2). This means that 'it is in the context of a territorially bounded group of the production team or village that most primary groups are most likely to overlap and have their most continuous influence on individuals and households. Within the same discretely bounded village, neighbours may be kin and friends at the same time.'[39]

At this local level, it also means that most of the cadres or village leaders will also be part of that network of kin and friends. While there are many advantages to such a system, such as a genuine rapport between leaders and led which makes for sensitivity on the part of decision makers to local conditions, it also leads to the situation where an aunt, say, despite her involvement in the Women's Federation, may be very unsympathetic to a nephew's desire to marry in defiance of family wishes. The nephew can no longer leave home, either. If the tensions between him and his parents become so severe as to affect the well-being or the productivity of the team, there may be pressure by all the kin and neighbours to resolve it. Locked in to a family-dominated local community, a young person who wants to do something outside the conventions must either persuade the entire community or submit.

Additionally, the state has been unable to implement or even to attempt a welfare system for the huge Chinese population. Education – except at the tertiary level, health care and provision for old age remain, primarily, the business of the family. 'The concept of mutual aid and support in the traditional Chinese family is as yet still indispensable and plays quite a significant role in the fulfilment of any economic plan.'[40]

This idea of mutual aid, and the inability of the state to provide alternatives, has contributed to family ties even in the cities, where otherwise there was a trend towards simple conjugal families. A lack of crèches has frequently led to one or other mother-in-law being brought from the country, on the birth of the child, to take care of it while its mother is out at work. 'Thus the fact that the mother worked could sometimes strengthen the solidarity between parents and grandparents.'[41] This was true of the 1950s, and it remains true today, when elderly parents remain among the few people entitled to migrate into the urban areas, to join the offspring who will support them.

In the circumstances, it is perhaps more remarkable that the Chinese family has changed as much as it has, than surprising that it has not changed more. Those commentators who saw the Party as determined upon the overthrow of the family were clearly misled; even those who have assumed that current family relationships in China are transitional and will fairly shortly lead to 'modern' marriages and family types may have been wrong. The traditional family has altered; authority and power within it have been somewhat redistributed among its members. But in some ways the institutional grip of the family upon its members, especially in rural areas, has actually tightened. The interventions of the state in family life are limited, until the state begins to take over more of those functions for which the family is as yet essential. Until recently, the state accepted the limitations of its influence in family life, preferring to attempt to alter 'feudal' relationships and behaviour through education and persuasion rather than through direct intervention. In the late 1970s, however, concerned with the effects of population growth in China's development, it began to intervene very strongly in one of the most basic aspects of family life: reproduction. As a consequence it has had to consider other interventions as ambitious as the introduction of pension schemes, and has also had to consider family policies as a priority equal to, though sometimes conflicting with, economic policies. The implications of this change in the relationship between the family and the state are the subject of much of the remainder of this book.

Notes

1. Yang, C. K., *Chinese Communist Society: The Family and the Village,* MIT Press, Massachusetts Institute of Technology, 1959.

2. Lang, Olga, *Chinese Family and Society,* Yale University Press, 1946.

3. Hsu, Francis L. K., *Under the Ancestors' Shadow: Chinese Culture and Personality,* Colombia University Press, 1948.

4. Brugger, William, 'The male (and female) in Chinese Society', *Impact of Science on Society,* vol. XXI,. no. 1, 1971, pp.5-19.

5. Mao Zedong, 'Report of an Investigation into the Peasant Movement in Hunan' quoted in Schram, Stuart, *The Political Thought of Mao Tse-tung,* Penguin Books, 1969.

6. Yang, C. K., op.cit.

7. Yang, C. K., op.cit.

8. Croll, Elisabeth, *The Politics of Marriage in Contemporary China,* Cambridge University Press, 1981.

9. Yang, C. K., op.cit.

10. Legge, James, *The Chinese Classics,* vol. IV, London, 1871, pp.306-7.

11. Lang, O., op.cit.

12. Croll, E., 1981, op.cit.

13. Davin, Delia, *Woman-work: Women and the Party in Revolutionary China,* Clarendon Press, 1976.

14. Davin, Delia, 'Women in the Liberated Areas' in Young, Marilyn S., *Women in China,* Michigan Papers No. 15, 1973.

15. 'Decisions of the Central Committee of the Chinese Communist Party on woman-work at present in the countryside of the liberated areas' (1948) in Davin, D., 1976, op.cit.

16. Hinton, William, *Fanshen,* Monthly Review Press, 1966.

17. Hinton, William, op.cit.

18. Marriage Law of the PRC 1950, quoted in Meijer, M. J., *Marriage Law and Policy in the Chinese People's Republic,* Hong Kong University Press, 1971.

19. Meijer, M. J., op.cit.

20. Croll, E. 1981, op.cit.

21. Myrdal, Jan, *Report from a Chinese Village,* Heinemann, 1965.

22. Tan Manni, 'Why New Marriage Law was Necessary', *China Reconstructs,* March 1981, pp. 17-23.

23. Quoted in Croll, 1981, op.cit.

24. Davin, D., 1976, op.cit.

25. Pan Yunkang and Pan Naiqu, 'Urban Family Structures and their Changes – a survey of a Tianjiu neighbourhood', *Bejing Review,* 28 February 1983, pp. 25-9.

26. Quoted in Meijer, op.cit.

27. Zhong Xiu, 'You should Value your Marriage', *Women of China,* No. 5, 1979.

28. Tan, M., op.cit.

29. Tan, M., op.cit.

30. Tan, M., op.cit.

31. Kang Keqing, 'Conscientiously study, actively disseminate and implement the new marriage law', *Survey of World Broadcasts,* 23 September 1980.

32. Kang Keqing, op.cit.

33. Kahn-Ackerman, Michael, *Within the Outer Gate,* Marco Polo Press, 1982.

34. Broyelle, Claudie, *Women's Liberation in China,* Harvester Press, 1977.

35. Wang Gungwu, *China and the World Since 1949,* Macmillan, 1977.

36. Myrdal, Jan and Kessle, G., *China: The Revolution Continued,* Pelican Books, 1973.

37. Bonavia, David, *The Chinese,* Allen Lane, 1980.

38. Croll, 1981, op.cit.

39. Croll, 1981, op.cit.

40. Meijer, op.cit.

41. Davin, D., 1976, op.cit.

CHAPTER TWO

CHINA'S POPULATION AND THE DEVELOPMENT OF POPULATION POLICIES

★★★

The History of Chinese Population

China is unique among the countries of the world in having made attempts to count its population for at least the past four thousand years. The first population count mentioned in Chinese histories is said to have taken place in some very remote period: perhaps around 2000 BC. Nothing beside the references to it remains. During the Zhou dynasty (1050-247 BC) the registration of people, and counts of those registered, became a routine part of the administration, although the data fragments which have been handed down from these early counts are too confused to tell much to a historical demographer.

From the time of the Western Han dynasty, however the records are somewhat better. Unfortunately, although the statistics appear in the table to give precise counts they are far from reliable (see Table 6). Moreover, the area that was included within the Chinese borders changed from time to time, so that the figures are not strictly comparable with those of modern China. At different periods, particularly when the government was weak, under-reporting reached massive pro-

46

portions. Various categories of people, such as women and female children, or minority peoples, were often left out of the count, and it is not always clear which groups were excluded from any particular count. As a result, there is much argument on the part of those who have studied the statistics about what they really suggest.

Table 6 Reported Population Totals: China AD 2-1901

Period	Year (AD)	Population
Western Han (Emperor Pingdi)	2	59,594,978
Eastern Han (Emperor Huandi)	156	50,066,856
Three Kingdoms	220-280	7,672,881
Western Jin (Emperor Wudi)	280	16,163,863
Sui (Emperor Yangdi)	606	46,019,956
Tang (Emperor Xuanzong)	742	48,909,809
Song (Emperor Huizong)	1110	46,734,784
Yuan (Emperor Shizu)	1290	58,834,711
Ming (Emperor Taizu)	1393	60,545,812
Qing (Emperor Shizu)	1661	21,068,609
Qing (Emperor Gaozong)	1757	190,348,328
Qing (Emperor Dezong)	1901	426,447,325

Source: Durand, John C., 1960 and Liu Zheng, 1979.

Nevertheless, there are some broad areas of agreement. It appears that during the Han dynasty (206 BC-220 AD), the population of China reached some 60 million. Until the Song dynasty (980-1223) the population probably fluctuated around a long term level of 40-50 million; the numbers of deaths varied wildly depending on the political situation and natural calamities. Over the period of about a thousand years 'there were too few periods of prosperity and stability to allow any long-term population increase'.[1]

From the beginning of the Song dynasty the trend is towards a gradual increase in population. Song dynasty reports give a household size of 1.4 to 2.5 people, presumably ignoring all females and perhaps some males, so that the exact amount of growth assumed depends on what assumption is also made on household size. Some authors suggest that in the eleventh century the population doubled to over 120 million as the result of a long period of peace, irrigation works which improved crop yield and minimized the effects of natural disasters like drought, as well as increased Chinese settlement in the fertile south. If, however, the population really did rise to over 100 million, then the period of rule under the Mongols, and the Yuan dynasty they set up (1280-1368), saw a serious decrease in China's population resulting from warfare and plague. Reported statistics during this period are more than usually defective, so that it is impossible to say with confidence anything other than that the population did not grow markedly during that dynasty.

The first emperor of the Ming dynasty (1368-1644) attempted to introduce more reliable reporting, with a census-like count which included listing the age, sex and occupation of each person. A system of grouping every eleven households into *jia* and grouping every ten of those *jia* into *li* made it possible for permanent household registers to be established. Unfortunately, it seems that the registers were seldom up-dated, or looked at, and the reports sent in to the Ming emperors merely repeated each other. No attempt was made to revise them and the consensus of historical demographers appears to be that the records are virtually useless after about 1400. There also seems to be agreement that the population increased slightly over time until the early years of the seventeenth century, when a series of wars, droughts and famines affected it. The records show a fall in the number of people from around 60 million to a mere 20 million (see Table 6) but most Western scholars assume only a slight fall, or even a slight increase (see Table 7).

The last Chinese dynasty was the Qing, ruling between 1644 and 1911. For the first hundred years of Qing rule, the statistics continue to be virtually unusable, but from 1741 population data were based on a refined version of the household grouping system. Called *baojia*, it has been described as: 'an ingenious mechanism for the execution of central policies at local levels, the maintenance of social stability, and the preservation of order and legality'.[2] Ten households formed a *pai* under the control of a *paizhang*, ten *pai* a *jia* under the control of a *jiazhang*, and ten *jia* a *bao* under the control of a *baozhang*. The differing levels of *zhang* were mutually responsible. The more obvious duties involved reports to the local officials of the Qing on the harbouring of criminals, gang activities, or the presence of strangers. However, it was the control of population in a more subtle sense that was the major contribution of the *baojia* organization to the operation of the vast Qing empire. Permanent domicile determined such critical matters as the payment of taxes and the allocation of quotas for the imperial examinations. Furthermore, the social class allocation of the household in the *baojia* placards and registers could not be changed casually.

The *baojia* system was abolished with the revolution of 1911, and reinstituted by the Nationalists in the 1930s when it became the pervasive system for local administration, protection against guerrillas, labour recruitment and population statistics. The post-1949 Communist government replaced the system with its own local-level administrative system of cadres and Party members.

The Qing officials who were supposed to collate the *baojia* totals and report them to the emperor appear to have been no more enthusiastic about the task than were their Ming predecessors. Once they had a figure on which to work, they simply added a more or less arbitrary number to that total or

Table 7 China Proper: Emended Series of Population Statistics, AD 2-1953

Dynasty	Year (AD)	Population
Western Han	2	71,000,000
Eastern Han	88	43,000,000
	105	53,000,000
	125	56,000,000
	140	56,000,000
	156	62,000,000
Sui	606	54,000,000
Tang	705	37,000,000
	726	41,000,000
	732	45,000,000
	742	51,000,000
	755	52,000,000
Song	1014	60,000,000
	1029	61,000,000
	1048	64,000,000
	1065	77,000,000
	1075	94,000,000
	1086	108,000,000
	1094	115,000,000
	1103	123,000,000
Song-Qin	1193-1195	123,000,000
Ming	1381	60,000,000
	1393	61,000,000
Qing	1751	207,000,000
	1781	270,000,000
	1791	294,000,000
	1811	347,000,000
	1821	344,000,000
	1831	383,000,000
	1841	400,000,000
	1851	417,000,000

Source: Durand, John C., 1960.

assumed a rate of growth each year. Whenever the emperor complained about these practices, many officials just upped the figures to imply greater population growth in a situation of rising prosperity. Under the *baojia* system, population totals rose from 143 million in 1741 to 432 million in 1851. Although the growth in total population looks dramatic, it implies a rate of increase of only around 1 per cent a year.

Much of Western Europe, which was also going through a period of growth between those dates, had rates which are not dissimilar to China's. Neither in Europe nor in China were growth rates in any way comparable to those seen in the developing world – including China – in the second half of the twentieth century. These have been of the order of 2 or 3 per cent a year. A growth rate of 2 per cent gives a population doubling time of thirty-five years.

While the Qing figures themselves are far from accurate, it is universally agreed that the later period of the dynasty was by the standards of the time one of considerable population growth, and that this growth took place most dramatically during the exceptionally peaceful and disaster-free period of the eighteenth century. (A revision of China's population statistics undertaken by one eminent Western demographer is given in Table 7).

Historical Views of China's Population

Until the revolution of 1911, mainstream perceptions of the Chinese population were that its size was an advantage, and that any increase in size was a sign of prosperity and a guarantee of China's power. There were exceptions to this viewpoint. One poet who lived about 500 BC commented on a contemporary boom in population:

In ancient times
People they were few and wealthy and without strife
People at present think five sons are not too many
and each son has five sons also, and before the death of the grandfather
there are already twenty-five descendants.

Therefore, people are more and the wealth is less;
they work hard and receive little.
The life of a nation depends on having enough food,
not upon the number of people.[3]

Contemporary with the English author of that major work on the theory of population, Thomas Malthus, was Hong Liangzhi (1744-1809), a Chinese scholar, whose essays contained grim warnings of the dangers of population increase. Hong was deeply pessimistic about the possibilities of doing anything about the problems he foresaw. Like Malthus he believed that a population growing at a geometric rate would outstrip the more slowly growing rate of food production. But while Malthus believed that the natural checks of war, famine and disease were the fundamental controls on population growth, and suggested late marriage and 'restraint' as alternatives to them, Hong Liangzhi saw that natural checks seldom counterbalanced the birth rate and had no alternative solutions to offer:

Does Heaven know a remedy? Flood and drought, plague and pestilence are what nature offers as remedies, though the percentage that die in natural calamities rarely exceeds one or two-tenths of the population.

Do emperors and state officials possess remedies? They can see to it that there is no uncultivated land and no unused labour in the realm. When land is reclaimed they can move people on to it to cultivate there. When taxation is unduly heavy, they may lighten it according to ancient precedent. They can forbid luxurious living and suppress speculation in land. In the case of flood, drought and plague they can open granaries and allow the treasury to relieve the masses. But that is all there is as to the remedies that could possibly be put into effect by the emperor and the state officials.

In short, in a long reign of peace, the emperor and his officials can neither stop human reproduction, nor are the measures they do dispose of adequate to provide the people with sustenance – no more at least than what we have stated.[4]

His essays were published in 1798; the same year that Malthus published his own theory, *An Essay on the Principle of Population*, in which he asserted that China had 60 per cent more population than the food resources could comfortably support.

However, Hong Liangzhi, like his poetical predecessor, was exceptional. On the whole, and especially after the coming of the Ming dynasty, a growing population was regarded as inherently desirable:

By the sixteenth century . . . there had developed a growing unreality in Chinese perceptions of all foreign nations. The limiting nature of the neo-Confucian language of politics and history had induced the Chinese leaders to foster views about China's centricity which must necessarily be the source of myth. What was beginning to take root was the idea of an invulnerable China, strong because of its cultural superiority, rich because of its large population, and self-sufficient because of its extensive cultivated lands. This myth reached its climax during the Manchu Qing dynasty (1644-1911) . . .[5]

In the second half of the nineteenth century, as the dynasty tottered, rebellions spread, and Western incursions into China proliferated, that myth was put under increasing strain. It was, however, easy to argue that what China needed was greater strength and greater numbers, in order to preserve its cultural superiority against a greedy world.

1911-1949: Population Issues

How large a population China had at the time of the 1911 Revolution was unknown. A first attempt at a more modern enumeration of the people, in 1907, was a failure; so too were the Republican government's effort in 1912 and the Nationalist one in 1928. Since neither government had the administrative apparatus necessary for a national consensus, and the period was one of political upheaval, the results of each of the two counts were defective and unreliable. Estimates made on the basis of small-scale samples were extremely varied. Some believed China's population had actually shrunk by the 1940s to around 350 million; others thought it might be as high as 600 million. The League of Nations used a rough estimate of 450 million for the whole of the time between the two world wars; the Nationalists in the 1940s assumed a figure of 475 million.

One Chinese demographer, writing in 1933, observed:

Many prominent scholars believe that China's population is not increasing and perhaps is even decreasing, and that China will have no problem of over-population at least until the time the unsettled area, especially in the north-west, is occupied. In general, there is a common opinion among most of the middle-class people of China, that the population of the other races and nations is increasing more rapidly than their own. Therefore a higher birth rate must be advocated or extinction will result.[6]

This was very much the view to which Sun Yat-sen had come around. In the 1890s, his writings included a number of statements on China's over-population relative to land and resources. At that time, it appears, he believed that the population was around 400 million. On reading a study by the American Minister to China in 1904, William Rockhill, which tentatively concluded that China contained only some 300 million, Sun Yat-sen began to consider the country's population decline as a dangerous symptom of 'racial extinction'. Looking at the growing size of other countries, he trembled for the future of China. The only reason that encroaching nations had not yet seized the country was that their populations were still smaller than China's. But given trends as he believed them to be, he predicted that in a hundred years 'China will not only lose her sovereignty but she will perish, the Chinese people will be assimilated and the race will disappear.'[7]

Even that early enthusiast for birth control, Chen Da (see Chapter 3), believed that China was only growing very slowly, at about 0.5 per cent a year. He pointed out, however, that this slow growth – unlike that of Western European countries – was the result of high birth rates being almost matched by high death rates. 'A quite different set of causes has been in operation, such as poverty and illiteracy, the lack of medical progress and public health, a low standard of living of the masses, and the absence of birth control.'[8] Chen Da was a member of the Committee for the Study of Population

Policies, set up in 1941 during the Sino-Japanese war, which concluded:

Facing poverty, ignorance, and the low living standards of the masses, the country should not and cannot encourage unconditional and universal increase of population. Increase should occur only where the individuals, as parents, are physically fit and mentally sound, where the families are able to give the children proper care and training, and where the social surroundings are favorable. The parents, after careful consideration of the interest of the family and of the community, may decide for themselves as to the proper number of children they should bring up. In addition, the number of children may also vary with the skill and income of the parents, as well as with the folkways and social wealth of the community. Thus viewed, some individuals may have children, others not; some communities may have population increase, others not. A differential rate of increase will therefore have to be worked out between individuals, classes and communities in the interests of all the parties concerned. Broadly speaking, such views are substantially in agreement with the theory of optimum population as first expounded in England and widely advocated of late in other regions of the world.[9]

The committee also called for better research into population issues, including eugenics; sex education; monogamous families with free-choice marriages; the social and economic development of minority peoples; and the encouragement of mixed marriages between the Han Chinese and the minorities to increase the population of the border areas.

The Revolutionary Government: Population and Policy

So far as questions of China's population size and growth rates were concerned, there seems little reason to doubt that the Communist Party and the government in 1949 shared the prevailing opinions about China's vulnerability and low growth rate. They were deeply distrustful of Western assessments of China's population, which many considered not merely overlooked the potential transformation of China's productive forces under socialism, but were open to a sinister interpretation.

Something of the flavour of their suspicion can be caught in the later reminiscences of Chen Changhen. In 1957, this former high official in the Nationalist regime took part in a seminar on population in Shanghai. He recalled:

[During the last reign] of the Qing dynasty, the Ministry of Civil Affairs conducted a census. Later, Rockwell, the American minister to China, sent his counsellor to get this set of preliminary figures from the Department of Interior of the Peking Government, and placed the number of households at about 70,000,000 in the nation as a whole . . . Rockwell thereupon arbitrarily multiplied this by 4, which he assumed to be the average size of the Chinese household, to obtain a total national population of 280,000,000. But, Walter Wilcox, Professor of Population Statistics of Cornell University, United States of America, borrowed the result of the 1920 U.S. Census that showed the average household size to be 4.8 in America and multiplied this by the number of households in China to place China's population at 300,000,000 at the end of the Qing. Actually, both Rockwell and Wilcox deliberately underestimated the total size of the Chinese population. The reason for this was that the United States was much opposed to Japanese immigration to Hawaii and mainland America: they therefore deliberately underestimated the total size of China's population in the hope that Japan would redirect its immigrants and aggression toward China. The year before the 18 September 1930 Incident, the Japanese Imperial Government invited the International Statistical Association to hold its annual conference in Tokyo. Wilcox attended the conference. At the meetings, various Japanese population statisticians presented papers of a more or less same vein to indicate how serious the Japanese population problem was . . . '[10]

Given this suspicion of Western motives, it was perhaps unfortunate that in August 1949 the United States government released a document on United States Relations with China with Special Reference to the Period 1944-1949, accompanied by a letter of transmittal by Dean Acheson, then Secretary of State. Towards the end of his covering letter, Acheson wrote:

Two factors have played a major role in shaping the destiny of modern China.

The population of China during the eighteenth and nineteenth centuries doubled, thereby creating an unbearable pressure upon the land. The first problem which the Chinese government has had to face is that of feeding this population. So far none has succeeded. The Kuomintang [Nationalists] attempted to solve it by putting many land-reform laws on the statute books. Some of these laws have failed, others have been ignored. In no small measure, the predicament in which the National Government finds itself today is due to its failure to provide China with enough to eat. A large part of the Chinese Communist propaganda consists of promises that they will solve the land problem.

The second major factor which has shaped the pattern of contemporary China is the impact of the West and of Western ideas . . .

By the beginning of the twentieth century, the combined force of the overpopulation and new ideas set in motion that chain of events which can be called the Chinese revolution. It is one of the most imposing revolutions in recorded history and its outcome and consequences are yet to be foreseen.[11]

Chinese leaders, one authority noted, repeatedly referred to this letter with 'unusual repugnance and bitterness' in subsequent years.[12] One of its more immediate effects, however, was to provoke a reply by Mao Zedong in the form of an unsigned article in the *People's Daily*:

Do revolutions arise from overpopulation? There have been many revolutions, ancient and modern, in China and abroad; were they all due to overpopulation? Were China's many revolutions in the past few thousand years also due to overpopulation? Was the American revolution against Britain 174 years ago also due to overpopulation? Acheson's knowledge of history is nil. He has not even read the American Declaration of Independence . . . The Russians made the February revolution and the October revolution because of oppression and exploitation by the Tsar and the Russian bourgeoisie, not because of any overpopulation, for to this day in Russia there is a great abundance of land as compared with people. In Mongolia, where land is so vast and the population so sparse, a revolution would be inconceivable according to Acheson's line of reasoning, yet it took place some time ago . . .

According to Acheson, China has no way out at all. A population of

475 million constitutes an 'unbearable pressure' and, revolution or no revolution, the case is hopeless . . .

It is true that 'so far none has succeeded?' In the old Liberated Areas in Northwestern, Northern, Northeastern and Eastern China, where the land problem has already been solved, does the problem of 'feeding this population', as Acheson puts it, still exist? The United States has kept quite a number of spies or so-called observers in China. Why have they not ferreted out even this fact? In places like Shanghai, the problem of unemployment, or of feeding the population, arose solely because of cruel, heartless oppression and exploitation by imperialism, feudalism, bureaucrat-capitalism and the reactionary Kuomintang government. Under the People's Government it will take only a few years for this problem of unemployment, or of feeding the population, to be solved as completely as in the Northern, Northeastern and other parts of the country.

It is a very good thing that China has a large population. Even if China's population multiplies many times, she is fully capable of finding a solution: the solution is production. The absurd argument of western bourgeois economists, like Malthus, that increase in population cannot keep pace with increase in production was not only thoroughly refuted in theory by Marxists long ago, but has also been completely exploded by the realities in the Soviet Union and the Liberated areas of China after their revolutions. Basing itself on the truth that revolution plus production can solve the problem of feeding the population, the Central Committee of the Communist Party of China has issued orders to Party organizations and the People's Liberation Army throughout the country not to dismiss but to retain all former Kuomintang personnel, provided they can make themselves useful and are not confirmed reactionaries or notorious scoundrels . . .

Of all things in the world, people are the most precious. Under the leadership of the Communist Party, as long as there are people, every kind of miracle can be performed. We are refuters of Acheson's counter-revolutionary theory. We believe that revolution can change everything, and that before long there will arise a new China with a big population and a great wealth of products, where life will be abundant and culture will flourish. All pessimistic views are utterly groundless.[13]

A more detailed refutation of those Western scholars who

were 'extremely pessimistic about China's ability to solve its population problem' was published by Chang Chih-i in December 1949. Chang, too, revealed an underlying suspicion of the motives for such interpretations:

Existing theories of overpopulation should be re-examined because of the misuse to which some of them have been put. Japanese militarists, it will be recalled, once invoked the theory of overpopulation to justify invasion of their continental neighbor, a country that can hardly be considered less 'overpopulated' than Japan. It suited their purposes largely to ignore possibilities of alleviating internal pressure by an attack on the problem of tenancy.[14]

He believed that the poverty of the Chinese was not caused by pressure on available land, but resulted from 'the social disequilibrium caused by the failure of productive techniques to keep pace with mounting needs' and that 'Rapid industrialization, together with modernization and eventual mechanization of agriculture, will raise the standard of living and thus, after the initial period of adjustment, effect a marked decline in the birth rate. The spectre of over-population will then cease to haunt China.'

If the note of xenophobia running through such statements appears to be somewhat strong, it is important to remember that at this period the government had taken over a country racked by years of internal strife and war with Japan; that the United States was still supporting the Nationalist claims from Taiwan; and that a mere handful of countries outside the Eastern European bloc were showing willingness to recognize the new government. (Burma and India did so in December 1949 and ten more countries, including Britain, the Scandinavian countries, Pakistan, Afghanistan and Ceylon in January 1950.)

The other consistent theme in such statements is the orthodox Marxist view of the relationship between people and production. This orthodoxy was the perhaps inevitable outcome of the past relationship of the Chinese Communist Party to the Comintern, and to the tradition of Russian advisers and Russian training of Chinese Party members, now much intensified as China's policy of 'leaning to one side' in international relationships brought the country closer to Russia, seen as the leader of world revolution. Mao Zedong later summed up this reliance on Soviet dogmatism: 'In economic work, dogmatism primarily manifested itself in heavy industry, planning, banking and statistics . . . Since we didn't understand these things and had absolutely no experience all we could do in our ignorance was to import foreign methods . . . our statistical work was practically a copy of Soviet work . . . The same applied to our public health work . . .' [15] Planning, statistics and public health were all areas which touched heavily on demography and population issues.

Following the Soviet lead involved, among other things, the abolition of departments and courses in sociology, political science and economics in 1952, when the curriculum of institutions of higher learning was reorganized. It was mainly within the context of such departments and courses that the early Chinese demographers had worked. From their later criticisms, it appears that scholars with a knowledge of demography or population issues were excluded from any significant role in the preparation of the 1953 Census.

There is a single tantalizing but unconfirmed report that in one instance Mao did refuse to follow the Soviet line – or at least, the suggestions of Stalin. A report in Taiwan claimed that in the original versions of Mao's 'On the Correct Handling of Contradictions Among the People' and another intra-Party document entitled 'The Problem of Birth Limitation' Mao remarked that when he first visited the Soviet Union in 1950 'Stalin advised that China had too large a population.'

While a large population has its contribution to the socialist construction, it will devour socialism if not handled appropriately. At the time he intended to implement a birth control program to cope with the population problem. But he did not take any measure at the time because he wanted to emphasize that the abundant population of the Sino-Soviet bloc was a guarantee of an eternal world peace and because it was during the Anti-American and Aid-to-Korean period. [16]

An early priority for the new government, however, was to discover what the population of China actually was. In 1953, the first modern census was carried out, and the initial results were announced in late 1954 (see Table 8).

Table 8 Total Chinese Population (Statistical Bureau) 1 Nov. 1954

Total population on the mainland by direct census registration	574,205,940
Estimates for border regions and other (minority nationality) areas where no elections and census took place	8,397,477
Taiwan (Formosa) according to figures published by the Nationalist government in 1951	7,591,298
Chinese settled overseas including students studying abroad, according to the Commission of Overseas Chinese Affairs	11,743,320
Total Chinese population (in the world)	601,938,035
Total population of the People's Republic of China (mainland)	582,603,417

Source: Chandrasekhar, S., 1960.

Table 9 Age Structure of China's Population 1953

Age Group	% Distribution
0-4	15.6%
5-9	11.0%
10-17	14.5%
0-17	41.1%
18-49	45.4%
50+	13.5%
All ages	100.0%

Source: Chandrasekhar, S., 1960.

The age structure of this population, with more than 40 per cent of the people under the age of eighteen (see Table 9), was typical for a country with high birth and death rates and low life expectancy.

The figure of 583 million for the total Chinese population, excluding Taiwan, was greeted with official approval. The *People's Daily* published an editorial with the heading 'Six Hundred Million People – a Great Strength for Socialist Construction'. Abroad, the result attracted more disbelief than anything else. The total number of people reported was so different from previous estimates by foreign specialists that many found it impossible to accept. It seemed to them inherently unlikely that a country so vast, which had suffered years of administrative disorder, civil war and war with Japan, could possibly have organized a census at all. Their scepticism was not dispelled by the information which gradually became available about how the Census had been conducted. Although it used a firm date for recording the population, namely 30 June 1953, it had been conducted over a year because there were not enough trained people to undertake a count all at once. It asked only five questions of the head of the household: full name and address, the relation of other household members to the family head, their sex, age and nationality. There were weaknesses in the design and handling of the data. An obvious one was the danger of over- or under-counting because of the difficulties of defining a household: each head was asked to report all family members regardless of their actual residence. (The State Statistical Bureau later explained that they had been forced to ask census questions this way 'because of the strong feelings of the traditional Chinese family ties'.[17]) A further problem was the reporting of age, for traditional Chinese reckoning of age makes the child a year old at birth, and from then on additional years are added each lunar New Year. Girl children tended to be under-reported because of their insignificance; boys might also be under-reported because of traditional Chinese fears that to indicate one's good fortune in having a son simply invited disaster. The data themselves were aggregated at three successive levels – the county, provincial and national levels – which compounded the possibility of errors.

Nevertheless, although the procedures were open to criticism, and both some Chinese and Western demographers believed that there might be a margin of error on all the statistics, most people eventually came to accept that a census had been carried out in China and that its results broadly reflected the population. Only a few eminent Western demographers continued to deny that there had ever been a field enumeration or a controlled registration of the whole population.

Today, much of the debate about the reliability of the Census figures seems somewhat academic. Perhaps the most important point which may be noted is that if, as one expert has suggested, the birth, death and growth rates for the 1950s, based on the 1953 Census and other registers, are too low, then 'China's progress in reducing fertility and mortality in subsequent years may actually have been underestimated'.[18]

Until 1958 the Chinese continued to release a little data from the Census, together with vital rates. (The total population and vital rates for the years 1949 to 1957 are given in Table 10).

Table 10 Population Totals and Vital Rates, China 1949-57

Year	Population – year end	Population – Census	Births per 1000	Deaths per 1000	Rate of natural increase per 1000
1949	541,670		36	20	16
1950	551,960		37	18	19
1951	563,000		37	17	20
1952	574,820		37	17	20
1953	587,960	582,603	37	14	23
1954	602,660		37.97	13.18	24.79
1955	614,650		32.60	12.28	20.32
1956	628,280		31.9	11.4	20.5
1957	646,530		34.03	10.80	23.23

Source: Aird, John S., 1982.
Note: These figures are from recent Chinese sources. They do not entirely correspond to the figures presented in 1960 by Chandrasekhar.

Statistics for the years before the Census may have been partially derived from what remained of the *baojia* registration system, but are thought to be largely estimated; they should thus be regarded with some caution. As has been noted, vital rates may well be on the low side because of under-reporting of both births and deaths, particularly the latter. It was not until 1955 that the State Council first issued a directive on the establishment of a regular household registration system. In January 1958 the 'Population and Household Registration Regulation of the People's Republic of China' was enacted, transferring administrative responsibility for registration from the Ministry of the Interior to the Ministry of Public Security.

The inherent strength of the registration system, compared with that of other countries, has been described as lying in:

. . . its integration with the rural collective economy and system of state employment, which, one way and another, touches virtually the entire population. Only through registration can one be legally part of a collective and partake of its economic benefits – grain allocations, private plots, cotton and other rations. Unlike other countries where registration defines legal residence, in China it defines livelihood as well . . . But the linkage between registration and the availability of economic benefits provided by the team, such as rations and private plots, is probably not as strict as intended because such internal allocations are decided by the team.[19]

There are economic disincentives to the registration of a death, and often delays in registering births. During the 1950s, as the systems were gradually introduced, errors and under-reporting were not uncommon.

Family-Planning Policy: the First Years

Apart from the concern for family health, which was a frequent subject of discussion in the 1930s and 1940s, there is no available evidence that the Communists had considered the provision of family-planning services prior to 1949. By August 1953, however, the Ministry of Health had been instructed by the State Council to help the masses to control reproduction, and the State Council had approved the Ministry's 'Revised Regulations on Contraception and Induced Abortion'. As has been pointed out, this implies that there had been earlier regulations in existence, and the work of revising them must have taken some time, so that it is reasonable to assume that agreement about the need to offer contraception was reached quite clearly in the life of the new government.

The primary reason for the government's acceptance of family planning seems to have been its benefits for maternal and child health, and possibly the greater opportunities it offered for women's development. Maternal and child welfare was certainly the primary argument put forward by Shao Lizu at the first meeting of the National People's Congress in 1954. While castigating Malthusian ideas, and reiterating that it 'is a good thing to have a large population' he did add that 'in an environment beset with difficulties, it appears that a limit should be set . . . If a child continues to be born to a mother every year even if she is no longer medically fit or when her burden has already proved too much for her, even if we disregard the sufferings of the mothers, it is no easy job for the state to place all the mothers under its protection.'[20]

A symposium on birth control was called by Liu Shaoqi in December of the same year, and resulted in the State Council designating responsible officials from various government departments to study the question of family planning and recommend ways of promoting it. Following this the Central Committee of the Chinese Communist Party announced in March 1955: 'Under the present historical circumstances and in the interests of the nation, the family, and the new generation, our Party seconds the proposition that reproduction be appropriately restricted.'[21] Zhou Enlai reported to the Eighth National Congress of the Party a year later that 'to protect women and children, and bring up and educate our younger generation in a way conducive to the health and prosperity of nations, we agree that a measure of birth control is necessary.'[22]

As maternal and child health facilities were established in the mid-1950s, at first mainly in urban areas, contraceptive advice was given along with the other services. Publicity, though largely restricted to written materials, emphasized the health benefits of family planning. The campaign was, in contrast to other health campaigns, a fairly low-key one, for a number of reasons.

First, it appears from careful analysis of family planning as a political issue that not all the policy makers were convinced that family planning was a suitable business for the state to involve itself with. At that time, only a handful of governments throughout the world were prepared to provide family-planning services. Contraception was a sensitive subject everywhere, as reports to the Health Ministry on the first campaign made clear:

Judging from the reports handed in, the main obstacle blocking the progress of birth control stemmed primarily from the lack of understanding of the important meaning of this program and the benefits of birth control to home and country on the part of leadership cadres in some places, as well as their disbelief in the possibility of extensively propagating birth control, with the result that this topic had not been put on the agenda. Although many of the masses, including cadres, felt the need for controlling births, they thought that matters concerning both sexes should not be brought up for discussion in public. They therefore would not talk about contraceptives and birth control. Nor would they learn skills and buy devices. This tendency must be reversed . . . [23]

Secondly, there was a shortage of contraceptives. To increase their supply and to 'provide preferential treatment' with a 'view to their general price reduction', imported contraceptive chemicals and devices were exempted from import and other taxes in 1957. In early 1958 it was stated that the local supply was only sufficient to meet the needs of just over 2 per cent of all couples in the child-bearing ages. Such contraceptives as there were had limitations: caps are seldom popular in overcrowded homes without sanitation; the oral contraceptive only went on general distribution in the West in 1960 (although the Chinese soon began to develop their own) and methods of male and female steriliza-tion were less sophisticated than they are today. Apart from condoms, the IUD was the one reliable and acceptable method available but it required insertion by a trained person, under hygienic conditions, and in rural areas in particular there was a lack of clinics and trained staff. There were, until 1957, restrictions on male and female sterilization which was only permitted to couples who had six or more children. Abortion regulations were liberalized in the same year, but initially the new rules were applied with caution and considerable reservations on the part of many policy makers and doctors.

In an attempt to cope with the shortage of contraceptives and to offer additional methods, as well as to integrate contraception along with other areas of modern medicine into Chinese tradition, the Ministry of Health began to collect recipes for traditional methods of fertility control. Shao Lizu applauded this initiative in a speech to the Third Session of the First National People's Congress in 1956, and quoted one method which might repay study:

Fresh tadpoles coming out in the spring should be washed clean in cold boiled-water, and swallowed whole three or four days after menstruation. If a woman swallows fourteen live tadpoles on the first day and ten more on the following day, she will not conceive for five years. If contraception is still required after that, she can repeat the formula twice, and be forever sterile.[24]

Widely reported outside China as a subject of comedy, the speech nevertheless marked an early effort to study systematically the possible value of indigenous contraceptives. Volunteers who tried out the various techniques were offered abortion if they became pregnant. Sadly, it appears that none of the traditional methods proved a useful addition to the range of fertility control techniques available.

Finally, it proved impossible to separate entirely the issue of contraception for maternal and child health from the issue of China's numbers. The latter issue was politically sensitive not only because orthodox Russian-dominated Marxism explicitly rejected the concept of population growth impeding development, but because of China's past and its current political preoccupations. In September 1954 the South-East Asian Treaty Organization had been established. Three months later the United States signed a mutual defence treaty with Taiwan. It was the time of the Cold War. Many countries still refused to recognize the Chinese government, and the Americans put considerable pressure on their allies and trading partners to refuse to trade with China. In such circumstances the beleaguered Chinese too easily equated strength with size, including population size.

Nevertheless, the concept of planned management of people had, during the 1950s, gained acceptance as part of overall socialist planning. Between 1949 and 1958, some 1,380,000 people were resettled in China's north-east and north-west provinces and in Inner Mongolia. They were encouraged and subsidized to go there partly to reclaim marginal land, which was done to the tune of some 9 million *mu* (a million and a half acres) a year over a ten-year period; partly to strengthen the border areas and promote conditions which would improve the development prospects of the various minorities; and partly to relieve what was seen as a population imbalance between the crowded eastern portion of the country and the rest. At the same time, China's cities expanded by about 35,350,000 between 1949 and 1967. Some of this growth was through the development of new towns and cities brought about by efforts to diversify the highly concentrated industrial centres of the country. City growth was, at least initially, seen as a matter for pride: as part of the attempt to develop and modernize China and to create an industrial nation. Even in this context, though, uncontrolled migration to the towns by under-employed peasants was frowned upon, and the rural areas were urged to develop small-scale industries and land reclamation schemes to keep their people at home. By the late 1950s, despite such efforts, it had become clear that stronger measures would have to be taken to ensure that urban population growth did not outpace industrial development in the towns.

Household registration was introduced together with various administrative controls to curb unplanned population movements. Urban dwellers were encouraged to move out: not, any longer, to the far borders where their contributions had been less than successful, but to the surrounding countryside. As the *People's Daily* explained:

So far as the question of the transfer of urban population to areas of reclamation is concerned, our experience during the last several years is that because the great majority of city residents have neither the habit nor the skill necessary for agricultural production, they should not participate in long-distance migration and reclamation work. They can, after apprising themselves of suitable opportunities, gradually move to nearby villages to take up physical labor and production.[25]

The city of Shanghai, that ultimate magnet for those seeking the bright lights and glamour of urban living, provides a vivid picture of the struggle to manage its population:

Due to political, economic and other factors, there have been great changes in population redistribution. These changes went through a series of reversals in direction which can be characterized as 'three rises and three falls' . . .
1. 1951-1954. In view of the restoration of national economy and the smooth implementation of the First Five-Year Plan, there was fast economic development and steady improvement in the people's living standards. Rural labourers and dependants of workers and staff members who previously resided in the countryside poured into the city in large numbers. The net inward migration in the four years mounted to 840,000. Coupled with the high rate of natural growth of the population, the population in the city proper increased sharply to 6,800,000.
2. 1955-1956. Shanghai made considerable efforts to disperse the population. In those two years, 1,180,000 persons moved out of the city and the net outward migration was close to 600,000.
3. 1957. Following the successful fulfilment of the First Five-Year Plan (1953-1957), quite a number of dependants of workers and staff members moved back into the city, and some of those who had gone to work elsewhere also returned. The inward migration that year numbered 380,000, causing the city population to increase to 6,340,000 . . . '[26]

If the efforts to redeploy the people and prevent unplanned urban growth were less than totally successful, they nevertheless did succeed in preventing the appearance of squalid slums lacking all basic amenities which grew up in many of the world's exploding cities, as well as in developing some of the under-used border provinces.

By 1957 Mao Zedong had accepted that the concept of planning for a population included not just the planing of its distribution, but of its size. In a speech to the Enlarged Third Plenary Session of the Eighth Central Committee of the Chinese Communist Party in October 1957, he said:

In my opinion, China must depend on intensive cultivation to feed itself. One day China will become the world's number one high-yield country . . . even with a fairly large population we still have enough food. I think an average of three *mu* of land per person is more than enough and in future less than one *mu* will yield enough grain to feed one individual. Of course birth control will still be necessary, and I am not encouraging more births . . .

There should also be a ten-year programme for family planning. However, it should not be promoted in the minority nationality areas or in sparsely populated regions. Even in densely populated regions it is necessary to try it out in selected places and then spread it step by step until family planning gradually becomes universal. Family planning requires open education, which simply means airing views freely and holding great debates. As far as procreation is concerned, the human race has been in a state of total anarchy and has failed to exercise control. The complete realization of family planning in the future will be out of the question without the weight of society as a whole behind it, that is, without general consent and joint effort . . .[27]

The growth of recognition that fertility control was important not merely to the health and well-being of families, but offered a potential aspect of planning a population, seems to have been an encouragement to those who felt China's population size or growth rate, or both, were in themselves a threat to rapid development and future prosperity. Coinciding as it did with the short-lived Hundred Flowers period when intellectuals were encouraged to debate a whole range of political and cultural issues, it persuaded many demographers that the time was ripe to push for a stronger population policy. Professor Ma Yinchu, President of Beijing University, and a member of the Standing Committee of the National People's Congress, had drafted a *New Population Theory* which he planned to deliver to the Congress in 1955; only to cancel his plan when the sub-committee to whom he had shown it for prior discussion proved markedly unenthusiastic. He said later:

All but a minority of the members either refrained from expressing any opinions, or disagreed with my views. There were people who asserted that my statements where the same as Malthus's. There were also people who maintained that, though my phraseology differed from that of Malthus, the essence of my thought was of the same persuasion . . . I therefore withdrew the draft of the speech and waited quietly for the time to ripen . . . [28]

Now, he felt the time was ripe: the speech was made to the Congress in March 1957, shortly after no fewer than twenty-five deputies to the Third Session of the National People's Consultative Committee had spoken in favour of birth control and had been reported fully in the *People's Daily*. The newspaper also carried an editorial, which stuck firmly to the middle ground in the emerging debate:

Because our industry and agriculture increase a lot faster than population, the level of living of our people has been assured of improvement year after year. But, if the growth of population is at a somewhat slower pace, then the improvement in the level of living of the people will be quicker. This is an obvious principle . . . .

We favour [the suggestion] that reproduction be appropriately restricted – this is fundamentally different from Malthusianism. The basic argument of Malthusianism is that life necessities can never increase as fast as population. Our country's realities have already proved the fallacy of this argument. But to point out the error of Malthusianism is not to say that early and closely spaced child-bearing is beneficial and necessary.[29]

Others, like the superintendent of Beijing People's Hospital, Zhong Huinan, went further. Entitling his assessment 'It is Necessary that We Restrict Reproduction According to Plan', he also warned that:

Some one has made a preliminary estimate that if we [had] to support only 500 million people, our nation's productive capacity would suffice and enable them to enjoy fine clothing and abundant food. As it is impossible for China's population to be reduced to 500 million, we have no recourse but to control reproduction. If we [could] manage to keep the population below 700 million within fifteen years, and positively fulfil our nation's economic construction plans, then in 1972 the whole people would be able to have a good life [with] fine clothing and abundant food.[30]

The distinction between 'it is necessary to control reproduction' and 'it is proper to control reproduction' is both subtle and serious. The latter viewpoint implied no more than that planning, of people as well as of production, was important for overall development. The alternative approach was infinitely more pessimistic, suggesting that whatever the efforts made to improve the economic base of the country, they would, at best, only keep pace with increasing numbers unless those extra numbers were strictly limited. Ma Yinchu himself inclined towards the pessimistic view, seeing population numbers as having a dominant impact on society's economic standing and development.

Such views were anathema to many, including some demographers. They seemed to question the very basis of the socialist revolution. Had not large strides been made in the national economy since 1949? 'This would have been inconceivable had there not been such a massive source of manpower . . . ' Given the existing increases in agricultural and industrial production, 'on the basis of the present rate our nation's population will increase by one-third but . . . food grain output can increase one and one-half times. During these fifteen years, it is estimated that industrial production will increase around tenfold.'[31]

It was inevitable, but unfortunate for the future of the population debate in China, that most of those who inclined to optimism were convinced Marxists while many of the pessimists were from the older generation of academics of a variety of political persuasions. During the Hundred Flowers, criticisms of the existing state of things came disproportionately from members of minority political parties.* In the repression which followed the brief period of open debate, six outspoken advocates of a stronger population policy were accused of being anti-Party, anti-people, anti-socialist, advocating anti-democratic dictatorship and harbouring political ambitions. The last charge may have stemmed from their demands that demography should be reinstated as a subject for study, and their claim that demographic research should contribute to national policy.

But there were other reasons why the question of population growth and its effects on China's development became so explosive as to be ignored for more than a decade. Professor Ma Yinchu himself was not purged until 1960: the pessimists were not all, and not merely, victims of the Hundred Flowers movement. One reason was that 1958 also saw the beginning of the Great Leap Forward, that ill-conceived attempt to turn the country into a powerful industrial nation almost over-night. In the climate of hope engendered by the campaign, it seemed that the possibilities for every pair of hands China could muster were limitless. And out of the Great Leap itself would come the conditions which would reduce the threat of unlimited growth. As an article in the *Peking Review* summa-rized it: 'With culture and scientific knowledge spreading on a mass scale, the prospect is that planned births will be progressively understood and accepted by the people.'[32]

Another reason for the rejection of the dangers of popula-tion growth was that the failure of the Great Leap coincided with three years (1959-1961) of natural disasters. The con-tinuing fragility of China's economy was revealed as the droughts and floods resulted in widespread disruption and famine. The Chinese government did not release the popula-tion totals for the 'three terrible years' and the years immedi-ately following them until 1982, but recently published population and vital rates for those years make it possible to gauge the extent of the disaster (see Table 11).

---

* As a 'People's Democratic Dictatorship' rather than a 'Dictatorship of the Proletariat' the Chinese People's Republic permits a number of non-Communist parties to exist.

Table 11 China: The Effect of the 'Three Terrible Years' 1959-61
(vital rates per 1000 population)

Year	Totals	Birth rate	Death rate	Natural growth rate
1957	646,530,000	34.30	10.80	23.23
1958	659,940,000	29.22	11.98	17.24
1959	672,070,000	24.78	14.50	10.13
1960	662,070,000	20.86	25.43	-4.57
1961	658,590,000	18.13	14.38	3.80
1962	672,950,000	37.22	10.08	27.14
1963	691,720,000	43.60	10.10	33.50
1964	704,990,000	39.34	11.56	27.78
1965	725,380,000	38.06	9.55	28.51
1966	742,060,000	35.21	8.87	26.34

Source: China Official Annual Report, 1982-83.

These figures may not be entirely correct. Given the magnitude of the disruption it seems probable that registration of births and deaths broke down to some extent, and that many were either not recorded at all, or only recorded later as some stability returned to the country. Thus, the very high birth rate for 1963 may represent some births recorded then which had actually taken place in the preceding years, as well as reflecting the births which replaced a previous child who died, or the births which were postponed in the hungry years, for example. If a substantial proportion of the under-reporting was never rectified, the death rates may have been even higher than they appear. However, the rates as shown are sufficiently dramatic to underline the point here: that far from being concerned about additions to China's population, the leadership was preoccupied with a major crisis one of whose effects was a soaring mortality rate.

All this took place against a background of increased international tension. In August 1968 the pace of the struggle against Taiwan was stepped up and China bombed Jinmen (Quemoy). Tibet revolted in March 1959 and a series of border disputes with India began, which were to intensify until the outright war began in October 1962. At this difficult and vulnerable time, there was a marked deterioration in

China's relationship with her major ally, the USSR, and in 1959, the Soviets withdrew their technicians and technical advisers from China, together with the blueprints of half-completed projects. In a situation in which a war looked possible, China's large population was among the few comforts left. Zhou Enlai is reported to have said that after the next war, there would be '20 million Americans, 5 million Englishmen, 50 million Russians and 300 million Chinese left'.[33] Following the Sino-Russian split, as Mao Zedong began to vie with Moscow for leadership of the world revolution, each side claimed to be the only true inheritor of Marxist doctrine (buttressed, in the case of China, by being called Marx-Engels-Lenin-Stalin-Mao Zedong Thought). In the circumstances, a rigid adherence to well-established socialist doctrine on the relationship between population and production was not surprising.

Finally, the establishment of people's communes was seen as the solution to a potential labour surplus. The communes, which began to be introduced at the same time as the Great Leap Forward, partook of the optimism which that movement generated, and with greater reason. Although they too suffered from over-ambitious planning, and many of the functions originally centralized at the commune level were soon returned to the team or brigade, they did produce opportunities for overall planning of local development – for the growth of local industries, for land reclamation through irrigation and terracing, and for such activities as local agricultural research stations – all of which mobilized and made better use of rural labour. 'The countryside', the Chinese said, 'is like a vast expanse of the sea in which the labour force is swallowed up.'[34] Here appeared to be conclusive proof of the need for development, not population control.

Nevertheless, the need for family planning continued to be recognized. Even during the height of the debate on population issues, there is no evidence that existing facilities were closed down; indeed, they continued to spread slowly, even beyond the cities. In 1963 Beijing introduced what appear to have been the first regulations designed to limit natural growth in the cities: people who married over the age of thirty were to get an increased clothing ration, while those having a fourth child would get no cotton coupons for that child. This regulation seems to have gone largely unnoticed and may never have been seriously implemented.

The Beijing initiative followed a Party directive in 1963 which recommended not just late marriage as in the past, but an optimum age of marriage of twenty-two for women and thirty for men. As before, it was argued that very early marriage was detrimental to the health of couples, their children and the population at large; that the country needed the time and energy of young people for the furtherance of socialism; and that it gave girls, in particular, the time to develop, to work and to become independent individuals.

A second educational campaign for family planning was also begun, this time aimed more specifically at the rural areas. Health facilities in those areas were improving and the death rates, after the 'three terrible years', resumed their steady decline, but infant and maternal death rates continued to cause concern. Because literacy levels in the countryside remained low and other channels of mass communication, like radios, were in short supply, this second campaign adopted a face-to-face approach, in which home visits and small group discussions involved maternal and child health workers, women pioneers, Women's Federation members and many others in a concentrated effort of individual persuasion (see Chapter 5).

Judging from the birth rates for the years 1966 to 1971 (see Table 12) it appears that this educational effort in the rural areas had little immediate impact.

Table 12 China – Vital Rates 1966-1971 (per 1000 population)

Year	Birth rate	Death rate	Growth rate
1966	35.2	8.9	26.3
1967	34.1	8.4	25.7
1968	35.8	8.3	27.5
1969	34.3	8.1	26.2
1970	33.59	7.64	25.95
1971	30.74	7.34	23.40

Source: China Official Annual Report, 1982/3.

Part of the explanation lies in the Cultural Revolution. Organized propaganda efforts, as well as the administrative structures designed to bring family planning to those who wanted it, were submerged in the factional disputes, the fighting, the disruption of all aspects of ordinary life, which affected China between 1966 and 1969. In the convulsions and the purges, family planning was just another casualty.

As life returned to normal, though, it became clear that the experience was not all negative. Large numbers of cadres, including doctors, were sent to the countryside for longer or shorter periods, for 're-education' or to keep them in touch with the realities of peasant life. They were often shocked at the conditions they found there. While the medically trained gave their services and set up new health structures, other cadres were able to spread the knowledge of family planning gained in the previous campaigns.

The recognition of the continuing gulf between rural and urban China, together with the post-Cultural Revolutionary emphasis on vocational practical training as opposed to academic studies, led to the creation of a vast corps of barefoot doctors. Contraception, being an area which requires little specialized medical expertise, was one of the subjects which they were considered well-fitted to tackle, and one of the seven chapters of a widely available barefoot doctors' handbook was thus devoted to the subject. The work of these paramedics was amplified by the establishment of co-operative medical services at the brigade level, financed with members' fees and from the brigade's public welfare fund, as well as by the building and improving of commune health centres. Contraceptive methods offered in those centres now included a wider range of alternatives as, during the 1960s, the Chinese developed their own oral contraceptives and intra-uterine devices. By 1972 it was estimated that China was largely self-sufficient in contraceptives. Abortion, too, became a more widespread back-up for contraceptive failure, with the invention in China of vacuum aspiration, making it possible for early abortion to be carried out cheaply and safely by staff with minimal training. The government, and most doctors, continued to see abortion as a necessary evil, rather than as an alternative to contraception or an addition to the range of methods of fertility control. Even today, abortion statistics are reported to the Ministry of Health, and not to the Family Planning Commission.

The Birth Planning Leading Group, as the Commission then was, had been re-established by 1969, together with regional and local birth-planning committees which had offices and a small staff to co-ordinate and administer family-planning work.

1970-1978: the Population Control Campaign Intensified

While the concept of population growth as a threat to development continued to be unmentionable, the early 1970s saw a considerable extension of the idea that population growth should be planned. Three ministries, including the Ministry of Public Health and the Ministry of Coke and Coal, produced a joint report recommending that population targets should be included in the Fourth Five-Year Plan (1971-5). Initially, it seems such targets were more for the administrators than for the general public, because although a target for a 1 per cent growth rate for 1980 was included in the Fifth Five-Year Plan (1976-1980) it was not widely publicized until 1977-8. More important for individuals, perhaps, were the local target growth-rates, which implied birth quotas for each area. From 1971, annual population-growth programmes, reflecting the population and age structure of each locality, were worked out. Such programmes were, inevitably, planned at the local level first, and the national programme was formulated on their basis.

The rationale for population planning was explained by the Chinese delegate to an international conference in Lahore in 1973. 'Our country is a country of socialist system, where economic construction and other undertakings are developed in proportion and in a planned way. This requires planned population-growth in order to have a population increase well adapted to the planned development of national economy . . . '[35] It was put more vividly by the delegation to the World Population Conference in 1974: 'We do not approve of anarchy, either in material production or in human reproduction.'[36]

At the World Population Conference, the Chinese continued to deny that population growth was on its own a serious obstacle to development, and claimed that if other Third World countries built themselves up through self-reliance and independence and tackled the problems of colonialism and exploitation by the rich countries, 'the future of mankind is infinitely bright'. Many observers understood this latter statement to be a rejection of population control issues, especially when it was reinforced by Chinese criticism of the idea of a World Population Plan of Action. In fact, as the delegation had made clear, China had no objection to population policies but only to the World Plan, on the grounds that it was for individual countries to make their own decisions, and that as demographic conditions varied from country to country, no uniformity could or should be imposed.

Increasingly, the policy within China itself was one of planning a limited growth. The Fourth Five-Year Plan called for an urban growth rate of 1 per cent by 1975 and a 1.5 per cent growth target in rural areas. The Fifth Plan, as has already been noted, called for an overall rate of growth of 1 per cent by 1980: it also included the long-term targets of 0.5 per cent growth by 1985 and zero growth by the end of the century. This reduction in growth was to be established through the policy summed up as 'later, longer, fewer' – delayed marriage, a longer gap between children, and fewer children. The parallel slogan, which expanded the message of 'fewer' into definite terms, was 'One is good, two is all right, three is too many.'

The shift in emphasis from planning growth to limiting growth was a gradual one, and the reasons for the shift have not been clearly established. It seems probable that more and more planners and policy makers were becoming concerned about the effects of a growth rate of more than 2.5 per cent each year. Additionally, China's isolation from, and fear of, the rest of the world was being reduced. Nixon had made his first overtures to China in 1969 and the 'ping-pong diplomacy' of 1971 marked the beginning of a new relationship with the

USA. In October 1971 China was at last admitted to membership of the United Nations; in that year and the one following, thirty countries established diplomatic relations with the People's Republic. International contact not only reduced Chinese fears of foreign aggression and the need for increasing numbers to meet it, but exposed the country to at least some of the increasing concern about population growth being voiced elsewhere in the world. That concern was to reach its height at the time of the World Population Conference: the calling of a conference itself showed how far the nations of the world had moved since their cautious acceptance of family planning as a basic human right in 1968.

It also seems probable that policy makers had decided it was now possible to take action in what had previously been seen as a rather private and delicate area. The cities had already reduced birth rates very considerably (see Chapter 3). The campaign of the 1960s in the rural areas might not have had dramatic immediate impact but it had created a climate in which intensified effort would not be met with massive resistance. The peasants had been educated over a long period in the importance of planning most aspects of their lives. The step towards discussing the anticipated number of births in a brigade or commune in the coming year, and their effect on the allocation of resources within that brigade or commune, was now not impossibly gigantic. (see Chapter 4).

One indication that public sensitivity to fertility limitation was decreasing can be found in the changing attitude to minorities. In 1949 many of the smaller groups among China's minority populations appeared to be more in danger of extinction than of a population explosion. The Dai minority had a saying: 'It is easy to see a pregnant woman, but difficult to see a child crossing the street.' Riddled with disease, including syphilis, and desperately poverty-stricken and backward even by the Chinese peasant standards of the time, they were also deeply suspicious of all attempts by central government to administer or control them. For many years, health policy towards the minorities concentrated on improving their conditions and making it possible for them to have children who would survive. By the early 1970s, this policy had been sufficiently effective for the larger and more assimilated minorities to be offered family-planning services as routinely as their Han neighbours. In 1975, one of the official family-planning posters included pictures of various minorities, in their national dress, around a central figure of a barefoot doctor holding a bottle of contraceptive pills. However, the minorities were exempted from any pressure to control their numbers; rather, it was emphasized that they should space their children for healthy births, and this remained the case until very recently.

Government intervention in what had previously been viewed as private choice can also be seen in the decision to offer contraceptives free of charge. Most medicines, together with most medical care, remained the responsibility of the brigade, the commune or the enterprise, and were commonly provided in part through the local welfare fund, but largely in return for a fee. The decision that the state should provide free contraception, together with free hospital care or laboratory tests where needed, was a major development of state responsibility. The state also offered sick leave to those in its own enterprises who had abortions, IUD insertions or sterilizations, and instructed the communes to provide sick leave with full workpoints for those members who underwent similar procedures.

In 1973, the Birth Planning Leading Group was reorganized again, this time with a strong composition of ministers as well as leading cadres. A campaign was introduced, as part of the overall movement to criticize Confucius and Lin Biao, to question traditional attitudes to fertility. As described in the *People's Daily*,[37] this 'three breaking-down and three establishing campaign' had the following themes. First, break down the outdated idea of 'attaching greater importance to sons than daughters and having both sons and daughters' and establish the new idea that 'times have changed, and today men and women are equal'. Secondly, break down the old concept that 'one will have more support and help if one has more sons and daughters' and establish the new idea that 'fewer children means better upbringing, and one should rely on the socialist collective economy'. Thirdly, break down the old concept that 'giving birth to and fostering sons and daughters is a private matter of minor importance' and establish the idea that 'family planning is something of major importance to socialist revolution and construction.'

In the same year, Zhou Enlai, in his report to the Tenth National Congress of the Chinese Communist Party, reiterated the need for young people to go to the country and be re-educated by the peasants, and affirmed the continuation of the policy. Between the beginning of the Cultural Revolution and the end of 1975, more than 12 million young people had been sent to the rural areas, and although some returned, the majority were expected to settle in the countryside for life. This continuing policy of population redistribution was designed not merely to limit the current growth of cities and reduce immediate pressure on urban services and infrastructures, but to reduce future growth by ensuring that the marriages made by these young people took place in the countryside, and that the children they produced had no entitlement to urban residence. Here again the experience of that urban magnet Shanghai is instructive:

1958-1965. The high birth rate in the 1950s, the large-scale movement of rural residents to the city in 1957 and the sharp increase in the number of workers and staff members in the course of the 'Great Leap Forward' led to a sudden sharp increase in the urban population. In the course of three years of readjustment of national economy the government adopted the general policy of 'readjustment, consolidation, filling out and raising standards'. It cut down a large number of workers and staff to reduce the size of the population. Workers and staff were mobilized to go in large numbers to work in the interior. Educated youths were sent to support agricultural production and construction in frontier areas. In the eight years 1,500,000 persons moved out of the city, and the net figure for outward migration amounted to 760,000.

In the 1968-1977 period, 1,080,000 educated youths went to the countryside. Over the same period, another batch of people were mobilized to move out to support construction work in the interior, agricultural production and construction in frontier regions. The net outward migration figure for the ten years was 1 million. As a result the population of the city proper recorded a rapid drop.[38]

Demographic statistics and research

The reconstitution of the Birth Planning Leading Group was followed quite shortly by the establishment of departments of population studies at a number of universities. The first, in Beijing, opened in 1974. After more than twenty years, demographic concerns were a subject for academic study once again. It is probable that the Leading Group was not only concerned about China's growth rate but about the paucity of information, and of the analysis of the statistics, which they were provided with.

Statistics had never been very good; there was a shortage of people at the local level with sufficient education and training to collect them carefully, and a continuing temptation to manipulate them to show good results in whatever campaign was currently active. During the Cultural Revolution the systems broke down almost completely, and during the early 1970s the damage had to be repaired.

Nevertheless, the belief common among Western analysts that the Chinese simply had no statistics and had no idea of the size of their own population was nonsense. It may have been true in 1971, in the aftermath of the Cultural Revolution, that as Vice-Premier Li Xiannian told a Cairo newspaper:

The officials at the Supply and Grain Department say confidently 'the number is 800m.' Officials outside the Grain Department say the population is 750m. only, while the Ministry of Commerce affirms that the number is 830m. However, the Planning Department insists that the number is less than 750m.[39]

In general, though, local statistics were kept and aggregated and the planners and policy makers had a reasonably accurate knowledge of the population.

The reason that so many outside observers doubted this and were later to question such figures as were released was that the government refused, after 1958, to give any statistics to the outside world. It was not until 1979 that China confirmed there had been a second census in 1964. Two papers on China's population prepared by the United Nations for the World Population Conference in 1974 had to be withdrawn following Chinese protests. Since 1978 an increasing volume of information has been released, or published inside China, to the point where one Chinese academic observed in late 1982: 'So much is being published now that I dare say it is almost impossible for any one person to know all that is being written on Chinese demography, a very remarkable change compared to only three years ago.'[40] But as late as the end of 1981, a Western demographer, in order to compile the first almost complete table of China's population totals and vital rates for the years between 1949 and 1979, had laboriously to collect this basic information from nineteen different official sources. In the circumstances it is not surprising that outside demographers during the 1970s simply made their own assumptions, and projected population totals which varied from each other, at times, by up to 200 million people. Their assumptions tended to reflect their own political bias, rather than anything the Chinese themselves said.

Table 13 Official Population Totals for China and the Banister Projections 1975-1981

| Year | Official figures (000s) | | Banister projections | |
	Year end	Census	Optimistic	Preferred
1975	919,700		928,000	937,000
1976	932,670		944,000	951,000
1977	945,240		960,000	974,000
1978	958,090		975,000	992,000
1979	970,920		990,000	1,011,000
1980	982,550		1,004,000	1,029,000
1981		1,008,175		

Source: China Official Annual Report, 1982/3; Banister, 1977.

Confirmation that the Chinese did keep reasonably good and consistent statistics came from a study in the mid-1970s by Judith Banister, who collected local statistics reported to a large number of visitors to the People's Republic, compared them with other local statistics released by the Chinese, and constructed population profiles for each province. She concluded that the data were fundamentally accurate, and constructed from them her own projections of the total population, the 'optimistic' one of which turned out to be remarkably close to the official figures, once these became available (see Table 13).

It is not difficult to understand why the Chinese govern-ment became reluctant to publish statistics after 1958. The failure of the Great Leap, and the disaster of the famine years, were not only a poor advertisement for the fledgling system, but would have revealed the country's real vulnerability at a time when, as has been seen, it was under severe threat from the outside world. It is also not difficult to understand how the policy was continued in the wake of the Cultural Revolution, when suspicion of, and hostility towards the outside world reached hysterical proportions.

Less easily explained, however, is the continued reluctance almost to the present time to share basic demographic information. It rests in part on traditional xenophobia; a feeling that it is nobody else's business. This was summed up in a Chinese statement to the UN Economic Commission for Asia and the Far East in 1974:

The formulation of population policy and target, census and the publication of statistics are internal affairs within the sovereignty of each country and should be handled by each government in accordance with the wishes of its people. It is inappropriate and unfeasible for the United Nations World Population Conference to lay down unified regulations.[41]

There was quite possibly too a reluctance on the part of Chinese demographers to reveal to the outside world their lack of sophistication in dealing with the data they had. Although demographic departments were set up, they were staffed by young people with little training, and by elderly specialists – some called out of retirement, others who had done little work on demographic issues since the 1950s, and who had been disgraced and sent to the countryside during and after the Cultural Revolution. Much of the time of these new departments was therefore spent on catching up with demographic techniques and theories, in the translation of basic undergraduate texts from around the world, and in trying to learn from each other. An illuminating example of the difficulties under which they have worked is an essay on urban population in a book on China's population which was translated by the Foreign Languages Press. This essay includes projections of the future population, and gives a careful explanation of how the calculation is done, together with an example: clearly for the help of other aspiring demographers.

A final contribution to the explanation for Chinese secrecy over population figures may lie in a fact which is universally acknowledged: that it is very much more difficult to get material declassified by a government than it was to get it classified in the first place.

1978 and After: Towards the One-child Family

The effects of the intensified family limitation campaign of the 1970s were visible from birth rates which were reduced from 33.6 in 1970 to just under 18 in 1979; growth rates fell from 2.6 per cent to 1.17 per cent over the same period (see Table 14). No other large country has achieved such remarkable reductions in such a brief period.

Naturally, the decline was greatest in the urban areas, but rural reductions in births were also impressive (see Table 15).

Between 1971 and 1979 some 210 million couples were sterilized or accepted IUDs, to say nothing of those who chose 'less permanent' methods, as the Chinese tend to describe Pill or condom usage.

Table 14 China: Population and Vital Rates for 1970-79 (population in thousands; vital rates per 100 population)

Year	Population	Birth rate	Death rate	Growth rate
1970	825,420	33.59	7.64	25.95
1971	847,790	30.74	7.34	23.40
1972	867,270	29.92	7.65	22.27
1973	887,610	28.07	7.08	20.99
1974	904,090	24.95	7.38	17.57
1975	919,700	23.13	7.36	15.77
1976	932,670	20.01	7.29	12.72
1977	945,240	19.03	6.91	12.12
1978	958,090	18.34	6.29	12.05
1979	970,920	17.90	6.24	11.66

Source: China Official Annual Report, 1982/3.

Table 15 Birth Rates and Death Rates in Rural and Urban Areas of the People's Republic, Selected Years, 1954-77

Year	Births per thousand population		Deaths per thousand population	
	Urban	Rural	Urban	Rural
1954	42.5	37.5	8.1	12.7
1957	44.5	32.8	8.5	11.1
1962	35.9	37.4	8.4	10.4
1963	45.0	43.4	7.2	10.6
1964	33.0	40.3	7.4	12.3
1966	21.7	36.7	5.8	9.5
1971	21.9	31.9	5.5	7.6
1972	20.1	31.2	–	–
1973	18.1	29.4	5.2	7.3
1974	15.3?	26.2	5.4	7.6
1975	15.3	24.2	–	–
1976	13.6	20.9	–	–
1977	13.9	19.7	5.8	7.1
1978	14.0	18.8	–	–

Source: Coale, Ansley J., 1981.

It was, however, becoming increasingly difficult to meet the growth-rate targets and as this became clear there is some evidence that especially in 1979, with the intensification of the population campaign, local units reverted to under-reporting of births to avoid having to admit that all their efforts had been unsuccessful. The hope for a future rapid reduction in growth rates was one which could not be fulfilled, simply because of China's age structure. The people who had been born in the birth bulge of the 1950s were now coming up to marriage; even if they had quite small families, the birth rate – the rate per thousand population – was bound to increase, because they were a larger proportion of the total population. In 1978, China's population was only a matter of some four years from the billion mark; ahead was the prospect of extra children resulting from the 1950s birth bulge, to be followed a few years later by those from the second bulge of the mid-1960s.

First efforts to deal with this problem concentrated on flattening the bulges, so that the difficulties of planning for a fluctuating population could be reduced and the fluctuation caused by the children of the bulge approximately twenty-five years later would be reduced also. Couples who, under the collective birth plans of their unit (see Chapters 3 and 4) were planning to get married were encouraged to postpone their marriages still further; those about to have their second child were also asked to postpone the child; for the first time the assumption that marriage would automatically be followed by the birth of the first baby within two years was questioned, and contraception immediately following the marriage suggested. Units were encouraged to make their own calculation for where the peak years of births would be in their particular circumstances, and to try to spread those births over a wider period instead.

Some of these ideas were spelled out in a book, *Renkou lilun* (Population Theory), put out in 1977 by a group of Beijing demographers.[42] This book was extremely significant, because it was the first attempt since the ill-fated ones in the 1950s to define a population policy for China in Marxist terms. Marxist and capitalist population theorists, the authors argued, differ not over the issue of who favours population increase, or advocates population control, but on the 'question of who stands on what class position, upholds what viewpoint, serves which class, and has what aims.' The production of scientific contraceptive methods, and fertility limitation, is not in itself Malthusian.

We view scientific contraceptive methods as the means by which to attain planned reproduction and to make possible planned population growth. But Neo-Malthusians use contraception and fertility limitation as a pretext by which to promote reactionary social doctrines, deliberately distorting fertility limitation into the fundamental way of solving the population problem to absolve the capitalist system of its criminal responsibility.

In support of the promotion of contraceptive methods, Lenin was enlisted and quoted as saying:

The freedom of medical propaganda and the protection of the basic democratic rights of men and women citizens are one thing. The social theory of Neo-Malthusianism is another. Awakened workers must always carry on a ruthless struggle to oppose the attempt to impose this reactionary doctrine ... Of course, this in no way hinders our demand for unconditional abolition of all anti-abortion laws, and also does not impede our support for the dissemination of medical writings on contraceptive methods, etc ...

The book also claimed that a population plan was the starting point for drafting a national economic development plan, as well as an important component of it. Thus 'Under our nation's socialist system, child-bearing is not only an individual and family matter, but also a major event that has a bearing on the scope and rate of increase of the population of the whole nation, and on socialist revolution and socialist development.'

Shortly after *Renkou lilun* was published, an irreproachable ideological basis for such a claim was discovered and explained by one of China's leading demographic policy experts.

If it is accepted that social production consists of both material and population production, it must also be recognized that the law of planned and proportionate development of the national economy calls not only for the planned development of material production, but also for planned regulation of population growth, and that the two must be co-ordinated and adapted to each other. Engels predicted that in communist society planned regulation can and must be exercised over both material production and population production. He wrote: 'If communist society should one day be compelled to regulate the production of human beings, as it regulates the production of goods, then it and it alone will be able to do this without any difficulty.'*

In China today, it is possible not only for individual families to practise planned birth control, but for society as a whole to exercise planned regulation over population reproduction in line with the needs of the developing social productive forces.[43]

---

* From a letter by Frederick Engels to Karl Kautsky on 1 February 1881.

As demographers began to analyse China's age structure and its relation to overall population size more carefully, the shift in emphasis from planned growth of population to planned reduction intensified. Although the aim of reducing the rate of natural increase to 0.5 per cent by 1985, and to zero by the end of the century, had been mentioned in the Fifth Five-Year Plan, it was now widely publicized, though the Director of the Birth Planning Leading Group, Chen Muhua, admitted it would be extremely difficult to achieve:

Firstly, our country's crude birthrate has already declined from 40 per 1000 to 18.34 per 1000 [in 1978]. To further reduce the crude birthrate substantially is comparatively difficult, in view of the large reduction that we have already effected. Secondly, at the present time, persons below 21 years of age account for half of the population. These people will reach the age of marriage and reproduction, successively, by the end of this century. Particularly, as the larger cohorts born in 1963, 1964 and two years in the late 1960s reach the age of marriage and reproduction, fertility will probably peak again. Thirdly, people living in rural areas account for over 80 per cent of our country's total population. Generally speaking, the task of controlling population increase in rural villages is much more difficult than in cities.[44]

The solution to the immediate problem of reducing growth despite the large cohorts of young couples was to eliminate the 30 per cent of births which were third or subsequent children. 'Births of third and higher parity probably amount to about 5.2 million of the 17.4 million in 1978. If we halve the multiparity rate, we will reduce total births by 2.6 million, thereby lowering the natural increase rate from 12.05 per 1000 to 9.4 per 1000 . . . ' If all third and subsequent parity births could be eliminated, she went on, the growth rate would be below 0.7 per cent by 1985.

But the only solution to the zero growth-rate target for the end of the century lay in one-child families. The proportion of one-child families was to be promoted by, among other things, 'a material reward, such as the provision of child health-care fees, extra workpoints, extra pensions for the old and retired. A second type of measure is an institutional guaranteed reward: in allocating jobs and housing in urban areas and private plots and housing lots in rural villages priority will be given to those couples who have only one child.' There would also be disincentives for those having more children, but those, she emphasized, were not the main focus of the policy:

As for those who insist on having several children in spite of patient attempts at persuasion and education, we will impose a multichild tax on them. Imposing the multichild tax by itself is not our goal. Nor is it our goal to increase the burden borne by the masses. Quite the contrary. We intend to implement the law in order to firmly control population growth, thereby reducing the burden on the state, the collective and families. In fact, if every family commits itself to not having multiple births, there will be no problem of a multichild tax.

Chen Muhua was encouraged in the introduction of this scheme by the promising results of trial one-child family measures which had been introduced in nine provinces as an experiment. On the basis of the results a law on the one-child family had already been drafted and was being sent around for discussion. The law was expected back for ratification at the end of 1979. It apparently met with so much opposition as to have been – for the time being – dropped. But, in the climate of increasing alarm about the effects of continued population growth on China's development plans, the government made amends to one of those who had earlier warned of the dangers. Ma Yinchu, then aged 98, was rehabilitated and given various honours, including being made Honorary President of Beijing University. He had lived to see China's numbers increase by 325,000,000 since the publication of his *New Population Theory*.

In the following year, 1980, the questions of what was a sensible growth-rate to aim for, and how to reach it, were complicated by the introduction of the issue of an optimum population for China. 'Optimum populations' – in which the population size is best matched with available resources – were a popular subject for Western demographers some fifty or sixty years ago but fell from favour as it was realized that so many assumptions have to be made about the future in working them out that the exercise is largely pointless.

Additionally, they involved awkward conceptual problems: optimum for what purpose (the economy, defence, or geographical distribution); and was one discussing optimum size or optimum growth? But the Chinese, having come across the concept and being unused to playing about with the future on a computer, were struck with the possibilities. A number of social scientists and natural scientists using cybernetics and systems engineering 'worked together to make projections of population size based upon quantitative studies of economic development, population food requirements, ecological balance and fresh water resources', concluding that 'the desirable population for China one hundred years from now should be between 650 and 700 million.'[45] The best way to achieve this, they added, would be to achieve universal one-child families by 1985 and keep things that way until the year 2000. Over the next twenty years, fertility could be brought back to replacement level of just over two children so as to stabilize in 2070 at 700 million.

Others have pointed out that too drastic a limitation on the number of children would result in a grossly distorted age structure, with small numbers of young supporting large proportions of old people. Yet other demographers distinguish between the single-child policy and the target growth-rate, explaining that the population can be kept to 1.2 billion people by the end of the century if average family size is around 1.5 to 1.7 children – i.e. if the proportion of single children rises to about half. Some demographers and policy makers admit to hoping for a 70 per cent acceptance of the policy; others believe that 30 per cent acceptance would be quite enough to reduce population growth substantially while not interfering too fundamentally with the population age structure or with people's wishes.

Government statements are themselves by no means clear. Hu Yaobang, the Party's General Secretary, has been quoted as saying that persuasive education, law and scientific measures are the three basic principles for improving birth-control work. By February 1983, the Family Planning Commission had already held two meetings since the beginning of the year to draw up a new plan for a family-planning law, expected to take effect in two years time. An editorial in the *People's Daily* summarized the contents of a March 1982 Directive from the Central Committee of the Party and the State Council which called upon Party organizations and people's governments at all levels to strengthen efforts to control population growth:

. . . except for certain special situations which have been specified, state cadres, staff workers and residents in cities and towns may give birth to only one child per couple . . . each couple in the rural areas is generally encouraged to give birth to only one child, but if certain people who really have actual problems want to have a second child, arrangements can be made after their cases have been reviewed and approved. Under no circumstances may a couple give birth to a third child. Although the policy towards the national minorities may be appropriately relaxed according to the actual situations, family planning must also be encouraged among the national minorities.[46]

But the April 1983 Party document on rural economic policies says only:

Family planning concerns economic development and the prosperity or decline of the nation, and must not be slackened in the slightest degree under any pretext. It is necessary through investigation and study to further improve policies and arouse the great majority of the masses' consciousness and enthusiasm about birth control. Attention should be paid to improving work methods and strengthening propaganda and education; coercion and commandism should be avoided. Such acts as female infanticide and injuring, and even killing of, the mother must be strictly prevented.[47]

Perhaps the most significant statement, because it was expressly designed to remove the confusion caused by these varying pronouncements, was that of Dr Qian Xinzhong, Minister in Charge of the State Family Planning Commission in 1982. His clarification, which can be summed up as saying that birth control is crucially important but that one-child measures can only be implemented so far as local conditions allow, suggests that, as in the past, provinces and even smaller units have considerable flexibility in population targets. Given the unpopularity of the policy, and the sheer impossibility of ensuring its implementation by every couple, such continuing decentralization is realistic. Family planning has been and largely still is outside the policy-making areas which have been subjected to political debate about more or less centralization.

Some comrades think that the family planning policy set forth in the 'directive' is more clement than that in the 'open letter'. Consequently, they slackened their efforts with the result of a rise in the second-birth rate and the rate of the third and subsequent births. Some other comrades think the other way round and have therefore become more rigid in carrying out the policy. Actually, the spirit of the 'directive' is the same as that in the 'open letter'. Based upon the experience gained from practice in different places in the past year, the 'directive' has made the policy more specific in accordance with the principles stated in the 'open letter'. The policy has set forth different requirements for government functionaries, workers, urban residents, peasants in the rural areas and people of minority nationalities. In order to carry out our family planning policy persistently, the policy itself must be feasible and would enjoy the support of the majority of the people after our work of publicity. This is an important issue which concerns the change of the passive state of family planning into a positive one. So long as we are practical and realistic and give specific guidance to suit different people and different localities, successful results can be achieved. There is the problem of how to understand and implement the regulations concerning the first, second and third births. Due to the vastness of China's territory, the political, economic, cultural and social conditions vary a great deal from place to place and the population distribution is also very uneven. In respect of strict control of the second births, the actual conditions should be well considered and there should be different requirements for different conditions. Things should not be done in an uninformed way. At present, many places have set a number of provisions in conformity with the actual conditions for allowing a second birth and the result is good. People there say that those who are allowed to have another child are at ease and those who are not have no more illusions and that family planning cadres now have more confidence in their work. The serious problem at present is that the rate of the third and subsequent births is still quite high in some provinces and regions. We must be resolute to solve and lower the rate of the third and subsequent births as soon as possible.[48]

To some extent, it can be said that there is no such thing as the one-child family policy. Instead, there are a number of prescriptions for controlling China's size, all of which involve an increased number of single children, but which vary in approach from the gradual, with a concentration on the urban areas, to the draconian, which envisage urgent application of the one-child family policy throughout China. All have one thing in common: a recognition that they are calling for an immense sacrifice from the people.

Family-planning programmes in the past, in China as elsewhere, stressed the advantages of a small family – the health benefits to mother and child, the fact that parents would have more time to devote to those children, the greater opportunities those children would have, and so on. A small family is promoted as being a good thing in itself. Nobody has attempted to suggest that the single child is intrinsically desirable: only that the situation is now so critical that unless individuals are prepared to do without more than one child for the sake of future generations and the community at large 'there is little hope of improving the people's living standards' as the CPC Open Letter to Party and Youth League members explained. The letter continued:

Then can the call for one-child families be realized? The goal can be achieved so long as all the people work conscientiously and with one mind. Between 1971 and 1979 China attempted to control population growth and reduced the probable number of births by 56,000,000. Responding to the Party's call, since 1979 several million young couples have volunteered to bear only one child. In 1979 alone, 10,000,000 fewer babies were born than in 1970. Facts show that the Chinese people have good sense and take the interests of the whole nation into account. They not only understand the State's difficulties but also consider the interests of future generations . . .

The achievement of one-child families is a major event which will change prevailing habits and customs. The Party Central Committee urges all Communist Party and CYL members, especially cadres at all levels, to pay keen attention to the future of the country, be responsible to the interests of the people and happiness of future generations, thoroughly understand the significance and necessity of this major event and set a good example in observing this call. Party members and cadres must take the lead in overcoming the feudal idea and erroneous concept that only a male infant can carry forward the family name. Young comrades must start from themselves while old comrades must educate and supervise their children in overcoming erroneous ideas. All comrades must actively and patiently persuade surrounding people, and all comrades in charge of planned parenthood must become propagandists by helping the masses solve ideological and practical problems and persist in and urge others not to resort to coercion or violate the law in order to correctly implement the State Council's call and promote the accomplishment of the four socialist modernizations.[49]

Ambiguities – about the potential role of a law, and about phrases like 'under no circumstances may a couple give birth to a third child', contrasted with the continuing insistence that no coercion may be used, about which target for compliance should be set and how realistic it might be, and about how far minorities are to be included in the policy – are made still more difficult by the conflict between the government's one-child family policy and its economic policies. The details of how current rural economic policies contradict efforts to reduce family size, and of the initiatives being taken to try to reduce the contradiction, are discussed in Chapter 4. Here, however, it is important to note that the 'four modernizations' – agriculture, industry, the armed services, and science and technology – are the corner-stone of the current government's programme. Every effort is being made to encourage the peasants to grow more, to diversify their crops and to increase both national and personal incomes. Such efforts involve incentives for individuals and families to become more productive and a reduction in the powers and activities of the communes and brigades. These liberal policies, as an article in the *People's Daily* admitted, work against the national birth-control campaign by encouraging peasants to have larger families to help them produce and earn more. Many peasants therefore see birth control as against their interests. At the same time, the government continues to stress that family planning is a major priority.

Given these contradictions it is not remarkable that many Chinese take the one-child policy with a pinch of salt. Even in the cities, a substantial proportion of those who have signed the one-child certificate can envisage the policy being relaxed and have signed in less than total acceptance of that policy (see Chapter 3). The Chinese have suffered much from the abrupt espousal and equally abrupt abandonment of policies in the past, and many are more than a little cynical about the prospects for the one-child policy. In 1981, sterilization numbers were reduced in many parts of China and the explanation almost invariably given was that even certificate-holders were reluctant to accept a measure which would make it impossible, if circumstances changed, for them to have a further birth. A renewed government campaign for sterilization is now under way.

The ambiguities, too, explain some of the excesses committed by individual cadres, caught between demands that they fulfil the policy and the difficulty of meeting it through persuasion alone. Again, this issue is discussed further in Chapter 4. The government, however, has continued to insist on 'mass voluntarism' and has publicized and criticized cases of coercion quite widely.

To some extent, the ambiguities can be understood as a part of the normal Chinese governmental technique of attempting to achieve results through the promotion of models or targets which are to be aimed for, rather than fully achieved. As one economist explained:

During the last three decades we have seen countless campaigns – a principal means of policy implementation in China – with specific targets. These goals play an important role in mobilizing the masses to move in the direction of those targets, but I doubt they are intended to be operational in and of themselves. In other words, I doubt that anyone ever sat down and estimated all the necessary requirements for achieving those targets or their consequences. Yet I do not deny that these targets are important and play a meaningful role in regard to motivations.[50]

Meanwhile, other aspects of a Chinese population policy continue with less interest from the outside world, but with considerable internal commitment. An agreement was concluded between the government and the UN Fund for Population Activities under which a considerable amount of population aid – US$50 million – was given to China, largely to help in conducting the 1982 Census. Census preparations began in January 1980 and involved the training of four million enumerators, a million supervisors, ten thousand coders, four thousand data processors and a thousand computer technicians, not to mention administrative staff and the installation of thirty-five computers needed to process the results. The Census itself eventually took place a year after originally planned, on 1 July 1982. To the surprise of many who contemplated this herculean task, the initial manual counts of numbers were published exactly on time, on 27 October 1982. Excluding the populations of the province of Taiwan, Hong Kong and Macao (which were however included in the official communiqué) the total population enumerated at mid-1982 was 1,008,175,288. The billion mark had been reached earlier in the year. The 1981 birth rate was given as 20.9 per thousand; the death rate as 6.4 and the growth rate 14.6 per thousand, or between 1.4 and 1.5 per cent.

The population of cities and towns had increased by 62.5 per cent since the 1964 Census, so that urban dwellers now make up nearly 21 per cent of the total population. Expansion of industrialization, and thus the continued expansion of urban areas, is still a central feature of the Chinese programme for overall economic development, but the strict control of migration to the towns is still a part of that policy. Employment is generally only made available for one child of a city-dwelling couple. Although most of those 'educated youth' who returned from the countryside in 1978/79 have now been found jobs (largely in neighbourhood workshops and co-operatives rather than the state sector) and there has been no return to the wholesale policy of sending large numbers of young people to the country, some city school-leavers continue to be redeployed to the rural areas. More important, perhaps, will be the gradual urbanization within the rural areas themselves. One Chinese demographer outlined the prospects thus:

But following the 4 modernisations, by the year 2000, the urban population may reach 30% of the total and if you include small towns, you may get 40%-50%. When our country is in the process of urbanising, lots of peasants will become city dwellers. How then can appropriate arrangements be made for the great quantities of labour which will be taken off the fields? This is something we must give much thought to. It seems very important to have a national plan for rationally allocating towns. The most important method should be a local solution; usually develop a small or middling town; develop labour intensive industries such as handicrafts or service industries and open up new employment.[51]

This same demographer, incidentally, considered the possibility that a part of China's population problem might be solved by migration to other countries. He came to the sad but inevitable conclusion that 'Even if you exported 10 million workers you still couldn't solve the problem of population pressure or production. Besides, which country could absorb several millions, or tens of millions, of foreign workers at one go?'

In 1981 the Birth Planning Office was up-graded to become the Family Planning Commission, a mini-Ministry in its own right, as a way of emphasizing the government view of the importance of its work. (This up-grading took place at a time when a number of Ministries were being merged, reorganized or even disbanded altogether). A few months before, a Family Planning Association had been formed to co-ordinate, in close liaison with the Commission, the work of all the various volunteers who supplement government workers at all levels of the programme: academics, doctors, as well as 'mass organizations' such as the Women's Federation and the Youth League. Late in 1981 the China FPA became an associate member of the International Planned Parenthood Federation, the co-ordinating body for voluntary Associations around the world.

Joining the Federation was an example of another shift in Chinese population policy: the increasing willingness to share information and expertise with other countries. The explosion of demographic materials inside China (many of which are now also available to outsiders) has been complemented by the willingness of Chinese officials and demographers to participate in international meetings, to exchange visits with other population experts, and even to be hosts to international population gatherings, such as the Asian Parliamentary Groups for Population and Development conference, which was held in Beijing in 1981. After years of isolation, such exchanges initially led the Chinese to a somewhat uncritical enthusiasm in adopting novelties from other family-planning programmes. Occasional concessions to internationalism, such as family-planning posters with the slogan in both English and Chinese, may have been counterproductive even if well-meant. All in all, though, the ending of China's isolation from demographers and policy makers elsewhere has not only provided others with a better understanding of what is probably the world's most successful family-planning programme, but has, at the same time, reduced the likelihood of sudden and drastic shifts of policy in an area where the effects of policies are only really visible in the long term.

Notes

1. Banister, Judith, 'The Current Vital Rates and Population Size of the People's Republic of China and its Provinces', Stanford University, unpublished thesis, 1977.

2. Taueber, Irene B. and Wang Naichi, 'Population Reports on the Ching Dynasty', *Journal of Asian Studies*, vol. 19, no. 4, 1960.

3. Quoted by Chen Da, 'Depopulation and Culture', The Phi Tau Phi Lecture Series, no. 11, Lingnan University, Canton, 1934, 16 pp.

4. Silberman, Leo, 'Hung Liang-chi: a Chinese Malthus', *Population Studies*, vol. 13, no. 3, 1960, pp 257-65.

5. Wang Gungwu, *China and The World Since 1949*, Macmillan, 1977.

6. Chiao Chiming, 'A Study of the Chinese Population', *Milbank Memorial Fund Quarterly Bulletin,* vol. 11, no. 4, 1933, pp. 325-341 and vol. 12, nos. 1-3, 1934, pp. 85-96.

7. Quoted in Chen Pi-Chao, 'The Politics of Population in Communist China: A case study of birth control policy 1949-65', Princeton University, unpublished PhD thesis, 1966.

8. Chen Da, 'Population in Modern China', *American Journal of Sociology,* vol. 52, no. 1, part II, University of Chicago Press, 1946, 126 pp.

9. Chen Da, 1946, op. cit.

10. Quoted in H. Yuan Tien, *China's Population Struggle*, Ohio State University Press, 1973.

11. Quoted in Chen, P., 1966, op. cit.

12. Chen, P., 1966, op. cit.

13. Quoted in Chen, P., 1966, op. cit.

14. Chang Chih-i, 'China's Population Problem: A Chinese View', *Pacific Affairs*, Vol. XXII, no. 4, 1949, pp. 339-56.

15. Quoted in Wang, G., op. cit.

16. Aird, John S., 'Population Studies and Population Policy in China', *Population and Development Review*, vol. 8, no. 2, 1982, pp. 267-97.

17. Yu, Y.C., 'The Demographic Situation in China', *Population Studies*, vol. 32, no. 3, 1978, pp. 427-47.

18. Aird, John S., 1982, op. cit.

19. Lavely, William R., 'China's Rural Population Statistics at The Local Level', *Population Index*, vol. 48, no. 4, 1982, pp. 665-77.

20. Tien, H.Y., op. cit.

21. *People's Daily*, 5 March 1967, quoted in Tien, H.Y., op. cit.

22. Zhou Enlai, 'Report on the Proposals for the Second Five-Year Plan for Development of the National Economy', Foreign Languages Press, 1966.

23. Reports on birth-control work submitted to the Ministry of Health, 1958: quoted in Banister, 1978, op. cit.

24. Quoted in Tien, H.Y., 'Sterilization and Contraception and Population Control in China', *Population Studies*, vol. 27, no. 3, 1965, pp. 215-35.

25. *People's Daily*, 24 March 1958, quoted in Tien, H.Y., 1973, op. cit.

26. Zhang Changgen et al., 'Shanghai: Population Developments since 1949', in Liu Zheng et al., *China's Population: Problems and Prospects*, New World Press, 1981.

27. Mao Zedong, 'Be Activists in Promoting the Revolution', *Selected Works of Mao Zedong*, vol. 5, Foreign Languages Press, 1977. It was not until after Mao's death that the outside world came to know of this speech: see Tien, H. Yuan (trans. and ed.), *Population Theory in China*, Croom Helm, 1980, for the full translation and comments on it.

28. Quoted in Tien, H.Y., 1973, op. cit.

29. *People's Daily*, 7 March 1957.

30. Quoted in Tien H.Y., 1973, op. cit.

31. Yang Ssu-ying, 'The Premise of Birth Control Advocacy is not Malthusianism', 1977, quoted in Tien H.Y., 1973, op. cit.

32. Zhang Huaiyu et al., *Outline of Population Theory*, Henan Publishing House, 1981.

33. Hsü, Immanuel C.Y., *The Rise of Modern China*, Oxford University Press, 1975.

34. Tien, H.Y., 1973, op. cit.

35. Li Xiuzhen, Statement to the International Conference on Population Planning for National Welfare and Development, Lahore, 25 September 1973, (typescript).

36. Speech by the Head of The Delegation of the PRC at the World Population Conference, 20 August 1974, (typescript).

37. *People's Daily*, 30 July 1973.

38. Zhang Changgen et al., op. cit.

39. MacDougall, Colina, 'China's Population: The Missing Millions', *Financial Times*, 15 July 1975.

40. Zhao Baoxu, 'Sociology and Population Studies', paper no. 5.002 presented at University of Texas, 1982, 26 pp.

41 'China's Position on the Population Problems Expounded', *Beijing Review*, 22 March 1974.

42. Liu Zheng et al., (translated and edited by Tien, H.Y.) *Population Theory in China*, Croom Helm, 1980.

43. Liu Zheng, 'Population Planning and Demographic Theory', in Liu Zheng et al., 1981, op. cit.

44. Chen Muhua, 'To Realize the Four Modernisations it is Necessary to Control Population Increase in a Planned Way' (translated by Chen Pi-Chao), *International Planning Perspective*, vol. 5, no. 3, 1979, pp. 92-101.

45. Song Jian, 'Population Development – Goals and Plans', in Liu Zheng et al., 1981, op. cit.

46. *People's Daily*, 14 March 1982 in *Population and Development Review*, vol. 8, no. 3, 1982, pp. 63-5.

47. CPC Central Committee, 'Some Questions Concerning the Current Economic Policies', *Summary of World Broadcasts*, 10 April 1983.

48. Qian Xinzhong, 'Family Planning is a Basic Policy of our State', *Hongqi*, no. 23, 1982. Translated and published in China: 'Population Policy and Family Planning Practice', China Population Information Centre, July 1983, Beijing, pp. 14-19.

49. CPC Central Committee, 'Open letter to all Party and CYL members on the question of controlling China's population growth', *Summary of World Broadcasts*, 25 September 1980.

50. Dernberger, Robert F., 'Economic Consequences and Future Implications of Population Growth in China', Paper no. 76, East-West Population Institute, 1981, 29 pp.

51. Sun Jingzhe, 'A draft of a preliminary analysis of the distribution of foreign workers in the World and the reasons for their existence', Dept. of Population Economics, Institute of Economics, Beijing, 1980, (manuscript).

CHAPTER THREE

FAMILY PLANNING IN URBAN AREAS

★★

It has long been recognized that family size tends to decrease in cities or urban areas earlier and more widely than it does in the countryside. Demographers often describe 'urbanization' as a major factor in fertility decline, but that overall term covers a wide range of social and economic processes which may or may not affect the choice of individuals about the number of children to have. This chapter explores some of the factors in, and policies affecting, Chinese cities which led first to the acceptance of small families and later to a very high incidence of one-child families.

Definitions of the word 'urban' are almost as difficult as definitions of a family. In China the difficulties are compounded by the overlapping category of suburban communes, which are generally grouped administratively within the sphere of the city or town; and also by the considerable mix of occupation and living patterns even within large cities. Nevertheless, it is clear that there is a distinction between Shanghai and the communes an hour or two away, or between a smaller town, like Chengdu, and its surrounding country. The Chinese define an area as urban if it has a population of more than 2000 at least half of which is working in non-agricultural pursuits. It is this definition which will be used here.

Historical Attitudes to Fertility Control

There is considerable evidence of the use of fertility control methods in China dating back over 2000 years. Some of the techniques involved contraceptive devices which may have been comparatively expensive; others were easily available local concoctions. Because the use of these methods persisted longer in the rural areas they are discussed in more detail in the chapter on family planning in the countryside.

There is, however, evidence that in the early part of this century questions of population growth and its effects, and of 'modern' contraceptive techniques, were being discussed among the educated urban Chinese. Sun Yat-sen referred extensively to population issues over the years; the fact that his views changed over time is in this context less significant than that he had views: it was a subject being discussed. Similarly, Chiang Kai-shek's repeated refutation of Malthusianism is of less interest than the implication that Malthusianism was in the air.

Only a few women, but two and a half thousand men, made a crowded audience at Beijing University for Margaret Sanger on her first visit to China in 1922. Her second, in response to a resolution passed by the Chinese Medical Association in favour of birth control in 1935, ended as soon as it began; a side-effect of the Japanese war. The writings of Marie Stopes are referred to as being available in China by Chang Chingshen, President of the Eugenics Society in Beijing, in his *Sex Histories*, and contraception is taken for granted in his discussions of the *Histories* themselves. It is only fair to add, though, that his book – an early attempt at sexology – was banned in Shanghai and Hangzhou in the 1920s.

A more ambitious attempt at sexology was the annotated translation of Havelock Ellis's *The Psychology of Sex*. Published in 1948, it contained many footnotes and explanations based on Chinese sources (from ancient history, diaries, novels and poems) added by the translator Pan Guangdan to make it 'an important work on the Chinese psychology of sex'.

During the late 1920s and early 1930s, various urban centres began to establish small family-planning clinics. An example was the 'Peip'ing Committee on Maternal Health', formed in 1930 by a group of volunteers, the majority of whom were Chinese academics or health personnel. Though the numbers it reached with one part-time paid case-worker were small, the committee also published an 8000 word *Population Supplement* as a section of the Sunday edition of the *Morning Post,* and a monthly column entitled *Birth Control News,* which appeared in another daily paper, *The Truth.* 'Its readers are mainly artisans, shopkeepers and the like', reported the committee.

One of its members, Chen Da, Professor of Sociology at Qinghua University in Beijing, visited Canton the following year, 1931, and gave a major lecture at Lingnan University on 'Depopulation and Culture' in which he urged birth control 'to the end that the population of this country will not increase so rapidly as to cause widespread maladjustment'.[1]

Chen Da was also a pioneering demographer, whose book on China's population has recently been reissued in China. In it, he noted the difference in birth rates between the rapidly growing city of Kunming (1939-41) and the rural areas around it. 'In contrast to these is Kunming city, where the processes of urbanization are proceeding much faster and the influence of city life on birth rates is more clearly seen. The number of surviving children per 100 married pairs in Kunming is only 165.1', compared with 203.3 to 220.4 in the surrounding areas.[2]

Looking at the city workers by occupation of the father and age of mother, he found that Party workers and government officials had the highest number of children: 216.2 per 100 couples. 'Other urban workers, however, have comparatively lower birth rates, such as retailers and workshop proprietors (195.1), big merchants and entrepreneurs (184.2) and educators (163.2). Classes of lower social strata have still lower birth rates, such as shop employees and pedlars (177.7), common labourers (149.8), skilled factory workers (148.5), servants (142.5) and handicraftsmen (118.4).'[3]

As Chen was talking about surviving children, rather than pregnancies, much of the differential reflects differences in survival due to income and education and health care as well as contraception. But he did point out that 'those who have gone to foreign countries for a university education, though small in number, are known to have practised birth control.

They therefore have the lowest birth rate of all, or 120 children per 100 married couples.' He implies that although less was known about modern birth control usage in other groups, some may have been aware of the techniques. The implication becomes more explicit when he contrasts Kunming with Chengdu – then a very remote town – and says that in the latter town modern methods of birth control were unknown.[4]

The poor continued, even in towns, to use the traditional methods of contraception and abortion they had always known. But the urban intellectuals at least were increasingly discussing issues of contraception and the impact of population growth or decline.

Simultaneously, attitudes to the family and to marriage began to change. In the Republican period, 'influenced by social practices in Europe and North America, the urban-educated younger generation had begun to demand the free choice of marriage partner or the non-intervention of parents or their parties, and the establishment of independent households on marriage.'[5] The young were defying their families. Although such conflicts may have been more common among the élite in urban centres, education appears to have been an important factor, enabling, for instance, Mao Zedong, the son of comfortably-off peasants, to refuse to accept his arranged bride.

Attitudes to marriage were changing among the workers, too, if less dramatically and visibly than among intellectuals. The factory woman 'has been brought in touch with modern ideas. She speaks with other women workers and sometimes even with men. She hears discussions of modern marriage and the advantages of a family without a mother-in-law. She learns that she is not legally obliged to surrender her wages to her husband or parents . . . Some women workers have used their independence to escape from an impossible situation at home. And even those who do not go to such extremes are no longer the obedient peasant wives of olden times.'[6] As pointed out in the chapter on the changing Chinese family, the factory women were likely to delay their marriages, sometimes to a very late age, just as their peers in the intelligentsia did. They had fewer children and had them later; some enjoyed a strong position in their homes without having any children at all. Among those who lived far from their husbands, abstinence broken only by a visit once or twice a year presumably limited fertility. The others relied heavily on abortion and traditional contraceptives to limit the number of children and to protect those they already had. Maternity leave seems to have been non-existent and a woman wanting to breast-feed and care for a new baby was seldom able to leave her job for the time needed. Those who could not breast-feed had in any case to work to buy substitute foods. Working mothers had to find a neighbour or relative with whom to leave the child and had to pay for the service.

Family Planning after 1949

The Chinese Medical Association, as has been noted, passed a resolution in favour of birth control in 1936. In the liberated areas, concern about women's health problems was frequently raised, although, in the circumstances of the Sino-Japanese war and the civil war, it had usually been subordinated to more urgent matters (see chapter 2). After 1949, the importance of family planning as a health and welfare measure was sufficiently well accepted by policy makers and doctors for the Ministry of Health to bring out 'revised regulations on contraception and induced abortion' which were ratified in August 1953. The regulations were designed to widen access to birth control as part of maternal and child health-care. Their immediate impact was limited, partly because of controversy within the Party about coming out officially on such a delicate issue and partly because of sheer lack of facilities.

Nevertheless, the regulations did exist, and by December 1954 a conference had been held to discuss birth control and the problems of implementing a programme, and the Second Office of the State Council appointed an *ad hoc* committee to study and submit recommendations on ways and means of expanding family planning. An internal Party instruction explaining official approval of birth limitation was circulated within the membership in May 1955. 'In all probability the instruction affected only those who either had already practised contraception, or desired to do so. This group of people, however, represented ... urban dwellers, professionals, intellectuals and Party cadres, for whom the socio-economic factors associated with the motivation to practise contraception had already existed.'[7]

At that time, such opinion-leaders had official and ideological support. Information also became more widely available: starting in 1955, contraceptive knowledge began to be disseminated through the mass media. Obviously, in a still largely illiterate population, written articles were most likely to have an impact in urban areas, where lived the majority of those who could read them.

Such concentration on the urban people was not out of keeping with overall Chinese policies towards the cities. The First Five-Year Plan, endorsed in July 1955 by the National People's Congress, selected key cities and some provinces for development in order to increase the country's industrial performance. Among the investments to be made were social ones: 'the development of public health and medical services plays a significant role in improving people's well-being ... in developing health and medical services priority must be given to improving the work in industrial areas ...'[8]

Work among women altered to meet the new priorities. Women's organizations changed the focus of their attention from land reform to work in the towns, where, according to the First National Congress of the Women's Federation, the most urgent need was the restoration of production. Women were organized on the basis of their occupation or residence, according to circumstance, and the initial concentration on getting women to work in handicrafts or industry was quickly supplemented by welfare, hygiene and literacy activities, as it became clear that without such attention women's contribution would be limited.

The development of family-planning propaganda and services was in keeping with this approach. The strategy – summarized as 'point first, space later' – has been described as having the following implications: concentrating efforts initially in densely populated areas, such as towns and cities; concentrating initially on the educated sectors of the community; and concentrating on pilot projects for later expansion.

As to how the approach actually worked, in the second half of 1955, cadres in government agencies and enterprises in the province of Hebei were the subject of a family-planning campaign. A year later, the campaign was extended to all urban dwellers, as well as to employees in industrial and mining enterprises. From 1957, the campaign was spread to the rural areas. In Hunan, by contrast, the campaign did not start in one region until 1957, when the Party committee of Ning County announced that organized efforts would initially be concentrated within cities, with villages being the last to be reached, while the persuasion campaign would be directed first to cadres and functionaries and then to the masses. One co-operative was chosen as a pilot project for an education campaign.

Given limited resources, the strategy was a logical one. Urban areas were those in which it was easiest to place services, for there was at least some existing infrastructure and it was comparatively cheap to introduce facilities in limited geographical areas with reasonable communications. There was an existing acceptance of contraception amongst the more educated people in the towns, and they might be expected to give their support to the campaign and help to spread it.

In the short term at least, the demographic impact of a strategy of this type was virtually nil, especially in a country where some 87 per cent of the population was rural. In the cities, however, as knowledge spread of the availability of family-planning services, and as those services were, from the start, closely linked with other health provisions – especially maternal and child health-care – it is probable that the number using contraception steadily grew.

Desire to exercise control over the number and spacing of children probably also grew together with efforts to raise the status of women and to bring more of them into the work force. Such efforts were uneven, and there was a period during 1956-7 when it seems that more women were trying to work than industry could readily absorb. Delia Davin's careful analysis of the frequently conflicting attitudes and pressures experienced by women during the 1950s nevertheless shows that the overall trend was towards a much greater involvement of women in the labour force, together with real efforts to encourage women to 'stand up' and take part in decision making both within the family and in the wider context of society and the Party.

In urban areas, again, it seems probable that these new roles for women offered greater opportunities, and were taken up more swiftly. The country's industrial base – badly undermined by the war – was sufficiently reconstructed by 1955 for the First Five-Year Plan to concentrate on industrial expansion: new jobs became available for the women to fill. By 1959, women workers and employees made up 18.8 per cent of all workers and employees; the increase in the number of women working was far greater than the overall increase in the total non-agricultural work force.

The Women's Federation, one of the primary tasks of which was the promotion of maternal and child health, helped to spread information about such matters as contraception and at the same time gave individual women strong moral support in challenging traditional family pressures.

Meanwhile, an increasing number of young people, in the cities especially, were receiving schooling (see Table 16).

This would not only have an impact on their own attitudes to family size and to contraception in due course, but meant that even where the parents in a family might have no education, their children were becoming able to read newspapers and propaganda to them and to others in the community including, inevitably, the discussions of the value of family limitation.

One traditional family pressure was marriage. The new Marriage Law of 1950 specified a minimum age for females of eighteen, and for men of twenty; in practice, considerable effort was made to encourage a later actual age. It has been universally agreed that the implementation of the Marriage Law itself was easier and quicker in urban areas, and that the policy for delayed marriage worked better in cities and towns.

Even in 1949, the percentage of urban women marrying at or above the age of twenty-three was in double figures. By 1965 it reached two-fifths. An indication, however, of the difference which continued to exist between urban areas and their suburban communes is provided in one study of

Table 16 Number of Female Students in Educational Institutions, Various Levels and Percentage of Enrolment, 1949-1958

	Higher educational institutions		Secondary specialized schools		Secondary general schools		Primary schools	
1949	23,000	19.8%						
1952	45,000	23.4%	158,000	24.9%	585,000	23.5%	16,812,000	32.9%
1957	103,000	23.3%	206,000	26.5%	1,935,000	30.8%	22,176,000	34.5%
1958	154,000	23.2%	397,000	27.0%	2,667,000	31.3%	33,264,000	38.5%

Source: Tien, H. Yuan, 1973.

Note: the percentages are for the females as a percentage of all students.

Shanghai. Here, the actual ages of marriage were higher than for China overall, given the long tradition of later marriage there among the textile workers, but the trends they show, and the difference between urban and suburban areas, are probably broadly representative (see Table 17).

Table 17 Average Age of First Marriage Among Women of Child-bearing Age (Shanghai Sample)

	Urban areas	Suburban areas	Overall
1950-54	20.9*	19.9**	20.4
1955-59	22.1	20.6	21.5
1960-64	23.3	21.1	22.0
1965-69	24.8	22.0	23.2
1970-74	25.5	23.2	24.2
1975-79	26.8	24.2	25.1

* According to data compiled in the Luwan District in the city proper.
** According to data compiled in the township of Chengxiang in Qingpu County in the suburban area of the city.
Source: Gu Xinqyan et al., in Liu Zheng et al., 1981.

A further factor during the 1950s which affected the numbers using contraception was the growth of the urban areas themselves. Between 1953 and 1957, the urban population grew from 71.6 to 94.4 million – a rate of increase more than twice that of the rural areas. Some 8 million of that additional 22.8 million was attributed to immigration but this figure is probably a minimum estimate. Government efforts to deal with this influx were somewhat spasmodic. Most of the increase must be linked with national efforts to develop industry in new as well as existing urban concentrations, though some of the increase was the result of individual families drifting voluntarily to the towns, despite periodic efforts to return such people to their rural origins.

The urban workers went predominantly into state industries, with fixed retirement ages and – more importantly perhaps – pension schemes. For this sector of the Chinese population, the old fears of dependency and/or starvation in old age were minimized: one of the great economic rationales for having several children (or at least several sons) had been significantly reduced. More men than women obtained jobs in state industries; women might well be working in neighbourhood workshops or co-operatives, where benefits were considerably less, but the existence of two incomes and at least a pension for the husband created a new financial security with which to contemplate retirement.

Women, too, no longer had to choose between working and having children. The introduction of paid maternity leave (generally 56 days for a worker, increased to 72 on medical grounds where necessary) meant she did not have to give up her job to care for the child; the introduction of crèches and co-operative child-care arrangements – more successful in cities than in the country – made it possible for her to go back to work after maternity leave. This, in turn, made it worth-while for the enterprise to offer her further training and career development. With a job to go back to, child-bearing ceased to be the only future for a married woman.

Urban growth presented planners and the town-dwellers themselves with problems. Housing stock already in existence was generally extremely inadequate: provision had to be made not only to improve it but to cater for a more than 5 per cent annual growth-rate. Communications, again historically poor, meant that getting food to the cities was difficult, and inevitably led to shortages and queues. Many other aspects of urban infrastructure – piped water, electricity, public trans-port, health facilities and so on, which showed ample room for improvement – were still further threatened by growth on this scale.

At the official level, the first introduction of a demographic factor into urban planning came in 1955, with an article in the *People's Daily* which told city planners to match demo-graphic expansion to economic plans and industrial construc-tion, and that having fixed these two the city must make every effort to control the population size, and prevent further influxes from the countryside. If the planners were concerned primarily with migration, rather than fertility, it is likely that the urban residents, suffering the effects of crowding in their daily lives, were also receptive to the birth-control measures now being offered them.

As new urban areas were opened up, and more cadres were trained, there was increased dispersal of families. Some rural families had members who worked in the cities; urban cadres were sent to the countryside, or to other urban areas, where their skills were needed. In 1957, the Minister of Labour estimated that of 24 million workers and employees in the state section of the economy, approximately 6 million were living apart from their parents or spouse or both. Among the effects of this dispersal (which was largely of the educated élite or the skilled proletariat) were both a further breakdown in the influence of the traditional family, and a considerable disincentive to have large families. Especially where the spouses were separated for long periods, and often both working, the difficulties of bringing up a family were much increased.

The family-planning campaigns themselves waxed and waned in intensity in China during the 1950s and 1960s. Sometimes they were overshadowed or even contradicted by other campaigns. The Great Leap Forward, for example, gave additional impetus to the idea that what China needed was more hands to take part in an economic breakthrough. Usually they suffered from their association with the linked debate over an ideology of population and the effects of population growth primarily on economic development (see Chapter 2). But the population arguments were largely over the total population – and in demographic terms that really meant China's peasants. The campaigns were also handicapped to some extent by the limitations of existing contraceptive techniques and the small number of contraceptives being manufactured, and during the 1950s, by the reliance on mass media for propaganda. None of these limitations was nearly so significant in the urban areas, where facilities did exist, distribution and medical support were better, and a substantial proportion of the population had some literacy. In addition, because the small proportion of the urban population made it a demographic irrelevance, arguments about the value of a larger population for China, or purges of 'Malthusians', had little impact on the provision of family-planning services.

From 1958, education in planned parenthood began to take

root and spread among workers in the factories. Unfortunately, statistics for this period are rare, and those which do exist – for Shanghai for instance – are subject to the usual reservations to be made about their relevance to the rest of China's cities, as well as to specific limitations because of migration. During the period from 1949 to 1958, Shanghai was characterized by very high in-migration, despite sporadic attempts to reverse the trend, and these migrants were presumably largely in the fertile age groups. Between 1959 and 1965 concerted efforts to reverse the flow led to a net out-migration of three-quarters of a million people. However, it is useful to compare the birth and growth rates for Shanghai with those for the whole of China (as shown in Table 18).

Table 18 Birth and Growth Rates, Shanghai and China (per 1000 population)

| | **Shanghai** | | **China** | |
	Birth Rate	Growth Rate	Birth Rate	Growth Rate
1950-57:				
All	42	33.7	35.56	21.35
City	41.4	33.4		
Suburban	45.7	35.6		
1958-63:				
All	28.7	21.6	30.44	16.6
City	27.3	21.6		
Suburban	31.3	21.6		

Source: Zhang Changgen et al., 1981; Kane, Penny, 1983.

With the exception of the growth rates for 1958-63, where the much higher growth in Shanghai can be explained by its comparative lack of suffering during the three years of drought, famine and flood, the rates seem reasonably consistent. Shanghai's birth rate fell further and faster than the rate for China as a whole, and the distinction between birth rates in the city and those in its surrounding areas are already visible.

Shangai introduced widespread sterilization facilities in

1963, and more than 4 million operations were carried out in three years. During the 1960s, average family size in the city declined to around two children.

Cultural Revolution and After

The effects of the Cultural Revolution on family planning – as opposed to its effects on implementation of a population policy – still require further study. Family-planning assistance continued to be in demand. Such evidence as there is suggests a rise in birth rates during the most disruptive period of the Cultural Revolution, notably in rural areas, but the figures are confused by the influx of large numbers of educated youth roaming the countryside. Some of them, in their rebellion against existing authorities, also made early marriages or sexual liaisons. Certainly it seems that during the most intensive period of struggle, communications, supplies and organizations largely broke down; but in most areas that period was comparatively short-lived.

But if the number of births rose during 1968-9, nevertheless some of the factors associated with the Cultural Revolution may have helped in the long run to reduce the birth rate. There was a questioning of traditional attitudes and values, which reached its culmination with the campaign to criticize Confucius and Lin Biao. This campaign, though not having women as its primary concern, did provide support and ammunition for women who were being pressured into accepting traditional roles, or into early marriage and child-bearing.

The slogan widely associated with the questioning of Confucian attitudes to women was 'women hold up half the sky' and, increasingly, they were likely to believe it. There was another upsurge in the number of working women. Few of them, after the late 1950s, could find jobs in the state sector, because the increase in that sector after the Revolution had resulted in a disproportionately young bureaucracy and labour force, with little attrition from retirement. Women in the cities went into neighbourhood workshops or factories, or into health and welfare work. During the late 1960s there was a massive attempt to widen the basis of medical care, through the creation of vast numbers of barefoot doctors, low-level medical stations and other facilities. This in turn led to a considerable increase in the number of women employed full- or part-time in the health services, which led to a substantial increase in the level of health care available to women. While it is true that the development of these additional forms of medical care probably had most impact in the countryside, where previously services were sparse, their effect among the poorer or less literate sectors of urban populations should not be under-estimated. Health stations in the neighbourhood, staffed by volunteer health-workers from that neighbourhood and perhaps also by a barefoot doctor, took on much routine work, including the distribution of contraceptives.

Some women may have found that while working, the opportunities for discussion and sharing of women's problems improved their knowledge of family-planning techniques; one thing is certain, that in the years of political campaign following political campaign, the difficulties of combining a family with the multitudinous other tasks were formidable. A nine-hour working day, six days a week, was supplemented by study and criticism sessions, often of great length and frequently organized to fill several evenings a week. After the fall of the 'Gang of Four', one of the most frequently heard criticisms of those years concerned the amount of time taken up in political study. Private household tasks were in turn supplemented by a share of the community tasks, such as street sweeping, or perhaps being responsible for some basic-level health care in the neighbourhood.

During 1971-2, the men and women workers of Shanghai began to discuss family planning in a more structured way. The idea of group planning of births began to be developed there, and later spread to much of China. Suggested target birth-rates were transmitted downwards by the city to the various residents' groups, or factories, in which those couples concerned met. There, they calculated the likely number of births among their number in the coming year: those just marrying, who thus expected to have a first baby; those whose family was not yet complete and who intended to have their next birth shortly; and so on. Calculations of the intended total were then looked at against the suggested target and

Table 19 Percentages of Contraceptors by Methods, Tianjin, 1978

Area	No. of contraceptors	Tubal ligation	IUDs	Orals	Injection	Vaginal methods	Others	Total
Urban	326,781	20.6	16.2	31.6	0.6	22.7	8.2	100
Suburban	135,254	17.2	37.0	28.0	0.5	11.3	5.7	100
Country	211,832	9.3	67.7	15.3	0.7	4.9	2.2	100
Total	673,867	16.3	36.6	25.8	0.6	14.8	5.8	100

Source: Lyle, 1981.

other community plans, such as proposed welfare fund spending on crèches, or priorities such as housing. If the number of intended births in the group was higher than the groups felt could reasonably be accommodated, or grossly out of line with the target birth-rate, its members attempted to agree on which of them had the greatest claim, and who could be persuaded to postpone a child, or give up the idea of an additional one.

Obviously, such plans could only work if there was a high level of acceptance of a small family as being desirable, and if there was a ready access to effective contraception. As an outcome of the increase in basic health-care, access to contraception now became extremely easy in the cities. Adequate distribution of contraceptives is too often taken for granted (though it exists in very few countries). In China too, the different patterns of contraceptive use between cities and the rural areas, with the latter far more heavily dependent on intra-uterine devices, reflect the greater difficulty in rural areas of providing access to the entire range of methods (see Table 19). Yet, given that each has limitations, personal preference within the widest possible number of options is likely to result in more effective contraceptive use. The development during the 1960s of oral-contraceptive manufacturing in China offered, at least to city women, a comparatively easy and reliable method, brought to their workbench or door by an informed neighbour.

By 1972, the results of widespread access to contraception, and of more than a decade of family-planning education, could be seen in the birth rates of cities, and in the contraceptive prevalence rates (see Table 20).

The often violent conflicts between the Cultural Revolutionary generation and their parents, and the travels of the young around China, gave them an independence and a refusal to take for granted the assumptions of their elders. Besides weakening familial pressures, their visits or long-term stationing in remote rural areas brought home to many the importance of family planning, both for the mother and child's health and welfare, and as a curb to population growth. Precisely because the spread of family planning was

Table 20 Family Planning Indicators for China and Three City Provinces 1977-80

Place & Year	Late marriage rate (%)	Birth limitation rate (%)	Planned birth rate (%)	Crude birth rate (per 1000 population)
China 1978		70*		18.34
Beijing municipality 1978				12.92
City proper 1978				9.73
Periurban counties 1978				16.72
Shanghai municipality 1979-80			80.0	
City proper 1978	90.0	85.0	85.0	7.4
Periurban counties 1978	80.0	80.0	75.0	15.3
Tianjin municipality 1978	95.0	80.6		15.42
City proper 1978	96.6	88.8	88.5	10.8
Suburban 1978	94.9	75.9	57.2	19.0
Rural 1978	93.2	73.0	63.6	18.9

Late marriage rate: Percentage of couples marrying in the year who marry at or after the ages set by the late marriage norm.

Birth limitation rate: Roughly, the percentage of married couples under age 50 using contraception. Use for any portion of the year is included in the numerator, and naturally infertile couples are excluded from the denominator.

Planned birth rate: Percentage of couples complying with all three birth-planning norms.

*Estimate based on regression equation derived from crude birth rates and birth limitation rates in selected areas of China.

not so advanced in the rural areas, it came as a shock to many urban refugees and this was, I believe, an important factor in their own choices about fertility. They are, after all, those who have been marrying and having children in the last ten years. Their ability to understand and sympathize with governmental warnings on the threat to China's development posed by its ever-increasing numbers was intensified by their experiences.

During the 1960s and first half of the 1970s, education was virtually universal in urban areas. Older students had their studies disrupted by the Cultural Revolution, but nevertheless there were few in the cities who could not read and write.

The importance of literacy as a factor in influencing attitudes towards family size is well known, though the relationship is inadequately understood. Figures from Hefei's West Side suggest not only an increased proportion of one-child certificate holders among the better educated groups, but a significant break in the pattern of acceptance when one compares those with junior middle-school education with those whose education went further. Above that level, more than half of the fathers were certificate holders; those with junior middle-school education who had taken up the certificate were in the minority. There were also significantly more mothers with more than junior middle-school education who had taken up the certificate.

This assumption is not confirmed by data from the sample fertility survey carried out across China in 1982. Junior middle-school appears, from this survey, to be the crucial level of education among the mothers: 40 per cent of urban women surveyed had completed junior middle-school, and some 22 per cent of those were holders of one-child certificates. By comparison, one-fifth of urban women surveyed had only primary schooling, and only 9 per cent were certificate holders. However, all the education figures need more study, based on information not currently available, because with increased levels of schooling over the years, those urban women who only attended primary school, for example, are probably largely concentrated in the older age groups and thus may be reflecting attitudes to family size of earlier generations.

Small-family Policy

The Birth Planning Leading Group was re-established after the worst excesses of the Cultural Revolution and in 1969 regional and local birth-planning committees again set up offices with small staffs. The themes which dominated family-planning propaganda during most of the 1970s were 'later, longer, fewer', and its parallel, 'one is good, two is all right, three is too many'.

After the fall of the 'Gang of Four', the Chinese began to look in more detail at the effect of China's current age-structure on future population growth. The new Constitution adopted in March 1978 stated for the first time that 'the State advocates and encourages family planning'. The target of 1 per cent growth rate by 1980, originally set in 1975, was now given wide publicity, and the drive for single-child families began shortly afterwards. The drive resulted at least in part from the experience of some of the larger cities, such as Tianjin, which from the beginning of 1979 offered 5 *yuan* a month subsidy for health care to all single-child families to last until the child was fourteen. The city also promised priority in kindergarten enrolment and medical care for such families, and the same housing space allowance as a family with two children.

Major eastern cities were among the pioneers of single-child family schemes because they already had a tradition of contraceptive use and very small families. Beijing introduced similar cash supplements in the autumn of that year and preferential admission to schools and priority in job alloca-tion were also promised to the single child, as well as priority in kindergartens and medical care. Beijing also decided that all urban single-child families would be allotted housing space as though they had two children, while suburban families would get private plots on the same basis. Thus the single-child family would have a bonus compared with a two-child family, while a larger one would be penalized.

Shanghai was comparatively late in introducing regulations for a one-child family; they were only promulgated in July 1981. This may have been because Shanghai already had a very high proportion of families with only one child so that additional incentives were felt unnecessary.

When the incentives were announced, they followed what was by now the familiar pattern of a 5 *yuan* health subsidy and priority in housing and the allocation of private plots, but they also included exemption from tuition fees and extras to the end of senior middle-school, and provision for additional maternity leave. The regulations also offered an extra week's leave to couples meeting the late-marriage requirements, while couples who did not register a marriage and went on to have a child would have to pay the hospital fees themselves, and were not entitled to full maternity-leave pay or workpoints. Couples who had a child outside the agreed plan, especially if it was a third or subsequent child, had to pay for the hospital, the child's medical care, lost out on maternity leave pay and might have to forfeit 10 per cent of salary or workpoints.

Table 21 Urban Families with Certificates as a Percentage of all Families with One Child

		1979	1980	1981
Beijing		70.0%	79.4%	85.0%
Shanghai				
	Urban	90.0%	82.0%	86.0%
	Suburban	75.0%	61.0%	
Tianjin				
	Urban	80.0%		
	Suburban	52.0%		
Harbin		85.0%		
Guangzhou				
	Urban		60.0%	
	Suburban		25.0%	
Suzhou			95.0%	

Source: Chen, P. and Kols, A., 1982; Goodstadt, Leo F., 1982; and Tien, H. Yuan, 1980.

Urban Responses to the Small Family

Such fragmentary information as is available for urban areas suggests that the take-up of one-child certificates was quite

Table 22 Urban and Rural Birth Rates, People's Republic of China, 1971-8 (per 1000 population)

	1971	1972	1973	1974	1975	1976	1977	1978
Urban areas	21.9	20.1	18.1	15.1	15.3	13.6	13.9	14.0
Rural areas	31.9	31.2	29.4	26.2	24.8	20.9	19.7	18.9
National average	30.7	29.9	28.1	24.9	23.1	20.0	19.0	18.3

Source: Chen, P. and Kols, A., 1982.

high during the initial stages of the campaign, although there are wide variations between different cities, and as one would expect, between urban and suburban districts (see Table 21).

There may also have been differences in the performance of different units, such as state factories, large and small co-operatives and departments of the bureaucracy. Once local regulations were promulgated, all organizations had to offer the same package of benefits and penalties to their workers, but the wealthier ones could increase the incentives, while those which involved prized work, like the state factories or government departments, had stronger opportunities to enforce the measures. The massive promotion of units which achieved 100 per cent success in signing up those eligible suggests that such differences did, in fact, exist: there is, however, no detailed information available about them.

Leaving aside the campaign for the one-child family, which only began in 1979, it is clear that during the 1970s the fall in birth rates in China was dramatic, both in urban and rural areas. In fact, the decline in rural areas was the greater, because of the much higher birth rates from which they started in 1971. The absolute level of crude birth rates reached by the urban population at the end of the 1970s was, however, extremely low, and could be compared with Western Europe (see Table 22).

City families in the 1970s were generally small. In Shanghai in 1978 only 10 per cent of births were of a third or subsequent child (in the city proper, the figure was less than 2 per cent). The previous year, Changsha reported the remarkably low figure of 5 per cent of all births being third or subsequent children, while Chengdu reported 15 per cent. By 1981, Beijing had reduced third-order births to just over 2 per cent, while Shanghai claimed that only 17 third births occurred in the city proper that year.

Some of the acceptance of the one-child family policy predates the policy itself. The report of a survey of Fusuijing residential area, in the West District of Beijing, describes the local campaign for one-child families which began in early 1979, before there were any official regulations. It appears that in the previous year the ratio of one-child families was already 19 per cent, or almost a fifth. Within a few months of the campaign beginning, the ratio of one-child families had passed 50 per cent, even before the regulations had been introduced and incentives or disincentives proffered. This large number of pre-existing one-child families appears to have been part of a longer-term trend. A survey carried out in urban and rural areas of Shanghai and Beijing in 1980, consisting of structured interviews with seventy-five households, found a high proportion of single-child families (see Table 23).

Table 23 Number of Children and Family Size, Shanghai and Beijing, 1980

Number of children	Urban Shanghai		Rural Shanghai	
	No.	Percentage	No.	Percentage
5	1	2%	-	-
4	-	-	2	3%
3	4	9%	5	10%
2	12	26%	22	42%
1	23	50%	18	35%
0	6	13%	5	10%
	46	100%	52	100%
	Urban Beijing		Rural Beijing	
	No.	Percentage	No.	Percentage
5	-	-	-	-
4	1	3%	-	-
3	4	10%	7	13%
2	18	46%	28	52%
1	16	41%	13	24%
0	-	-	6	11%
	39	100%	54	100%

Source: Croll, 1980.

Even more interesting, perhaps, is the table for the number of single children by the age of parents (Table 24). Leaving aside the youngest age group, in which many of the urban sample are childless because of very late marriage, it seems that single children are quite well represented at all ages, implying that some women at least had been content with a single child well before the campaign began. The table also suggests that this trend was intensifying during the 1970s, as other statistics confirm.

Table 24 Single-child Families, Beijing and Shanghai, 1980, by Age of Parents

Age of married persons	Urban Shanghai		Rural Shanghai	
	No.	Percentage	No.	Percentage
40-49	8	35%	1	5%
36-39	5	22%	1	5%
30-35	9	39%	5	28%
25-29	1	4%	11	61%
	23	100%	18	100%
	Urban Beijing		**Rural Beijing**	
	No.	Percentage	No.	Percentage
40-49	4	25%	-	-
36-39	2	12%	1	8%
30-35	10	63%	5	38%
25-29	-	-	7	54%
	16	100%	13	100%

Source: Croll, 1980.

In Shanghai the proportion of single children increased steadily throughout the 1970s. Half of those women from Shanghai proper who married in 1970 have had only one child. It is true that Shanghai is not only an 'exemplary' city as far as birth planning is concerned, but somewhat exceptional. However, lest it be thought that such a trend applies only in the 'advanced' cities of Beijing and Shanghai, comparison can be made with a survey of single-child families carried out in Hefei's West Side district, in the province of Anhui. Among the one thousand families who had applied for a one-child certificate, half of the fathers were thirty-six years old or older, and 84 were over fifty. Of the mothers, 267 were over the age of thirty-five including six over the age of fifty. While

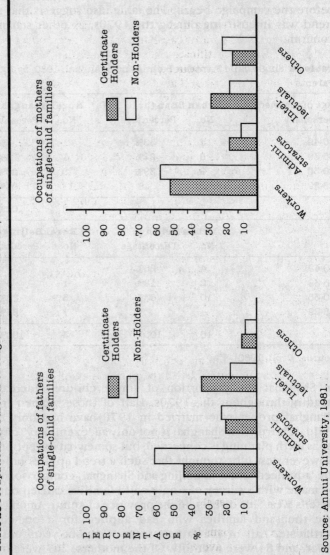

Table 25 Occupations of Parents of Single Children – West Side, Hefei, 1979

Occupations of mothers of single-child families

Certificate Holders

Non-Holders

Others · Intel-lectuals · Admini-strators · Workers

Occupations of fathers of single-child families

Certificate Holders

Non-Holders

Others · Intel-lectuals · Admini-strators · Workers

PERCENTAGE %

Source: Anhui University, 1981.

some of these couples may have been hoping for another child before the single-child campaign was introduced, given their ages it is probable that a high proportion had already chosen to have one child in any case, and merely decided to avail themselves of the certificate, and the consequent incentives, when these were introduced. Hefei's West Side contains several universities, as well as factories, and the proportion of cadres and intellectuals is high, particularly in the older age groups. (A breakdown of the occupation of the certificate holders and non-holders is given in Table 25).

In recent years, in addition to the factors already discussed, there have been others which have helped to intensify the trend. One which is often forgotten due to the myth of the 'extended family' is that in any traditional society with high death rates, the number of generations living together – and the numbers within those generations – tends to be quite small. As was noted in Chapter 1, data from one field survey between 1929-31 suggest that nuclear families accounted for more than three-fifths of the total households, and that over three-quarters of all family members in the sample were heads, their wives and children.

Substantial falls in the mortality and concomitant increases in life expectancy, which overall by 1975 was estimated to be 63.2 years for men and 66.3 for women, mean that families have become units of several generations. In the three municipalities, which are the only cities for which separate figures were calculated, life expectancy is even higher.

Table 26 Life Expectancy at Birth 1973-5

	Male	Female
Tianjin	69.9	72
Shanghai	69.2	74.8
Beijing	68.3	70.8

Source: Rong Shoude et al., 1981.

These longer life-spans have contributed to crowded housing conditions. Urban average living-space per head actually declined from 4.5 square metres in 1952 to 3.6 square metres in 1977, as a result of lack of housing investment aggravated by population growth. In principle, housing is allocated by the municipal authorities to a young couple on their marriage, although where there are housing shortages – as there are in many of the larger cities – the couple may be forced to live for a while with the parents of one or other partner (usually the groom). Once they have managed to get a home of their own, they are likely, at a later date, to have to take in a widowed parent. If there are no other close relatives to take care of the parent or parents left in the rural area, the couple can bring them in to their home; this despite the overall very strict controls on in-migration.

Thus, a recent study of urban family structures in Tianjin showed an actual increase in the numbers of city couples living with a parent among those born after 1951. Housing problems, economic and social support for the old people, and the need to have somebody to take care of children and housework, were identified as the main factors contributing to this situation. Those factors are often enough to counter the opposing trend, which the study also noted: the desire of the financially independent young couple to be independent in living arrangements; the stresses of communal living – not least, stresses between mother and daughter-in-law – and the 'generation gap'. The force of the desire for nuclear families was stronger, the authors concluded, than old lineal traditions.

Where three generations live together in increasingly cramped conditions, the benefits of extra hands, extra help with the child and so on are possible outweighed by the irritation of parents-in-law demanding deference and, increasingly as they age, care. In those circumstances, too, a mother-in-law's traditional yearning for grandchildren around her feet may well become muted.

Housing shortages are widely admitted as a major – perhaps the major – problem in Chinese cities, and lack of investment in this sector has been complicated by the coming to marriage age of the cohorts from the previous baby-boom. The very high age of marriage in Tianjin is attributed partly to the difficulty in securing housing – a particular problem in that city where the 1976 Tangshan earthquake wrecked much of the existing stock as well.

While, unfortunately, the West Side Hefei study only looked at housing-space allocation among those families which did have a one-child certificate, the report states that 'there is general tension in housing among the families surveyed. This is an important factor affecting the steadiness of thought among the parents of the certificate-holding families.' Among certificate holders the single most frequently expressed demand was that the government should do something about housing conditions (40 per cent), and housing was the second-greatest priority for the non-holders, too.*

A further complication in the housing situation over the past four years or so has been a growth in bride payments and a tendency for them to be spent on bulky furniture. The groom may have to pay out 2000 *yuan* on furniture, from a monthly salary of perhaps 45 *yuan,* and I was assured by city women that a three-piece suite was the essential accompaniment to marriage, no matter how it was fitted into the tiny space allocated for the couple. This has resulted from official policies in favour of higher disposable incomes and a greater availability of consumer goods, although the furniture fashion seems to be a phenomenon largely confined to urban areas.

One reason for the later age of marriage in cities may be that the costs of the marriage and establishing a household are now generally the responsibility of the young couple, rather than of the family. The savings may be augmented by small gifts in cash or in kind from kin, friends and fellow-workers, but the main burden falls on the couple. In the circumstances it is understandable that many would prefer to postpone child-bearing and its additional responsibilities for a while, and enjoy the luxury of being able to spend more of their combined salaries.

Inside the home, while the numbers of meetings and criticism sessions which reduced free time have diminished, life is still arduous. It is well expressed in the following Chinese account:

---

*But their greatest demand from the government – 50 per cent of them expressed it – was to stop having to fill in forms! It appears almost as if those who reject the one-child family are expressing a protest at the world's largest and oldest bureaucracy, rather than the policy itself.

In cities, both husband and wife work to get enough money for the family to live on. They work six days a week, eight hours a day, plus one to two hours of travelling back and forth for those who live far from their working units. They have to do washing, cleaning, queuing for shopping, cooking etc. on their days off. Life for working couples is tiring and exhausting, and it will be more so if a couple has more children. Problems like waking up at night to feed the baby, more washing to do, not being able to go out because of young babies, nutrition, health, education and many other things all have to be dealt with. These are all time- and energy-consuming. Conflicts may even arise between couples over taking care of children. Bringing up children is not always an easy thing to do, especially in cities where life is more hectic when both husband and wife are working.[9]

Confirmation of this description comes from a survey carried out into the off-duty activities of Shanghai's workers, the results of which were announced in 1983. Household chores such as cooking, washing and commuting took an average of 6 hours and 45 minutes a day. 'Moreover, the situation with women, who account for one-third of the city's 4.7 million workers, is even worse, as they are traditionally considered responsible for childcare . . .'[10] As a result of the survey, Shanghai is encouraging enterprises to set up service facilities for their staff, including laundries, sewing and clothes-mending shops and repair shops for household equipment. Vegetable markets are now accepting orders, to obviate the need for queuing, and the housing departments in twelve districts have arranged apartment exchanges for couples so that they can live nearer their work units. Finally, nurseries in work units are being asked to allow babies to be boarded for up to forty-eight months, instead of the previous eighteen, to free their mothers from the demands of a toddler. But these are very new initiatives, and in most cities a young couple's week remains extremely tiring.

Further amplification comes from a 1980 survey of the Chinese household and its economy. In urban Shanghai and Beijing, average daily shopping time took over three-quarters of an hour and half an hour respectively. Cooking took an hour and three-quarters in Shanghai; an hour and twelve minutes in

Beijing. Rural Shanghai and Beijing spent still more time on cooking, but in rural areas the men appeared to be more active in helping to do it. Where the household does not have a resident grandmother (and overall, 35-45 per cent of the working women had to undertake these tasks), shopping and cooking add appreciably to the length of the working day.

The baby booms of the 1950s and 1960s, combined with post 'Gang of Four' efforts to rehabilitate some of the young who had been banished to the countryside, resulted by 1979-1980 in a severe employment problem. It was one which affected cities disproportionately – partly because under-employment is easier to accommodate in the rural sector, and partly because of the return of the educated young. Up to 10 million young people had to be found jobs each year during that period, and although most of the backlog of returnees from the countryside has now been accommodated, new employment must still be found for some 5 million entrants to the job market each year.

Jobs in the state sector, with its coveted benefits including retirement pensions, are generally available only through inheritance. (This does not necessarily mean that the daughter of a stevedore has to become a stevedore too, but that her father's unit will be responsible for finding her some job within the unit.) Thus, unless both parents were lucky enough to work in state industries, they became acutely aware during the 1970s that a second child was unlikely to be able to look to the state for employment. In the late 1970s, many cities followed the examples of Beijing and Shanghai and intro-duced regulations which refused to guarantee employment to any child beyond the first, even where both parents did work in the state sector. Some of these regulations preceded the one-child family policy and seem to have been as much a response to employment problems as strictly designed to limit families: yet a smaller family must have been one of the effects. More recently, regulations to encourage the one-child family announced by the cities specifically state that the single child will have priority in job allocation; this may be designed to reduce the fears of the parents that an only daughter will not get the coveted state job, because of the lingering preference of some factories to give apprenticeships to young men. In the long term, then, the urban family knows that extra children will not be much of an investment; in the short term, there seem to be few opportunities for urban children to earn, whereas in rural areas the development of the production responsibility system may mean that even quite young children can contribute to the family economy, as they do in other Third World countries.

The Chinese woman quoted above expressed it as follows:

In cities, children are more an economic liability than an asset. They need care, they need food, clothing and education. But they cannot provide much help to the family when they are small. In the Chinese circumstances where salaries are universally low, the average salary for working people in cities is about $25-35 a month, which is just enough for a person to live on with not much surplus. When a young couple start thinking of having a child, they must be prepared to have a lower living standard than before. When the baby is born, more expenses are involved, and the economic situation in the family becomes tighter for the couple. It will be more difficult to have another child without further decline in the living standard of the family.

The cost of living in cities is much higher than in the countryside. There are few means of income generation outside wage employment, and wage increases are dwarfed by inflation. Therefore, bringing up children involves more economic difficulties for people living in the cities.[11]

Inflation, I would suggest, has probably had quite an impact on the acceptance of the single-child policy. Until the late 1970s, deliberate management of the economy meant that many prices had been stable for almost twenty years. The government's decision to allow many prices to rise produced considerable shock among a population cushioned for so long. In their perception, at least, such rises more than outweighed additions to their salaries: the result was a kind of unease, a feeling that the ground was slipping from beneath their feet, which those from countries used to soaring inflation as a part of life find it difficult to imagine.

Children born to urban families have also lost some of their value for their parents as a long term investment for security in old age. Those working in the state sector are entitled to retirement pensions of 60 per cent of their previous salaries. Shanghai offers a 70 per cent of final salary pension for those who have only one child, and Beijing and other cities give 100 per cent of salary pensions to the childless. Tianjin and Beijing began in 1979 to experiment with workpoint pensions for the old in suburban communes, giving such pensions initially to the childless or those who had one child. In Shanghai, suburban communes began to introduce pension schemes at around the same time, spurred on by the fact that the factory workers among them – and in suburban communes this may be half the labour force – were getting 60 per cent of their previous salary as pensions, so that the peasant half of the population were seen to be losing out. By mid-1983, 71 per cent of the peasants in Shanghai's suburbs were in receipt of pensions: their number had risen by a quarter in the previous six months. These suburban peasant pensions are considerably lower than the factory ones; the Shanghai average was 113 *yuan* a year, or a quarter of the peasant average cash income, but they are a start which may help to diminish the differences in family-planning acceptance between the cities proper and their suburbs.

Pensions begin to loom larger in the calculations of families not merely as they spread to more categories of worker, but as the proportion of those who have worked, and are thus eligible for a pension, increases. About 45 per cent of retired persons in the household surveys of rural Beijing and Shanghai had no pensions and were largely supported by their families. All but one of these people were elderly women or housewives who had never had a formal income. The vast majority of the men and women whose daughters are now coming into marriageable age have been and are workers, and are likely to be able to look forward either to a state pension or at least to reasonable savings for retirement from a second income.

Meanwhile, the immediate benefits to the individual child from reducing overall numbers are spelled out by the authorities. Shanghai, which in the 1960s had a two-shift system in schools, with a teacher/pupil ratio of 1/37, publicizes the fact that is has managed to improve the situation considerably because of falls in the number of school-age children; so does Beijing. Overall, kindergartens can only cater for about a fifth of the children in the under-six age group – which, given two working parents, must add to their difficulties, even when there are grandparents to help. Even in Anhui, which had 40 per cent of infants in kindergartens, lack of qualified staff and facilities was a major criticism emerging in the survey of West Side Hefei: parents seem to be willing to reduce their families in return for a better future for their children, but they want to see visible evidence that the sacrifice is being matched by advantages for the single child.

In the absence of sufficient child-care facilities, and also given the reluctance of some parents to entrust a child – especially the precious only child – to outside care, an alternative has been to offer extended maternity leave so that the mother can look after the baby herself. A factory in Shanghai offers a year's maternity leave to single-child mothers, granting full pay and an assurance that neither their promotion prospects nor wage increases will be jeopardized as a result. This experimental scheme was explained on the grounds that not all families had a grandmother living with them who could help to take care of the child; that the factory's three-shift system, and the commuting problems of its workers, made it difficult for women with babies to work; and that the baby's health was best safeguarded by its being at home with mother, rather than in a crèche picking up infections.

Shanghai's family-planning regulations in any case provide for maternity leave of up to a year for single-child mothers, on 80 per cent salary. Shaanxi offers four to six months' maternity leave for a single-child mother. Many individual enterprises offer similar incentives; there is six months' maternity leave at the Beijing Normal University, for instance.

The assumption by outside observers that in cities there is still strong family pressure for more than one child put upon the marrying couple may itself no longer hold good. The women who are coming up to marriage age now are the ones whose mothers were sterilized in the early 1960s; there exists a generation of actual, or potential, grandmothers who were in the vanguard of contraceptive use. A substantial proportion, especially amongst the opinion-forming cadres and intellectuals, were themselves the parents of only one child, so that they are – or are about to be – the grandparents of a second-generation single child.

The family seems, in any case, to be a less all-pervasive influence in urban areas. Many of the functions of the family and the clan have been taken over by the unit, and ubiquitous as that unit may be, its concerns and demands are different. A unit *(danwei)* is the place in which one works, or the district in which one lives. It has 'taken over many functions formerly fulfilled by the extended family and which in Europe have been handed to an impenetrable state bureaucracy: for example, child care and education, social welfare and social control . . . just as the extended family insists on the right to have a say in all important decisions faced by its members, so the unit today has a fundamental influence on the personal and professional destiny of those who belong to it.'[12] Thus the unit can forbid marriage if there are 'strong political or medical reasons against this', and it supervises behaviour 'in accordance with political and moral norms'. But those norms are more likely to be the ones acceptable to the Party than those acceptable by tradition; the unit is more likely to be on the side of late marriage, of stopping at one child even if that child is a girl, or of a married woman continuing to work, than are the family networks of the village.

In addition, the unit will try to overcome the fears of young people that they will be left on the shelf if they do not marry in their early twenties – a fear which is held to be the biggest deterrent to late marriage in urban areas. The unit will offer young people a chance to meet in socially approved work or recreational activities, and so have a wider choice of partners than is available to most rural young. The unit will probably support the desire of young people who have met in this way to marry, unless there are remarkably strong reasons why they should not. Alternative parental desires and family alliances seldom seem to be reasons a unit would accept as justifying intervention, to judge by the increasing practice of free-choice marriages in the cities.

Information gathered from case studies on marriage formation shows that 'peer groups in the urban areas were more autonomous and influential and that young people from the urban areas are as likely to take the advice or follow the example of friends, peers, fellow members of class or political associations as of kin or neighbours. They will even be influenced by abstract categories or role models . . .'[13]

There is some evidence that traditional familial values – whether inculcated by the family or the unit – are in any case breaking down. In the wake of the Cultural Revolution, many of the young have become disillusioned with politics, and their search for alternative life-styles has been fuelled by the 'open door' policy pursued by the Chinese government since the late 1970s, which has exposed people to a far greater variety of foreign influences. The Tianjin family structure survey noted that 'older people are generally conservative and practical, while younger ones like to break away from set rules and are more idealistic. The two have different interests and preferences . . . Furthermore in the past few years Western bourgeois ways of life have spread to China through various channels, and have affected young people. Therefore, in looking at life, work, and society, the two generations have different views, resulting in estrangements between them, and even disruptions of families.'[14]. Interviewing all the young workers in a neighbourhood factory, the survey concluded: 'By the time they become economically independent and reach marriageable age, each naturally hopes to organise a nuclear family in which what they say counts . . . These are factors accounting for the dwindling in family size. This demand mainly comes from the younger generation.'

Pre-marital pregnancy is said to be on the increase, and a hospital survey in Tianjin indicated a possible 398 illegitimate births out of a total of 110,237 in 1978 (though the proportion – 0.4 per cent of all births – is nevertheless extremely small).

The first pre-marital family, sex and eugenics counselling service was set up in Beijing in February 1981, with others planned to begin shortly afterwards. The expressed rationale for such a move was partly to provide health check-ups for young couples, and identify potential medical or genetic problems, and partly to enable those getting married to delay their child-bearing through effective contraception. But an official from the service also referred to the low level of knowledge among young people about family planning, and said that in the Xuanwu district where the hospital is situated, half of those who had abortions in the previous year had had no knowledge of contraception. The implication appears to be that the service is at least partly designed to prevent pre-marital pregnancy. The introduction of sex education in schools (see chapter 5) is also stated to be necessary because of growing pre-marital sexual activity.

Whether or not there has been pre-marital sex, a young couple who have married late and who have chosen each other may be beginning to find other satisfactions in marriage, and in their lives, than simply the family round: '. . . more and more workers are using their leisure time and earnings to improve their educational and technical levels, to take advantage of the mass media, and to engage in creative work, sports and cultural activities. This suits the needs of modern-ized production and modern society. It will also influence social behaviour patterns and lead to a further decline in the population growth rate.'[15]

The Impact of One-child Policy Measures

As has already been indicated, the introduction of municipal or provincial packages of incentives during 1979 and early 1980 accelerated the trend to the one-child family dramati-cally. In 1981, 33 per cent of all married urban women aged 15-49 had only one child. This percentage was heavily distorted by the increased number of marriages that year, together with the young age structure of the population. Of much greater significance was the fact that nearly 78 per cent of those urban women had signed the one-child certificate, compared with 31 per cent of the much smaller proportion of single-child families in rural areas.

Of this age group of urban married women, 14.4 per cent were certificate holders. It is impossible to guess the propor-tion of older women in that group, who had decided to stop at one before the new policy, but the figures given earlier in this chapter for the large number of single-child families which predated the one-child policy suggest that the proportion might be quite large. All that can safely be said is that the urban take-up of the certificate is approximately four times that of the rural areas. It is less clear, though, that the acceleration will be permanent. The Fusuijing survey divides those who have taken out one-child family certificates into three groups. The first (about 60 per cent of the total) really only wanted one child or were at least quite happy to stop at one in the interest either of their careers and pressure of work, or of population control. A further 30 per cent were ambivalent, conforming to 'social expectations'. They were prepared to go along with the policy if it remained unchanged, in many instances, but would have a second child if there were any signs of official relaxation of policies. Others felt they could not afford a second child but if their circumstances changed they would have one – and, presumably, be willing to pay back the benefits from certification. The remaining 10 per cent felt they had been pressured to take the one-child certificate.

The survey of West Side Hefei did not ask questions in a comparable form, but, interestingly, it too gathered a rather similar figure of 9 per cent who were not at all sure they had done the right thing in accepting a one-child certificate. More than half of the doubters had expected more welfare benefits or better housing than they actually got; they tended to be the poorest families and were clearly more influenced by the prospect of incentives than genuine conviction about the need for sacrifice.

There seems little reason to doubt the reliability of these surveys. Obviously, the demographic success of the measures in cities will be quite considerable if most of the 60 per cent reported in Beijing as being content with the decision to stop at one child stick to their pledge. There is no way of knowing how many of the remainder will backslide, but there are indications of potential problems.

The rapidly increasing number of abortions being performed may both indicate a problem – the ambivalence of many couples about the policy – and itself give rise to further problems. There is no published analysis of the abortion information from the sample fertility survey, except for some data on the reason for the pregnancy occurring: half of those who had an abortion were not using contraception, and among the remainder, the biggest proportion of pregnancies came about as the result of the failure or expulsion of an IUD.

A household survey of married women under fifty in one of the five administrative districts of Xi'an, Shaanxi, however, found that the average number of abortions obtained by women aged 25-39 was 74 per cent higher in 1981 than it had been in 1977. Between 1973 and 1978, only 32 per cent of the women who had undergone an abortion had that abortion after only one live birth. Between 1979 and 1981 the proportion increased to 71 per cent. Xi'an now has an incidence of induced abortion which is comparable to the highest levels known of anywhere in the world.

There is, unfortunately, nothing to suggest that Xi'an is an exceptional case amongst Chinese cities. The increased reliance on abortion indicates that many women are being pressured into terminating a second pregnancy which they really want. The long-established pattern in cities, of women making a sensible choice about contraceptive needs, and using contraception to limit a family, with abortion as a back-up for contraceptive failure, has been transformed. This is not only a tragedy for many individuals, but, as the study points out, the very high number of abortions being performed puts considerable pressure on badly-needed medical facilities and personnel. It also transforms the family-planning worker from the assistant helping couples to achieve reasonable fertility choices into a punitive agent of the state. These are very large prices to pay to reduce still further the very low urban fertility-rates.

In addition, it seems very unlikely that the authorities can rapidly fulfil the pledges on housing, nurseries and so on for which those who have a one-child certificate have priority. The West Side Hefei survey indicated that even with a lower take-up of certificates, 40 per cent of those who held them had not got the improved housing they had hoped for. Those concerned with the Fusuijing study concluded:

We must urge the departments concerned to actively support and create the right conditions for family planning and to strictly enforce the policies and regulations related to family planning. We must help the families with one child to locate day-care centres and schools for their children, to get medical care, and to find jobs and housing. We must help single-child parents resolve their domestic problems, so as to relieve them of whatever anxieties they may feel about their family life . . .[16]

If such measures cannot be provided, considerable resentment may build up among certificate holders.

Further grounds for dissatisfaction may arise from the differentials in incentives at the local level. West Side Hefei reported:

Take the bonus system for instance: there is no unified standard and large disparity exists between different units even within one city; the bonus standard is different from factory to factory, from factory to schools or administrative units, from state units to collective units. The people are very dissatisfied. Some of the more profitable factories or commercial enterprises provide bonuses to single-child parents amounting to as much as over 100 *yuan*, or in the form of commodities such as woollen blankets, transistor radio-sets, brocade sheets, etc. But other units, such as administrative organizations, having no special funds for family planning, can only take money from the general welfare funds; bonuses are as low as 10 or 20 *yuan* or only a couple of towels, a thermos bottle, some toys, a washing basin or even nothing at all.[17]

The factory in Shanghai, already quoted as offering a year's leave to all women having their single child and taking the certificate, pointed out that this experimental incentive could not be imitated in many other Shanghai factories, such as cotton mills, where most of the workers were female: the disruption would simply be too great.

In some areas, the authorities have asked units to avoid giving incentives which are widely out of line with what others are offering. In others, units seem to have been left to their own devices. So far there has been no overall attempt to regulate incentives and disincentives provided by individual units, although some prominent policy-makers, while pointing out that a unified system would be difficult to implement because of varying local conditions, nevertheless believe that the state should have some basic requirements and limitations.

In the long run, the most serious danger of the one-child

family policy may result from its success in China's urban areas, compared with the level of acceptance in the country-side. Priority in education, in health care, in employment and in other areas of life for the single child is likely to widen still further the gap between the privileged town-dwellers and their rural counterparts, at least in the medium term. And the creation of an urban élite in itself may make it difficult, in the course of time, to ensure across-the-board national development.

Notes

1. Chen Da, 'Depopulation and Culture', The Phi Tau Phi Lecture Series, no. 11, Lingnan University, Canton, 1934, 16pp.

2. Chen Da, 'Population in Modern China', *American Journal of Sociology,* vol. 52, no. 1, part II, University of Chicago Press, 1946, 126pp.

3. Chen, D., 1946, op. cit.

4. Chen, D., 1946, op. cit.

5. Croll, Elisabeth, *The Politics of Marriage in Contemporary China,* Cambridge University Press, 1981.

6. Lang, Olga, *Chinese Family and Society,* Yale University Press, 1946.

7. Chen Pi-Chao, The Politics of Population in Communist China, PhD. thesis, 1966.

8. Quoted in: Tien, H. Yuan, *China's Population Struggle,* Ohio State University Press, 1973.

9. Qiao Xinjian, 'Possible Obstacles to the Realization of the One-Child Family', extended esssay, David Owen Centre for Population Growth Studies, July 1982, in partial fulfilment of a postgraduate diploma.

10. *Xinhua,* 21 May 1983.

11. Qiao, X., op. cit.

12. Kahn-Ackermann, Michael, *Within the Outer Gate,* Marco Polo Press, 1982.

13. Croll, 1981, op. cit.

14. Pan Yunkang and Pan Naiqu, 'Urban family structures and their changes: a survey of a Tianjin neighbourhood', *Beijing Review,* vol. 26, no. 9, 28 February 1983.

15. Sun Jingzhi, 'Economic Development — A Major Solution to Population Problems' in Liu Zheng et al., op. cit.

16. 'One-Child Family Becoming Norm in Beijing West District', Beijing *Renkou Yanjiu,* no. 1, January 1981.

17. Anhui University, 'A Survey on Single-Child Families of West-Side Hefei, Anhui Province, *Anhui Population,* 1981.

CHAPTER FOUR

FAMILY PLANNING IN RURAL AREAS

★★

Traditional Fertility Control

The number of children in a traditional Chinese family was, as noted in Chapter 1, quite small. Very high death rates among infants and children were one cause, but it is also known that the Chinese, in common with people throughout the world, attempted to avoid unwanted pregnancies. Such efforts at fertility control are better documented for China than for many other countries because written records exist, and because of the systematic collection of traditional recipes by the Chinese government in the 1950s.

References to contraceptives such as condoms or caps made of paper and even tortoise-shell occur in classical literature. Other traditional methods were handed down from one generation to another among herbalists or midwives in the same family. The belief, for example, that silkworm eggs could serve as an oral contraceptive dates from the seventh century. (A selection of herbal contraceptives is shown in Table 27.) While it is possible that among the concoctions used there were some which had at least a slight contraceptive effect, others produced severe toxic symptoms in the mother, and were probably abortifacients.

The majority of couples in old China who wanted to avoid a

birth probably practised abstinence, or *coitus reservatus*, or relied on prolonged breast-feeding of the existing baby. Buddhists and Taoists believed that abstinence would prolong life, which was an additional benefit. It was also widely believed – probably from before the Han dynasty which began in the year 2 AD – that while a man's health and longevity were improved by his absorption of vaginal secretions, they were lessened if he ejaculated. Very early handbooks on sex therefore stressed the importance of *coitus reservatus* as a health measure for men. This was the easier to do because of an assumption consistent in all the early texts that sex was for enjoyment as well as for procreation. Breast-feeding was recognized as tending to reduce fertility, though its limitations were drily indicated by a woman pioneer in Liu Ling, Shaanxi, in 1962:

Certain of the families don't use any contraceptives at all but only simple techniques. A lot of women still believe that they can't become with child as long as they are suckling. And each time they are as surprised as ever when they find they are pregnant again . . . [1]

Table 27 Contraceptive Recipes

ONE
Ingredients
Brassica rapa (4 mace), Angelica polymorpha (3 mace), Conioselinum univittatum (½ mace), Rehmannia lutea (3 mace), Paeonia albiflora (1 mace).
Preparation and dosage
Place all ingredients in an earthenware pot. Add about 2 cups of water and simmer 30 minutes. Strain to obtain a first decoction of about ½ cup. Add another 2 cups of water to the ingredients. Repeat the process to obtain another ½ cup of decoction. Combine both decoctions. On the day of cessation of the menstrual flow, drink ½ cup each after lunch and dinner. Prepare and take two additional recipes in the same manner on the two following days. Repeat the whole process at end of the menstrual flow during the next 2 months.
Claimed contraceptive potency
Permanent

Promoting agent or agency and source of information
Shanghai Municipal Bureau of Health. *Da Gong Bao* (Tianjin), 22nd July 1956. Reprinted in *Chongqing Daily*, 26th July 1956; *Hubei Daily* (Wuhan), 2nd Aug. 1956; *Xinhua Daily* (Nanjing), 23rd Aug. 1956; and *China's Women*, no. 9, 1st Sept. 1956. *Harbin Daily*, 2nd Aug. 1956.

TWO
An antidote to the above recipe
Ingredients
Adenophora verticillata (3 mace), Dioscorea japonica (3 mace), Alisma plantago (3 mace), Bark of Paeony (3 mace), Cornus officinalis (3 mace), Pachyma cocos (3 mace), Shu fu kuai (3 mace)**, Ze yu kuai (3 mace)**.
Promoting agent or agency and source of information
Da Gong Bao (Tianjin), 22nd July 1956.

THREE
Ingredients
Mung beans.
Preparation and dosage
Pulverize 10 to 20 fresh beans. Swallow one preparation each day for 3 days after the termination of the menstrual flow.
Claimed contraceptive potency
1 month
Promoting agent or agency and source of information
Zhejiang Daily (Hangzhou), 12th Aug. 1956. Recommended by Gao Deming of the Zhejiang Institute of Women's Health.

FOUR
Ingredients
Canarium album (Chinese olive)
Preparation and dosage
Soak in Kaoliang spirit for 10-15 days. At the end of menstruation, take 7 of the prepared olives each day for 3 days.

Claimed contraceptive potency
1 month
Promoting agent or agency and source of information
ibid.

FIVE
Ingredients
Black muer (an edible variety of thallophytic plants) (20 mace)**,
Fresh tili (40 mace)**, Steatite (20 mace).
Preparation and dosage
Add water to the ingredients and simmer. Drink the decoction on 3
successive days immediately after the menses.
Claimed contraceptive potency
1 month
Promoting agent or agency and source of information
ibid.

SIX
Ingredients
Persimmon stalks
Preparation and dosage
Place 7 stalks on an earth tile. Bake dry on fire, but no metal utensils
should be used to touch them. Do not burn stalks. Pulverize.
Swallow one whole preparation with yellow wine (millet wine) after
the menses. Do not drink yellow wine excessively. (Antidote:
persimmons.)
Claimed contraceptive potency
1 year
Promoting agent or agency and source of information
Hengyang News (Hunan), 25th Aug. 1956. This and the following
three recipes were presented in the name of the editor of the *Hengyang News*. In all cases an endorsement was given by the Hospital of
Traditional Chinese Medicine, Beijing.

SEVEN
Ingredients
Melilotus officinalis (2 mace).

Preparation and dosage
Place the leaves in water. Boil. Drink 1 cup on the first day after the cessation of the menses.
Claimed contraceptive potency
1 month
Promoting agent or agency and source of information
ibid. Reprinted in *Chongqing Daily*, 29th Aug. 1956; *China's Women*, 1st Sept. 1956.

EIGHT
Ingredients
Xanthoxylum piperitum (10 mace).
Preparation and dosage
Boil in water. Cool and wash feet in the solution after the menses.
Claimed contraceptive potency
1 month
Promoting agent or agency and source of information
ibid. Reprinted in *China's Women*, 1st Sept. 1956.

NINE
Ingredients
Solanum molongena.
Preparation and dosage
Take 14 flowers just before blossoming, sun dry and then place on an earth tile. Bake on fire. No metal instruments should be used. Pulverize. Swallow with yellow wine after the first menstrual flow following childbirth. (Antidote: eggplants.)
Claimed contraceptive potency
Indefinite
Promoting agent or agency and source of information
ibid. Reprinted in *Chongqing Daily*, 29th Aug. 1956. (Side-effects: menstrual irregularities during the 3 following months, and a tendency to gain weight.)

TEN
Ingredients
Brassica rapa (3 mace), Artemisia keiskeana (3 mace), Vaccaria vul-

garis (3 mace), Angelica polymorpha (3 mace), Carthamus tinctorius (8/10 mace), Gypsum (3 mace).

Preparation and dosage

Place all ingredients in an earth pot. Add 2 cups of water. Follow the instructions for recipe no. 1. Starting on the third day after the menses, drink ½ cup each time after lunch and dinner. Repeat on the next 2 days.

Claimed contraceptive potency

1 month

Promoting agent or agency and source of information

Chongqing Daily , 29th Aug. 1956. Reprinted in *China's Women*, 1st Sept. 1956 and *Health News* (Beijing), 31st July 1956.

ELEVEN

Ingredients

Bombyx mori (3 mace of eggs).

Preparation and dosage

Roast, but do not burn. Swallow with aged wine on 3rd, 5th and 7th days following delivery.

Claimed contraceptive potency

Permanent

Promoting agent or agency and source of information

From Sun Simao's *'Thousand of Gold Prescriptions'*. Sun lived in the Tang dynasty and died in AD 695. This and the preceding and following recipes (nos. 9, 10, 12) were formally introduced at the First Symposium on the Treatment of Women's Diseases, sponsored by the Traditional Chinese Medical Society of Hebei Province.

TWELVE

Ingredients

Semen plantagiuis (2 mace), Lotus stamens (2 mace), Xanthoxylum piperitum (½ mace), Calcareous spar (1½ mace), Melilotus officinalis (1½ mace).

Preparation and dosage

Mix and grind the ingredients into fine powder. After menstruation take 1 mace each, 3 times a day, until the supply is gone. Or, divide the preparation into two equal portions, take one portion immediately after the menses, and the other 15 days later.

Claimed contraceptive potency
1 year
Promoting agent or agency and source of information
Introduced by a herbalist in Hebei; *China's Women*, 1st Sept. 1956.

THIRTEEN
Ingredients
Verbena officinalis (5 mace), Caprifolium (5 mace).
Preparation and dosage
Cook in water. Drink the broth all at once as soon as the menses cease. Repeat for several days.
Claimed contraceptive potency
?
Promoting agent or agency and source of information
Hangzhou Daily, 18th Oct. 1956. Introduced by a herbalist at a symposium attended by some 25 doctors of both Western medicine and traditional Chinese medicine.

FOURTEEN
Ingredients
Angelica polymorpha (1 mace), Conioselinum univittatum (5 mace), Rehmannia lutea (6 mace), Paeonia albiflora (3 mace), Pachyma cocos (3 mace), Alisma plantago (3 mace), Radix liquiritiae (3 mace), Bignonia chinensis (5 mace), Verbena officinalis (5 mace), Hydrargyri sulphidum rubrum (1½ mace), Calcareous spar (3 mace), Atractylis ovata (5 mace), Calomel (1 mace), Semen areca (2 nuts), Su xiong (3 mace)**, Cun xiang (¹⁄₁₀ mace)**.
Preparation and dosage
Wrap calomel in very thin paper, and burn into ashes. Combine all ingredients, pulverize and sift with fine cloth. Add honey. Roll into small balls of about 3 mace each. From the day after the cessation of the menses take 1 pill each time before sleep until the supply is exhausted. (For women who have just given birth to a child, wait until 30 days after the delivery.) No other drugs should be ingested at the same time; otherwise, the effect of the pills will be nullified.
Claimed contraceptive potency
10 months to 1 year

Promoting agent or agency and source of information
Recommended by a herbalist in Hebei Province. *Hebei Daily* (Baoding), 4th Dec. 1956.

FIFTEEN
Ingredients
Arsenic monosulphide (½ to 3 mace), Calcareous spar (3 mace).
Preparation and dosage
Pulverize. Swallow with water. One preparation should suffice. To assure success, take two additional doses. The three preparations may be taken separately; starting on the day after the menses, take one dose a day. No intercourse within a week after the last dose.
Claimed contraceptive potency
9 months
Promoting agent or agency and source of information
Anhui Daily (Anjing), 30 Aug. 1957.

---

* 1⅓lb = 1 catty, which has 16 *liang* or 160 mace.
** English transliterations of the Chinese names of the ingredients, the identities of which have not been established.
Source: Tien, H. Yuan, 1965.

Women in that village suckled their babies until they were two or three years old. 'Many go on even longer, especially if it is the last child, or if the mother wants to avoid having any more children for a time.'

When preventive measures failed, the women would try abortion. Traditional Chinese law dealt with abortion in only two kinds of circumstances. Abortion as the result of assault was considered a relatively light offence, 'only a little more serious than breaking a limb or causing permanent blindness in one eye'.[2] Where an abortion resulted in the mother's death, an abortionist was subject to penalties, but there was no law which prohibited women from seeking an abortion or penalized her if she achieved one successfully. 'Not only was she not prohibited from seeking to abort; it may actually be inferred that the law extended some marginal protection to her when she did so.' A foetus was apparently not considered as a potential human being until it was ninety days old, and then because the life of the foetus was integrated with, and derived from, the mother, she had a far greater degree of freedom to abort than did her Western sisters. 'There was a far more flexible and situational and a far less moralistic approach', although the woman was subject to her husband and her mother-in-law and did owe an obligation to her husband's ancestors to procreate.

In 1910, however, the tottering empire introduced a new penal code modelled on Western and Japanese laws. Under the code, any woman who attempted to procure an abortion, and any person who helped her to abort, had committed an offence; no allowance was made for therapeutic abortion until 1935, when the code was revised. However, given the turbulence of China during the first part of the century, and the almost complete breakdown of national control, it is unlikely that this aspect of the new code impinged much on the ordinary peasant.

Indeed, there is evidence that it did not. After 1949, while abortion continued to be prohibited, many women nevertheless attempted it and some died from the dangerous methods they used. 'For what was perhaps the first time in Chinese history, these cases were reported in the Press in their grisly details, and a heated debate took place . . .'[3]

Traditional abortion techniques were clumsy and all too often fatal to the mother. Women desperate enough might 'try to bring on a miscarriage by taking drugs or beating the womb with a stick. Or they'll get an abortion done with a big hook or pressure on the belly.'[4] The alternative, or the next step if the abortion failed, was infanticide. Although infanticide has been practised in many societies throughout the world, it seems to have been unusually widespread in China. This may have been because of the low status Chinese children had, and their absolute subservience to parents and family. Additionally, still births and child deaths were common and largely ignored. A demographer in the 1940s wrote: 'The registration of deaths at Cheng Kung [Yunnan] does not include still births, for in rural communities such items are considered misfortunes and are therefore avoided in ordinary conversation. Nor does it include miscarriages which occur after the completion of six months of pregnancy. Both instances are, according to the Chinese laws, required to be registered. However, the observance of the law in these matters will take some time . . . '[5] In this area, except for infants, 'the use of a coffin for the dead person is quite general' but the same could not be said of Shaanxi even in the 1960s:

Children under twelve may not be buried in their family's burial ground. The older people say: 'Children under twelve have not got fully developed souls. It would bring bad luck to bury them in the family grave.' So they are buried without ceremony up on the hillside. Children under seven are buried without coffins. They are thrust into some natural crevice or hole in the rocks near the village and covered with earth and stones to keep wild animals from getting at them. The older people say that any other way of burying those who die so young is unthinkable. 'It would bring great misfortune upon the entire family.'[6]

Infanticide was safer for the mother than abortion, and, in many instances, the child would have died of starvation anyway. The great Chinese Red Army general, Zhu De (1886-1976), recalled that his mother 'bore thirteen children in all. Only six boys and two girls lived. The last five children were drowned at birth because we were too poor to feed so many mouths.'[7] In the first two decades of this century, following the Boxer uprising (1900), Catholic missionaries began to open orphanages in Shaanxi, including one in the village of Longbow:

Because the peasants lived from year to year on the verge of starvation and in bad years often died themselves, it was impossible for them to raise all their children. Boys, when they grew up, stayed home to help support their parents. Therefore every effort was made to save them. But girls, after twelve years of feeding, could only be sold for a few bags of grain, or given in marriage for the equivalent of a few dollars. Therefore in times of distress girl children were sometimes abandoned or even killed at birth. The orphanage in Long Bow was built specifically to care for such abandoned children. From picking up babies in the streets and fields, the custom developed of accepting babies directly from their parents, or even of paying modest sums for girl children in order to encourage their mothers to part with them[8].

So widespread was the practice of infanticide that in some villages in Anhui there were in the 1930s still 'baby ponds in which unwanted girl infants were drowned at birth'.[9] One woman's experience in the same period was recounted by Han Suyin from the hospital where she worked:

There was the countrywoman who came a long way from Chingsien, eight *li* or more, to be delivered of her tenth child, because all the others had been daughters; and a neighbour of hers had been to the hospital and had acquired a son; this woman thought she too could obtain a son by coming to be delivered at our hospital. She rode in a rickshaw all the way and this must have cost a good deal; and as she lay on the obstetric table she told Mrs Hsu what had happened to her baby daughters: the first was alive, and also the third; but the second had been strangled at birth by the husband and so had the fifth and sixth; the seventh had been born in a bad year, a year of famine when her belly skin stuck to her spine, and the husband had smashed her skull in with his axe; at the eighth female child the husband had been so angry that he had hurled it against a wall; the ninth was a year old and had been given away to a neighbour and now here was something in her belly . . . oh let it be a son, a male child.[10]

Changing Attitudes to Women and Children

By 1948 the Central Committee of the Communist Party, in the Liberated Areas, recognized in a Resolution on Women the need for legislation to stop infanticide, as well as education on the equality of the sexes. Land reform, by reallocating land on an individual basis, and allowing women separate title deeds if necessary, did help to improve the status of women. It also provided, for some poor peasants, an object lesson in the advantages of having a large number of children, each of whom was entitled to a share of land.

But land reform was a single intervention. Once completed, it left the poorer peasants and the landless, at least, better-off, and a little more able to support the children they had. If it increased the desire for children, especially sons, to inherit that land, the move to advanced co-operatives and communes in the late 1950s made that ambition pointless. More important, probably, in shaping attitudes to family size and to the relative value of sons and daughters, were the gradual introduction of work teams, and of women into the labour force. Peasant children in the past had not made a major contribution to the family budget; a survey of 15,316 farms in the period 1929-32 indicated that children carried out 7 per cent of farmwork. (In the cities, children's contribution seems to have been much greater, presumably because of the greater opportunities to beg, do piece-work, and so on.) Most of this farmwork was carried out by boys, from the age of seven. Girls of that age began to help with the housework, take care of smaller children, and by the age of ten it was expected that 'a girl ought to be able to help her mother unpick quilted jackets and trousers and wash them, and she should also be able to wash vegetables and cook a meal. The girls mend clothes and help their mothers do the washing in the river.'[11]

As families began to pool their labour, the value of the contribution made by small boys declined still further, so that in Liu Ling in 1962 they did little more than collect wild grass for the pig. Thus, as schools were opened it does not seem to have been difficult to persuade peasants of the need to send the boys to learn to read and write and do arithmetic, at least.

The situation of small girls may have been rather different. As their mothers increasingly worked outside the home, their role in helping with household tasks and the care of younger children may have actually increased, especially where the family did not have a resident grandparent. A report from Anhui in 1955 illustrates the problems of working mothers in looking after young children:

In this district *(xiang)* there are 24 co-operatives and three mutual-aid teams. In 581 households there are 455 children under six needing care. Some mothers get grandparents or elder children to care for them, and others make exchange agreements with neighbours. This has taken care of 332 of the children. Eight old ladies between them care for 28 more of the children. Thus, 216 mothers go to work with easy minds.

For 95 other children there was no solution; either their mothers did not work or they worked and worried that their child would get up to mischief and have accidents.[12]

A family in which there was no mother-in-law, or no daughter of a suitable age to take care of younger children, had to pay for the childminding carried out by somebody else. This additional expense lessened the family's gain from a working mother, although it may, at the same time, have been seen as an addition to the costs of children.

Even where there was a mother-in-law, she was, as noted in Chapter 1, far from enthusiastic at the prospect of taking on new responsibilities, when she had expected to shed those she already had on the arrival of her son's wife. Childminding was not such a problem: even some of the grandfathers were reported as being prepared to take that on. The real labour was in housework.

Housework, in a society without labour-saving devices, was hard and burdensome. Even collecting the water for washing and cooking involved heavy labour, clothes and sometimes the cloth and thread themselves were made at home, cloth shoes which took two days to make lasted only five or six months, and food for the winter all had to be pickled and preserved. The value of a daughter in the home was apparent and quite often outweighed appeals from cadres, the Women's Federation and other officials to send the girl to school. There was no law to reinforce their appeals: education, though strongly encouraged by the government, remains non-compulsory.

The Liu Ling Basic School had 109 boys and only 68 girls in 1962 despite the fact that the villagers seem to have been quite enthusiastic about the idea of education, and despite the struggles of many adults to achieve literacy. As an adult woman worked in the team and collected workpoints, and as her daughter helped to make that possible by her contribution in the house, the status of both may have improved but that did not, especially at first, lead to equality of opportunity for girl children.

As women undertook a greater share of farmwork, the difficulties of combining heavy agricultural work with child-bearing became apparent. Articles in the press in the 1950s reported miscarriages among women working in the fields and warned work-team leaders to be careful of the special needs of women. Co-operatives which arranged for women to have days off or to be given lighter duties during periods and pregnancies were praised. Women were often shy about discussing such matters with a male team-leader while some, perhaps, were keen to prove themselves the equals of the men with whom they worked, particularly in the early days, when their emancipation was the subject for teasing. Whatever the causes, combining work with pregnancy continued to be a problem for some years, until the practice of offering lighter work and maternity leave with workpoints spread widely within communes. That, in turn, depended not only on official propaganda and encouragement for the idea, but on the income of the collective and its ability to set up a large enough welfare fund to meet the expense.

The contribution of women in agriculture first peaked in about 1958-9 when their participation rate may have been over 80 per cent. This was partly the result of the introduction of co-operatives, which did away with the dividends which had previously been paid to team members for their share of the land, tools and animals. Now, a family's income depended entirely on its members' labour and the participation in the work-force of as many family members as possible. At the same time, the work available outside the busy farming seasons was not always sufficient for a work-force which had been expanded by the inclusion of women. Irrigation, tree planting and flood-prevention works organized by the communes or even larger units – county or provincial – offered additional opportunities, but for women who wanted to earn there were probably greater possibilities in sideline occupations and handicrafts set up by the Women's Federation, or in marketing co-operatives. Here, furniture, baskets and other everyday items were made for local sale; and workshops for the repair of tools and farm machinery were established. Some household chores, such as making clothes, were undertaken on an institutional basis too, lightening the load of working women but lessening the visible profit from their earnings. In some communes, women won the fight to have their earnings not

Table 28 Proportion of Days Spent in Productive Labour by Women in the Main Geographical Areas, 1957

Area	Percentage of total labour force		Average labour days worked		Percentage of total working days	
	Males	Females	Males	Females	Males	Females
North-west and Inner Mongolia District	60.1	39.9	170	88	74.5	25.5
North-east District	65.3	34.7	185	60	85.5	14.5
Central District	55.8	44.2	195	84	74.6	25.4
Southern District	54.3	45.7	226	133	66.8	33.2

Source: Salaff, Janet W., 1972.

only recorded separately but paid to them, rather than to the family head; in others – perhaps the majority, judging from an accountants' handbook from Hunan Province of the early 1970s – although the workpoint recorder recorded individual amounts, workpoints were periodically totalled and entered in the accountant's books by household and paid to the household head. This latter practice did not necessarily affect the woman's status (she was, after all, seen to be a contributor by the family) but it may have limited her independent use of the money she earned.

More demoralizing, probably, for women torn between the demands of family and work was the question of equal pay. Equal pay for equal work was a fundamental tenet of the Party, but defining and evaluating 'equal work' was not so simple. Agriculture in China was, and largely remains, unmechanized. Cultivation requires backbreaking toil with primitive tools; loads may be carted but those carts are still frequently pulled by people, not animals. Youth, health and above all strength are inevitably valued even above skills: women, especially in the early days, possessed few farming skills in any case to offset their average lesser strength. Sometimes this meant that they were just allocated to lighter, lower-paid jobs; in some communes women got a lower assessment in terms of workpoints whatever they did. Given that women worked fewer days of the year, partly because there was not always enough work to go round until local industries were developed and partly because of household responsibilities, it is remarkable that by 1956 women should have earned a quarter of the total workpoints that year. But statistics for the number of days worked by women suggest that women put in more work time than the workpoints alone imply (see Table 28).

The increasing value of women as earners had to be balanced against their role as mothers. In Liu Ling, reported Myrdal: 'The most serious thing one can say about anyone is: "He has been so bad and behaved so immorally that he has no young generation." To die without anyone to continue the family is the most dreadful thing that can happen to anyone.'[13]

Family Planning in the 1950s and 1960s

Children were not only the inevitable consequence of marriage, but – as everywhere in the world – a major rationale for it. Children gave women, especially, their standing as full members of the community. In the late 1950s and 1960s, as death rates and especially infant death-rates fell, the number of children each couple reared increased. A recent survey carried out in Hubei Province[14] suggests that women born in 1932-41 (aged 40-49 at the time of the survey) gave birth on average to 4.9 children and brought up 3.9 of them. A similar pattern prevailed among those ten years younger: the average number of children they bore was 4.7 of whom 3.4 survived.

Among the women aged fifty and over, of an average of 5.5 children born only 3.8 survived at the time of the survey. Thus, the older women lost about 31 per cent of their live births, whereas those aged 30-49 lost about a quarter.

In the years from 1956 onwards, condoms, spermicides and sterilization facilities very gradually began to be provided in the rural areas but, as one peasant pointed out, 'those who live too crowded together often find it difficult to use contraceptives'[15] – or at least, the only contraceptives which were then available. Vasectomy was recommended in preference to female sterilization, as the easier and safer operation. Zhou Enlai's discussion on this topic with a young couple working in a factory in Manchuria was widely publicized:

Li Ying then told the Premier, 'Two years ago, the father of these children had a vasectomy so that there would not be any more births . . .' The Premier asked: 'Was that what you two were willing to do?' Said Li Ying 'This was our wish.' The Premier seemed pleased; he praised them for doing the right thing, especially the husband . . .

The Premier further inquired about the economic circumstances of their family as well as his physical condition after the surgery. Sun replied that he is now Vice-director of the factory . . . He and Li Ying earn a combined income of a little over 200 Yen monthly, and so their family financial situation is not bad. They practised planned parenthood, not because of economic considerations. What is more important is that it is in the interests of their work and the health of the mother and children. As to whether vasectomy would affect health, Sun told the Premier that there have been no inimical effects on his health or on their marital life.

The Premier was pleased to hear this . . . and also said that in the matter of planned parenthood, the Sun Yen-wen couple has set a good example, especially the husband who voluntarily assumed the burden of planned parenthood and deserved emulation by other people.[16]

The lack of easy-to-use and reliable methods and the novelty of the idea that modern contraceptives could be more reliable than the old village techniques led to a kind of fatalism. In Liu Ling a young woman pioneer was admired by all the other women 'because she has always decided exactly when she is or is not to have children. Chi Meiying says "I am not like Li Kueiying. We too tried to be clever and plan, but it went wrong and so I had my last child. Not everyone can be as decided as Li Kueiying." '[17]

Ambivalence about the possibility of successfully planning one's family lasted well into the 1970s in the countryside, when even the woman team-member responsible for birth control might, rather frequently, reply that 'she hadn't taught herself well' when asked about her young family of three or more children.

A report from a field medical team which went from Guangzhou into the Renhe commune in the Guangdong countryside in the mid-1960s provides a lively illustration of the attitudes of the peasants in an area where 'certainly the majority of people had never heard about birth control'.[18] After the initial educational campaign that situation had changed, but most people 'still had some doubts. They said "It is useless just to hear about something; it only has reality once you see it." ' Shown samples of intra-uterine devices, they were relieved. One said 'I thought it would be as large as a bracelet' and another, 'If even a foetus can be hidden in the womb, how can such a small device be uncomfortable?'

'Fears that birth control would harm health or affect marital life were very widespread' and particularly intense, it seems, where vasectomy was concerned. This may explain why, in Liu Ling, the men were adamantly against permanent birth-control although they were prepared to agree to their wives' using a method to postpone a birth. Women there, and in

Renhe, were more eager than men to use contraception, although some in Renhe later wanted their IUDs removed when 'they encountered their husbands' strong disapproval'. Others had second thoughts because they feared there would be inadequate future medical supervision after listening to 'sarcastic remarks such as "There's nothing to having a device inserted now but in eighteen months, when something goes wrong, there will be no medical team to take care of it . . . " '

Some peasants remembered only too well that in the past their babies had died of starvation, infection and disease, or had been killed because their existence posed a threat to the already destitute family. Talk of limiting the number of their children frightened them. ' "What", they said, "Does that mean that bad times are coming again?" '[19]

Table 29 Insertions of IUDs in Rural Women, Shandong Province 1963-5, by Number of Children and Age of Women

Insertions of IUD in 1528 rural women, by parity

Parity	Percentage of women
1	5.2%
2	10.6%
3	19.4%
4	25.6%
5+	39.1%
Total	99.9%

Insertions of IUD in 2170 rural women, by age

Age	Percentage of women
21-25	8.5%
26-30	18.4%
31-35	31.1%
36-40	28.6%
40+	13.2%
Total	99.8%

Source: Salaff, Janet W., 1972.

Exactly how widespread the efforts were to educate the peasants about family planning between the mid-1950s and the end of the Cultural Revolution is still unclear. The situation seems to have varied enormously from area to area. One study of local and national newspapers between 1956 and 1958 suggests that the first campaign was pushed more vigorously along the coastal provinces, especially Hunan, Jiangsu, Hebei, Fujian and Zhejiang, and in the Yangzi valley (the most populous areas). But by 1962 the Liu Ling peasants of backward Shaanxi were quite knowledgeable about contraception, if not very apt practitioners, while Renhe in Guangdong was entirely ignorant three or four years later. Han Suyin reports that the city of Kunming was just beginning to offer family planning in 1964; Sichuan claims that there was no programme before 1970.

From Shandong, where it was claimed that by the end of 1957 the campaign 'had generally reached the overwhelming majority of lesser cities and villages'[20] there are some interesting statistics on the insertions of IUDs in rural areas between 1963 and 1965 (see Table 29). These figures suggest that the IUD was welcomed only after the birth of the fourth or fifth child, by women who, given the average marriage age of just over nineteen, had been married for more than ten years.

Unfortunately, there are no provincial figures available which give the birth, death and growth rates for each province during the pre-1970 period. There are, however, figures for the overall growth of Chinese provinces which help to give some indication of the effects of the spread of family planning. Where there are extraordinarily high rates of growth for some provinces, these are probably due to internal migration, especially in border and inland areas (such as those starred in the table). Others, such as Shandong and Henan, lost people to these provinces. Overall, however, the growth rates in the eastern provinces between 1963 and 1964 reflect the impact of reduced death rates and continuing large numbers of births.

Of the ten provinces with a growth rate somewhat above the national growth rate in that period, seven had rates after 1964 which were lower than the national average. All but one of those provinces with below average growth were in the eastern coastal and Yangzi valley belt of provinces which were earliest exposed to contraceptive methods and propaganda (see Table 30).

Table 30 Provincial Population Growth 1953-64 and 1964-79, in percentage (excluding the three municipalities)

Region and Province	1953-64	1964-79
TOTAL	17.6	41.6
NORTH-EAST		
Heilongjiang	68.7*	48.2
Jilin	41.9*	(22.1)
Liaoning	32.5*	(16.7)
NORTH		
Hebei	24.8	(23.2)
Shanxi	27.3	(34.4)
Shandong	10.8	(30.2)
Henan	14.6	42.9
EAST		
Anhui	2.9	53.7
Jiangsu	16.1	(32.4)
Zhejiang	23.8	(33.9)
CENTRAL		
Hubei	21.3	(37.4)
Hunan	11.9	40.5
Jiangxi	25.6	53.3
SOUTH		
Fujian	27.5	48.0
Guangdong	23.1	(32.7)
Guangxi	6.5	66.5
SOUTH-WEST		
Guizhou	14.0	59.3
Sichuan	3.5	43.8
Yunnan	41.7*	52.9
Xizang (Tibet)	−1.6	46.4

Table 30 cont.

Region and Province	1953-64	1964-79
NORTH-WEST		
Nei Monggol	63.7*	54.3
Shaanxi	30.8*	35.1
Ningxia	31.7*	68.5
Gansu	12.0	50.0
Qinghai	27.4	73.8
Xinjiang	49.3*	72.8
Years in period	(11)	(15)

Total includes the municipal provinces of Beijing, Shanghai and Tianjin which have been excluded here.

* Heavy internal migration

Source: Tien, H. Yuan, 1983.

This does suggest that the most populous areas of China, where the family-planning campaigns had been concentrated in the earlier days, were the quickest to respond to the renewed efforts carried on after 1969. They were also, of course, areas which had received the bulk of the increase in health facilities and educational provision, and were the ones where the overall living standards were higher than else-where. Additionally, they had received the majority of the exiles from the cities.

These came in various guises. Beginning in the 1950s, city cadres were regularly sent to the countryside for a fixed period, to pass on their skills, such as literacy, and to learn what the life of an average Chinese was like. Such voluntary physical work (*laodong*) was intended to prevent the growth of intellectual arrogance among officials, but it also offered opportunities to help the peasants with such things as reading and writing, or simple bookkeeping, as well as in spreading the Party's messages about the need for female equality, for example.

In the later 1950s their numbers were supplemented by city dwellers in larger numbers. These were the people for whom no jobs could be found in the towns, or who were among the many dependants of those who had managed to get an urban post. Many were ex-peasants; during the period 1953-8 it was estimated that some 8 million people flocked into the cities. Apart from these rural migrants,

the high rate of natural multiplication of our 89 million urban population generates an estimated addition of some 2 million annually to the labor force for whom employment must be found . . . [And], there are still unemployed persons left over from old society. Thus, in the cities the number of persons desirous of employment exceeds that of jobs available, resulting in a labor surplus . . . The principal way to [resolve this] will be to have them participate in agricultural production on the basis of an overall arrangement and appropriate regard for all. For, only the vast rural region can absorb the ever-increasing labor force.[21]

The introduction of the communes led to large-scale and divergent rural projects, such as irrigation works, more intensive farming and the development of local factories and enterprises which actually led to labour shortages in many communes, so that the migrants were absorbed without too many problems. The ex-peasants among them had, in any case, farming skills, and were often returned to their original community. Many of these resettled city-dwellers had been exposed to new ideas and influences in their urban environment; some would have been practising family planning, while others were at least aware that it existed, and had heard discussions about it.

During the Cultural Revolution the numbers of cadres taking part in *laodong* increased enormously. It became routine for people from the cities to spend shorter or longer periods in the countryside, to help with the harvest or to undertake some specific project. Schools and factories developed links with particular communes; groups of specialists, such as doctors, spent months at a time helping to set up medical facilities in rural areas or formed teams which went to particular areas at regular intervals. Many were shocked by the conditions they found and genuinely anxious to help improve them. Among their functions was the spread of birth-control information and supplies. In addition, there were those cadres from closed-down universities and elsewhere who were rusticated for years at a time. They were usually separated from their families and all too often their banishment was seen by themselves and the peasants as disgrace and punishment.

Finally, the number of ex-urban migrants was swelled by the *xiaxiang* youth: the urban products of middle-school who were sent 'up the mountains and down to the countryside' in their millions between the mid-1960s and 1978, although the movement itself began in the mid-1950s. They were expected to settle in the countryside for life and to marry into peasant families. Some were later sent back to the cities to get further training and others got to university and from there obtained jobs in the urban sector, but the majority were expected to stay put. Some of these young people, especially those sent to the remoter areas, found genuine satisfaction and stimulation in a pioneering role. Others felt like lonely exiles. Most of them in fact were sent to communes fairly near to their original home town.

Exactly what effect these various groups of urban migrants had on their peasant hosts is unclear. Some commune leaders today look back on them as having been merely a nuisance, especially the *xiaxiang* young, who often arrived in large numbers (several hundred might be employed in one commune) and had no practical skills. They were sometimes arrogant and certainly reluctant to marry into a peasant family. Where peasant and former city-dweller regarded each other with equal contempt, if for differing reasons, it is unlikely that the mutual transfer of knowledge was particularly fruitful.

All the same, it is probably fair to say that 'organised movement to rural areas, whether temporary or permanent, has acted as a catalyst in the diffusion of modern knowledge to the backward Chinese countryside,'[22] One of the areas in which this effect was most important was the status and role of women, as can be seen from an assessment by Liu Ling village in 1969:

The young intellectuals have been a great help. These young women from Peking, particularly, have influenced the brigade's young women. They sing and laugh and aren't a bit shy. They get up and make speeches. The most active women here are those who are

Table 31 Demographic Data of Selected Communes, China, 1972

Commune	Number of households	Population	Number of production brigades	Number of production teams	Crude birth rate	Crude death rate	Crude rate of natural increase	Number of married women of repro- ductive age
Shajiao, Shunde County, Guangdong	15,200	66,000	22	296	27	7.32	19.68	6977
Qiyi, Shanghai	4122	16,965	11	88	13.2	5.2	8	2496
Dongding, Wu County, Jiangsu		45,000	30	237	17.6	5	(13)	6000
Nanwan, Beijing	9473	39,000	16	135	25			3500
Nanying, Shanghai	6800	27,000	17	164	14	4	(10)	3500
Bayi, Shenyang, Liaoning	4400	20,853	15	73			17	
Sizhiqing, Hangzhou, Zhejiang	4656	21,890	10	105	16	2	14	3328

Source: Chen Pi-Chao, 1975.

between thirty and forty. The young girls find it harder to speak in public. But they, too, take part . . . [23]

Although a *xiaxiang* girl was unlikely to know much about the mechanics of contraception she was usually well aware of the arguments for family planning – its value for maternal and child health, the importance of late marriage for health and for women's work, and the need to achieve planned population growth. Older, married cadres also knew those arguments, and in addition could talk from personal experience of contraception. The young helped to make the subject mentionable; the cadres could assist in making birth control a practical reality.

Later, longer, fewer: the 1970s

The decline in the birth and growth rates in China in the 1970s was dramatic. The country's overall decrease in birth-rates, from 33.6 per thousand in 1970 to 17.9 in 1979, was greatest in rural areas, where birth rates which had been around 34.6 during the second half of the 1960s declined to 18.8 by 1978. No other large developing country has achieved such a decline so rapidly. During this period, the Chinese refused to reveal national statistics, which caused much debate abroad about whether the local rates which were reported to visitors were true, and, if true, whether they were representative or isolated freaks. As more evidence became available to suggest that they did at least indicate a real trend, the debate began to focus instead on what it was about China's experience – and particularly the experience of Chinese peasants – which made the family-planning campaign so successful.

Naturally in a country so huge, there was wide variation in the rate of decline in births, reflecting local priorities and local conditions. A selection of statistics for different units in different parts of the countryside indicates that variation. Information collected on seven communes in 1972 is shown in Table 31.

Table 32 Birth and Growth Rates of Guangdong Province, Taoyuan County, Hunan Province, and Rural China, 1962-77

	Guangdong (pop. 1977: 55,019,000)			Taoyuan (Hunan) (pop. 1977: 889,845)			Rural China (pop. 1977: approx. 756,192,000)		
	Birth rate	Natural increase rate	Death rate	Birth rate	Natural increase rate	Death rate	Birth rate	Natural increase rate	Death rate
1962	43	37					37.4	27	10.4
1963							43.4	32.8	10.6
1964				49	36	10	40.3	28	12.3
1965	36	30	6						
1969	36	30	6	31	19	12			
1970	29	23	6						
1971	29	23	6				31.9	24.3	7.6
1972	29	23	6	29	19	10	31.2		
1973	27	21	6				29.4	22.1	7.3
1974	24	18	6	22	13	9	26.2	18.6	7.6
1975	21	15	6	16	10	6	24.2		
1976	19	13	6	16	10	6	20.9		
1977	19	13	6	14	6	8	19.7	12.6	7.1

Source: Chen, P.C., 1979; Liu Zheng in Coale, Ansley, 1981.

These seven communes were in areas fairly near to major cities, and in fairly 'advanced' areas of the country. Nevertheless, the Guangdong commune's birth rate is only two points below the rate for Guangdong as a whole in 1972 (see below) which in turn was two points below the average birth rate for the entire country of 31 per thousand in the same year. The seven communes also provide a useful indication of the variety in the size of communes in different areas, and thus of the number of brigades and teams within each. Average household size varies from 3.9 members in Nanying, Shanghai to 4.7 in the Liaoning and Zhejiang communes.

In 1977, incomplete time-series data were acquired for two areas – a province and a county – which amplify the single-year information which is available for many communes (see Table 32). They show, again, considerable differences; compared with Taoyuan, Guangdong's birth rate fell more slowly, and never as far. Although no death rates were originally provided, the evidence of the other vital rates suggests that Taoyuan had deaths which were considerably above the national average until the mid-1970s while Guangdong appears to have stabilized at around six deaths per thousand ten years earlier: a number nearer to the urban rates reported for China than to the average rural ones. (This is not altogether surprising because Guangdong is the wealthiest of China's provinces, with a per capita income higher even than Shanghai's, as a result of high agricultural fertility, boosted by remittances from relatives abroad.)

Guangdong's rather slow progress in reducing its birth rate, and Taoyuan's faster reduction, suggest that it was not simply a reduction in overall death rates which encouraged people to have smaller families. Naturally however, official propaganda for family planning stressed (and continues to stress) that it was no longer necessary to have as many children as possible in order to make sure that some survived.

It is possible to look at the effect of reductions in death rates on the success of the family-planning programme by comparing the provinces which had achieved a growth rate of less than 1 per cent in 1978 (see Table 33) with those which had an above-average life expectancy according to a retrospective study of deaths between 1973 and 1975. (This study is discussed in more detail in Chapter 5.) In the period since 1949, average life-expectancy at birth had more than doubled by the mid-1970s, to around 63.6 years for men and 66.3 years for women. Two of the eleven provinces which had less than 1 per cent population growth rates in 1978 were not included in the mortality study. Of the nine which were, however, seven had above-average life expectancy for men and women. The exceptions were Shaanxi and Sichuan; in the latter province in particular, life expectancy was well below the national average.

Table 33 Provinces with a Natural Growth Rate below 1 per cent in 1978

	Life expectancy at birth		Life expectancy at age 5	
	Male	**Female**	**Male**	**Female**
Sichuan	59.16	61.08	62.49	64.08
Shaanxi	63.96	65.18	63.18	65.21
Shanxi	65.33	68.00	63.8	66.13
Hubei	n/a	n/a	n/a	n/a
Hebei	67.11	70.17	65.38	67.07
Beijing	68.34	70.77	65.17	68.49
Tianjin	69.93	71.96	66.62	68.58
Shandong	n/a	n/a	n/a	n/a
Jiangsu	65.10	69.34	64.69	69.02
Shanghai	69.24	74.84	65.68	71.13
Zhejiang	66.44	70.52	64.89	69.54
National average	63.62	66.31	64.22	66.75

Source: Rong Shoude et al., 1982; Chen Pi-Chao, 1979.

Life expectancy at age five provides some indication of the level of infant and child mortality. If it is greater at five years than it was at birth it suggests high death rates in early childhood. On average in China in 1973-75 life expectancy at age five was higher by 0.60 years for boys and 0.44 years for girls than at birth. Because of the under-reporting of early childhood deaths, the figures are probably over-optimistic. Nevertheless, there is so much variation reported from different provinces that the statistics for each probably do give an indication of real differences in controlling infant and child mortality. Of the nine provinces with a growth rate below 1 per cent in 1978 for which there are life tables, male life expectancy at age five was lower than at birth in eight, implying a low level of infant and child losses. Female life expectancy at five years was also lower than at birth in seven provinces (although for one province, Jiangsu, by less than the national average). The exceptions were again Sichuan for both sexes and Shaanxi for girls.

The comparison suggests that while reductions in the death rates, especially in the rates of death in early childhood among boys, has been a factor in the acceptance of family planning, it is not the only one. Sichuan, after slow start, managed to achieve one of the most remarkable rates of decline in birth rates – from 40.7 per thousand in 1970 to 13.6 in 1979 – despite its continuing comparatively high levels of child mortality.

Reductions in the death rate also indicated overall improvements in health. Health care and family-planning work within the health care system are discussed in Chapter 5. Here, it is sufficient to note that by 1965 it was claimed that all of China's 2000 counties had one health centre or hospital with some in-patient facilities, and that during the late 1960s and the 1970s a very large number of para-medical and medical personnel were trained, dispatched to the countryside and given further training at intervals. Such people provided immunizations for children as part of their heavy orientation towards maternal and child health; emphasized the importance of hygienic measures such as boiling drinking water and ensuring careful storage and handling of night-soil (still the most important fertilizer in China); and took care of the day-to-day illnesses and injuries within the community. They were people who came from the community they served; were known to and often related to the villagers among whom they worked; and indeed had been chosen by them to receive medical training.

Thus the barefoot doctors, in particular, were well suited to the promotion of family planning and the distribution of contraceptives. Not only were they aware of the circumstances of their patients and able to tailor arguments for family limitation to those particular circumstances, but, living and working among the community, they were easily available to deal with worries or side-effects, or to refer couples for more specialist advice. At least one barefoot doctor in a brigade medical centre was expected to be a woman, able to discuss matters of contraception, pregnancy and childbirth with the traditionally shy peasant women.

The efforts of the barefoot doctor in family planning were supervised and supplemented by an even greater number of unpaid activists. A Birth Planning Leading Group in each commune, consisting of the commune's first Party secretary and members from the commune's Party committee, the commune management committee, the public security station (which keeps the basic population statistics), the local branch of the Women's Federation, the Young Communist League, the militia, the school system, the commune health centre, and so on, was responsible for co-ordinating family-planning activities. They worked within the general framework laid down by the provincial Birth Planning Leading Group, whose members came from various government departments and from the provincial universities and the mass organizations such as the trade unions, the Youth League and Women's Federation. The provincial Leading Group also included full-time family-planning workers.

Day-to-day work at the provincial level – research, co-ordinating local efforts, organizing conferences, running a variety of courses for different audiences and providing information and publicity – was undertaken by the paid staff of the provincial Birth Planning Office.

Below the commune level, each brigade also set up its Leading Group, usually including a doctor, if the brigade had one. The brigade Leading Groups supervised the work of the barefoot doctors, part-time birth attendants, maternal and child health workers, or health aides at the team level. The health aides – women from within the team, chosen by the Women's Federation – delivered the contraceptives to women's homes, accompanied women to the commune health centre for sterilizations or abortions, and were supposed to keep their friends and neighbours motivated to use family planning. There might be several such aides in a village depending on its size, each serving perhaps twenty households.

Many of these volunteer women were mobilized through the Women's Federation. In some cases the local Women's Federation representative might spend up to 80 per cent of her time on family-planning matters. Their work was described thus:

They need to know the number of women of eligible age, the number of children they have, their menstrual cycles, which contraceptives they use, what attitude they have to contraception, their health, and their work. A hundred days after the birth of the first child, they will try to persuade the woman to use contraception. Should an IUD be expelled, they will advise the woman on using an interim method. They also advise on interim methods after childbirth. Leaders and cadres are expected to set a good example, to marry late and postpone births; if they are past childbearing, they should encourage their own children to accept family planning. In a village people look to local cadres and copy their example. So cadres should also persuade their brothers and sisters to stick to the approved number of children, so that they and their family can be seen to practise what they preach.

They talk to the local people and may also get theatre groups, slides and so on. They tell them that boys and girls are equal, and teach people about population and resources, to make simple calculations about the effects of population changes locally, to compare the past with the present . . . The women's leader also works on the husband and the grandparents, arranges medical examinations for subfertility, accompanies women to the hospital for contraception or other matters, stays with them there and arranges for alternative help in their homes. She helps to set up kindergartens, and crèches, and to provide support for mothers with young children. She also helps to arrange support for old people without children: help in the housework, or the running of a home for the aged.[24]

Family planning is not seen as a question simply of providing contraceptives but of offering a complete infrastructure, from attacks on 'feudal' attitudes to women through to home help and care for the childless aged.

The number of unpaid family-planning promoters at the different levels is extremely high. In Sichuan alone it has been estimated that one million people are involved, or one family planner for every hundred of the population. If those people for whom the message has no relevance are excluded – for example, the 36 per cent of the population under the age of sixteen – it is clear that the number of individuals to be contacted by a volunteer is very much smaller.

During the 1970s, each community became involved in a more positive sense in discussions on family planning and population growth, through the formulation of collective birth-plans. Peasants in each village met routinely in their team assemblies to decide a wide range of issues ranging from farming decisions to the disposal of the collective income, or to discuss a new project, like the establishment of a co-operative medical station. In these meetings, it was normal to consider priorities and make plans: if a medical station were to be set up, for example, who might make a suitable barefoot doctor and would need to be sent for training? Who might take over his or her existing work while the training was taking place? What was the need for a medical station, compared with the need for a schoolroom?

In such a context of planning for production, income distribution, investment and social welfare, it was almost inevitable that local demographic questions would also be raised. For how many children in which age groups would a schoolroom have to cater? Was the need a temporary one, or did the village contain a number of young people coming up to marriageable age who would shortly need provision for their children? If there had been a recent large number of marriages was a crèche a more urgent priority? It was not a difficult step to move from consideration of such questions to the adoption of group birth-plans, as the idea of such plans spread.

Typically, the commune committee, acting on plans from the county or province, would suggest that the crude birth rate should be brought down slightly from the previous year. This served as a reference point rather than an instruction for the production teams, which then met to consider the target. The team would calculate the number of births which would yield the proposed rates, based on the members' knowledge of who was marrying in the coming year, who had already married but was not yet pregnant, who had a first child and would shortly be hoping to become pregnant with a second, and so on. If the total potential number of births in the team was above the target they might decide to try to allocate the births, giving priority to the newly married and those with only one or two children, or to those whose youngest child was near to five years old. Each team couple would be asked to give their own plans for the next few years; where such plans conflicted with the targets, or with the 'later, longer, fewer' message, the group would attempt to persuade them to modify their intentions.

Once the team had drawn up its plan, it would be forwarded to the commune and put together with plans from the other teams. If the total number of births from these aggregated plans was out of line with the suggested target, renewed discussions would take place between the commune and the teams – each of which might have slightly different demographic characteristics such as age structure. It was reported that it usually took three 'up and down' consultations before a master plan was agreed.

The master plan could seldom be strictly adhered to. Some couples failed to conceive in their planned year; others had accidental pregnancies; yet others were faced with radically changed personal circumstances as, for instance, when a parent developed a terminal illness and wanted to see a grandchild before he or she died. Sometimes the team would simply accept the changes; in other cases two couples might agree to swap their allocated year for child-bearing so that the overall plan remained unaffected. Given the size and variety

Table 34 Late Marriage Rate, Birth Limitation Rate, Planned Birth Rate, and Crude Birth Rate for the People's Republic of China and Selected Provinces, 1977-1980

Place & Year	Late Marriage Rate %	Birth Limitation Rate %	Planned Birth Rate %	Crude Birth Rate (per 1000 population)
China 1978		70*		18.34
Gansu Province 1979	92.0	83.7	60.8	16.6
Guangdong Province 1980	87.6	73.0	66.2	20.2
Hebei Province 1977	93.0	83.0	77.0	15.0
Jiangsu Province 1977	88.5	83.7	60.8	15.99
Shaanxi Province 1980		86.1	.9	14.0

Planned Birth Rate: percentage of couples complying with the late marriage, birth spacing and family limitation norms.

* Estimate.

Source: Chen Pi-Chao and Kols, Adrienne, 1982.

of China, too, it was natural that different areas and different communes should develop variations on the approach to communal birth-planning described above. But, while it is not known how comprehensively group planning was adopted, the evidence suggests that it became in one form or another quite widespread (see Table 34).

About 70 percent of Chinese couples of child-bearing age were estimated to be practising contraception in 1978. About half of those using contraception were using an IUD; in the countryside that proportion was generally much higher, because the oral contraceptive was little used. Some peasants were reported to find the Pill especially valuable in busy times like the harvest, when they took the contraceptive without a break throughout the month, to avoid bleeding and cramps: the medical profession, however, disapproved of this 'initiative'. Generally, the greater use of IUDs in rural areas in the 1970s may have reflected administrative convenience and distribution difficulties in supplying the Pill, rather than individual choice.

Sterilization was the second most widely used method with female sterilization continuing to be more common than male in a ratio of three to just over two, despite continuing education efforts to stress the greater simplicity and safety of vasectomy. A few provinces were exceptions, with Sichuan for example reporting nine vasectomies to every one tubectomy between 1971 and 1979.

Abortion, still regarded as a remedy for contraceptive failure or unplanned pregnancy rather than as contraceptive method itself, was also widely used, and in 1978 there were an estimated 318 abortions for every 1000 live births.

The administrative records on fertility and contraception for four areas within communes were collected and analysed in 1979, and results showed considerable variation in the proportion of methods used, not just between different communes, but between different teams even within a single brigade. An important ingredient in the acceptance of family planning may have been that all the major methods of contraception were available, and that individual preferences for one or another method were met.

Table 35 Differential Use of Contraception among Rural and Urban Women Aged 15-49 years (percentage*)

	Sterilization		IUD	Pill	Condom	Other
	female	male				
Urban	20.30	2.77	38.86	18.99	9.68	9.41
Rural	25.73	10.09	49.96	8.36	2.06	3.80
Han minority	14.05	7.15	56.62	11.00	0.11	11.06

* percentage distribution of users

Source: State Family Planning Commission, 1983.

However, overall there were some significant trends. Users of the contraceptive pill were largely aged less than thirty-five and some 70 per cent of them had two or fewer children. Women who used the IUD were also predominantly under the age of thirty-five and of these, too, nearly three-quarters had two children or less. But there was an interesting difference between them and the Pill users: 44 per cent had two children and 28 per cent one child, while among Pill users the situation was reversed, with 39 per cent having one child and 31 per cent having two. This suggests that more people chose the Pill as a spacing method between their recommended two children, but that having had their second child many switched to the more 'permanent' IUD.

These trends were confirmed by the findings of the fertility sample survey in 1982. Oral contraceptives and condoms were most popular amongst the younger age groups, and those with fewer than two children. The IUD reached almost 70 per cent use amongst women aged 20-24 and gave way gradually to sterilization, generally of women, which peaked among the age-group 35-39. There were quite considerable differences in the type of contraceptive used by rural and urban women (as Table 35 shows). Interestingly, there are also differences between rural Han women and those from the minorities, even though both groups live in the countryside. Minority women showed a greater preference for the Pill, and much lower levels of sterilization. The survey also showed that use of contraceptives of different types varied from region to region of China, with sterilization being used far more in the south-west (43 per cent of eligible couples). That high figure in the south-west is largely due to Sichuan, where in the case of more than 30 per cent of the eligible couples, it is the man who has been sterilized, compared to 13 per cent of women. The north and north-west regions had far more Pill users, at 18 and 12 per cent respectively, than the average of the rest (6 per cent) and also had the lowest sterilization rates.

Taken together, the figures suggest that women in China as in other countries with good family-planning programmes tend to choose different methods at different stages of their reproductive life to meet their different needs, or depending on how satisfied they have been with the original method. This, in turn, implies a good level of contraceptive understanding on their part, and of flexibility on the part of those advising them about family planning.

There were a number of other reasons for the success of the campaign to limit population growth in the 1970s. By that time, the peasants had not only had quite a long exposure to the idea of contraception, but had been living for a number of years in conditions of greater stability than many had previously known. The post-war convulsions caused by land reform and increasing collectivization had, after 1962, been replaced by a fundamentally stable, group-oriented existence. The excesses of the Cultural Revolution affected the peasants far less than the townspeople. Local committees of management were renamed and to some extent reconstituted to include more young people, and there was considerable politicization of the villages together with a greater emphasis on austerity and on 'service to the people' instead of material rewards. These were, though, small changes in the routine of agricultural life. Increasing control over the environment of China — Mao's continued emphasis on storing grain; the commune-organized building of canals, dams and flood barriers; the expanding ability of the government to switch resources from one part of the country to another to meet an emergency — must have given the peasants a new confidence, that in a stable situation their lives too could be planned and managed. 'We are the masters now; we decide the way things will go' was a common response in the mid-1970s to a variety of questions about possible future problems or prospects.

In such a mood of confidence, it was comparatively easy to grasp that several sons were no longer necessary to provide a family with protection. It was also apparent, in many places, that one threat to a comfortable future was increasing pressure on land. One study of villages in Guangdong, based on information provided by refugees in Hong Kong in 1973–4 noted that 'Where there is less land per labourer, the planned birth campaign is reported to be a success and there are also fewer children per mother'. One informant explained why, in his village, the campaign had worked:

No one opposed the movement — they have learned their lesson. Before, the brigade population was 600, but now it is 1400 plus. So there had been an increase of over 100 per cent in recent years, and everybody understands the need. The economic difficulties of actual life persuade them. Now people don't think that many sons will pay off later . . . Now the concept of 'more sons — more wealth' is already undermined by practical experience. Women, in particular, are increasingly afraid of having many kids.[25]

Besides the pressure of land, the peasants were afraid of the need to keep a balance between the number of earners in the family and the number of consumers. The same study reported that although factors like private sideline activities affected the picture:

. . . in general the families with the highest 'labor-mouth ratio' tend to be the most prosperous in the team. In rural China the typical peasant family seems to have 42.5 per cent of its members in the labor force. In our interviews more than two-thirds of those households with more than half their members working in the team's fields were judged to be more prosperous than their neighbors by our informants, while about two-thirds of those families with fewer than a third of their members in the labor force were judged to be poorer. In other words, a careful balancing of births, deaths, ages and illnesses is critical to family security, and these considerations weigh heavily on peasant minds.

It was not only the total number of children which affected the labour-mouth ratio, but their timing. A woman who married during the 1970s at the average age of 21.5 and had her first baby a year later was likely to be a mother-in-law in her mid-forties. This mother-in-law and her husband (given increasing longevity, both were quite likely to be around) would continue to work for a few more years, so that the household might consist of three or four working adults supporting the first couple of children, at least for five to ten years. However, should the son's wife continue to have children, her in-laws would retire in all probability at about the time of the fourth birth, leaving herself and her husband to cope with six dependants.

Of course, the more children a woman had, the less able she was to contribute to the family's economy. By the 1970s, her contribution was taken for granted. Following the Cultural Revolution, women's involvement in the labour force reached even greater rates than it had before the collapse of the Great Leap Forward.

'In the rural areas, access to and organization of women's labour is necessary for each household in order to combine the three sectors of the economy: the income-earning contribution from the public or collective sectors of the economy, the sideline activities of the private sector of the economy, and the non-economic earning contribution within the domestic sphere.'[26] In a 1977 study of Jiang village in Guangdong, all but one of the women worked in agriculture, in the production team, and except for a few older women who worked part-time, all the women worked a full day. Another study — a household survey — indicated that in the rural suburbs of Beijing and Shanghai, well over 70 per cent of agricultural field-workers were women. This study also drew attention to the ratio between dependants and wage-earners as being one of the main determinants of household income.

Because it has been impossible to hire labour in China, the only way a family could recruit an additional pair of hands was through marriage. Wives, in general, have continued to earn less than their husbands in the villages, partly because agricultural field work earned fewer workpoints and partly because the women continued to work fewer days of the year. Moreover, it has been the men, predominantly, who have gone into the rural industries and other non-agricultural activities that paid higher wages. (Rural women surveyed in the 1982 fertility sample survey were overwhelmingly farm workers; of 23,565 women only 210 were workers, 146 were cadres, and 243 were grouped as having 'other' occupations or no occupation.) Nevertheless, the working wife has become universal, and her contribution to the family budget is essential.

The greater poverty of a household with many dependants was being reinforced, at least in some areas of China, by financial disincentives for having additional children. In just under one-third of the villages in Guangdong from which the refugees surveyed in 1973–4 came, the fourth child was ignored in the distribution of various products produced by the teams. Additionally, no regular grain ration might be allocated to it, which would have meant that the parents would have to pay cash to make up any deficit in their supplies. (This may have been less important than it sounds, because the household survey of Beijing and Shanghai indicated that households did not consume their total grain ration.) Other Guangdong sanctions were that the fourth child got no cotton ration, no sugar, oil or fish distributions from the team's production, and no extra private plot allotment. In some villages, cadres 'announced that if extra children pulled the family into debt, the team would not loan money'.

There was, however, little emphasis on disincentives during most of the 1970s. Where villages introduced them, they seem to have done so on their own initiative, rather than at government urging. Efforts to persuade people to plan their families and to have smaller ones rested instead on the development of group understanding of the issues, through publicity, political discussions and persuasion, and on personally-tailored talks with individuals. Indeed, family-planning workers were usually hesitant to describe any particular approach through which they worked, saying instead 'there is a key to fit every lock', which meant that every woman, and every family, was approached with arguments to fit the particular circumstances.

In all, it seems that official concern with China's population growth-rate, and about the need to plan reproduction as well as production, may have been slower to develop than the peasants' own demand for family planning. The authors of the study of Guangdong refugees summed up their findings:

The birth rate reductions which appear in official reports and interview data have preceded the recent heavy administrative pressure. The birth control campaign may become even more intensive in the future, but to this point peasants in Guangdong seem to have responded more to the changing cost-benefit ratios of collective living, the realization that fewer children are needed now to provide the family with surviving sons, the presence of more midwives and doctors who provide contraceptives, and to such factors as the shortage of available land.[27]

The Peasant and the Single Child

In 1979 the government instituted a call for the single-child family. It was meant to apply to the peasants as well as to city-dwellers, for it was considered that the vast mass of China's peasants must be persuaded to reduce their fertility still further to contain what the government perceived as a demographic crisis.

However, if the peasants wanted to plan and to limit their families, it was within certain limits. A 1981 survey in Hubei found that of 728 women in the child-bearing years, 51.2 per cent wanted two children; 28.4 per cent wanted three and 15.5 per cent wanted four. The peasants wanted a son above all, but preferably children of both sexes. One-third of the 710 peasants who had two sons still wanted a daughter; almost two-thirds of the 747 who already had two daughters wanted a son.

The same survey asked why people wanted children: 51 per cent said they were needed as security for old age, a quarter said they were necessary to carry on the family, and a fifth said to provide additional labour. A few (3.5 per cent) just liked children and had them 'for the sheer enjoyment and happiness'.

The desire for children as security in old age is a common one in societies without national social-security systems. It may be even stronger in China, paradoxically, because many of the other basic needs are taken care of. Educational facilities, at least to lower middle-school level, are wide-spread. Three-quarters of all Chinese are in a collective health scheme. Unemployment is rare, despite the employment problems of 1979–80, caused partly by the 'birth bulge' generation and partly by the return of the *xiaxiang* youth from the country. Food, clothing and housing, if at a fairly basic level, are within almost everyone's means. But the system remains based on providing for each according to his or her contribution: there is not a sufficient surplus to provide according to need. Thus, once the elderly retire they are dependent upon their families. Even control of the family finances escapes them, now that they live so much longer, for on retirement they generally hand over that control to the working son living at home.

A few homes for the aged who have no family to support them do exist, although they appear to be looked upon with the same dislike which the elderly of other countries feel for them. From the founding of the People's Republic, the elderly were promised the 'five guarantees' — adequate food, medical care, clothes, shelter and burial — but anecdotal evidence suggests that those who have to claim them find them humiliating. According to refugee informants in Guangdong, recipients of five-guarantee support were allocated staple food and clothing needs by the production team, as well as a small amount of cash, depending on the wealth of the team. A more secure living could be had with the addition of income from sideline activities such as growing vegetables on a private plot, or keeping chickens. The numbers of those without family support are currently extremely small, but it is easy to understand peasant fears of being left alone and destitute.

In most instances, the main source of family support for an old person is a son who will marry and bring his bride to the home. From the 1960s, official propaganda made much of cases where, with no son in the family, a daughter brought her husband into the home. This was not an entirely new concept: it had been known to happen in the old China but it was, and remains, unusual:

Wang Hanchen, an ageing commune member of Chencunying Village in Dingxian County, was left with an only daughter when his wife died. For years, the thought that he would be alone and uncared for once his daughter got married made him unhappy and listless, not caring if the house needed any repairs or if the courtyard wall collapsed. He could often be found musing at his wife's tomb.

The matter took a turn for the better when his daughter got married and brought her husband home to live with him. From then on their lives have been improving daily. They have built five new rooms and planted fruit trees in the courtyard. The young couple have bought bicycles and a hand cart. They also bought a radio for the old man.

Wang Hanchen always looks happy these days. He never misses a day in collective labour. He's a changed man now![28]

While such well-publicized cases may have helped to make the peasants feel that a daughter was not automatically lost to her family on marriage, the effect has been undermined by calls for a one-child family. Whichever home they move into, two single children marrying would find themselves responsible for two sets of ageing parents.

As a result, there have been increasing demands for a national pension scheme. In the past, suggestions of an old-age pension were rejected out of hand: an economy such as China's, it was said, would simply collapse under the strain. Many cadres, and some policy-makers, continue to assert that pensions are an impossibility. But, now that population growth is seen as the major threat to improved living standards, pension provisions are being seriously discussed. There were requests for such a scheme made at the National People's Congress in 1980, and in 1981, when two Sichuan deputies proposed an insurance fund into which peasants would pay each year towards a pension. A few communes have instituted their own pensions, with a variety of approaches, but most of these have been in areas around the larger cities (see Chapter 3). It is improbable that the majority of the brigades could introduce provision for old age without state backing: a survey in 1982 of some 3500 brigades in eleven provinces and municipalities indicated that only 1 per cent of men aged sixty-five and older, and women aged sixty and older, were receiving pensions of 10-15 *yuan* a month paid by the community.

Currently, the government has gone no further than to encourage and publicize those communes which have introduced pensions. At the same time, however, the People's Bank is undertaking feasibility studies, and the People's Insurance Company even small-scale experiments, on the possibility of a national old-age insurance scheme.

The dilemma is not only one of resources but of ideology. The Chinese road towards socialism has, so far, encouraged collective thinking and collective initiatives at the local level, allowing considerable autonomy with the state stepping in only to provide additional basic health or education facilities, for example, in areas demonstrably too poor to provide for themselves. To provide a national pension scheme would weaken the economic base of the local collective, and would be a step towards unprecedented expansion of state responsibility for welfare.

Without some widespread pension provision, on the other hand, it seems unlikely that the peasants will be willing to reduce family size much further, let alone embrace the concept of a one-child family. Pensions are not, however, the only concern. A second economic dilemma for the government has been the need to encourage productivity — which means giving greater incentives to individuals — while at the same time trying to persuade the peasants that more hands do not mean more wealth.

Under the new responsibility systems, the peasant family or, more rarely, a group of families or an entire work team, contracts to produce a certain amount each year. Anything produced above this is then sold to the state, at a higher price. Additional earnings, from private plots, sideline activities and so on, are encouraged, and private 'peasant markets' for the sale of vegetables, meat and handicrafts have opened. There seems to be no doubt that as a result peasant incomes have increased quite considerably although it is likely that the more substantial gains have been made in areas near to a city or large town which provides a demand for such goods.

Under the new systems, peasants not only earn more but are faced with rather different demands on their labour resources (see Table 36).

As has been noted, the men of the household were already working disproportionately in the rural industries and other non-agricultural activities, while the women were heavily engaged in field work. That field work has now achieved greater importance, for it is no longer just a question of reaching a quota but of exceeding it for a profit. Thus one would expect that women would spend more time, if anything, on the land and in earning extra income from handicrafts. Much of the work in sideline activities — growing vegetables, tending a few pigs, and so on — can be delegated to children, and so can at least some of the housework. There

Table 36 Demands on Labour Resources of Peasant Households

	Collective		Domestic	
Before 1978	Production	Sidelines		Servicing
	cropping	private plot		cooking
	livestock	livestock		childcare
	rural industries	handicrafts		sewing
				laundry
				cleaning
	Collective		**Domestic**	
After 1978	Production	Production	Sidelines	Servicing
		for the	as above	as above
	livestock	collective	but expanded	
	rural industries			

Source: Croll, E.J., 1983.

may be a new temptation to keep children away from school and bring them into the labour force of the household. Once in the labour force, their contribution to the family economy makes it difficult for family-planning workers to stress the costs of children.

With the majority of children — an estimated 80 per cent — receiving at least primary education in the 1970s, the number of years in which a son was a net contributor to the budget was quite small, assuming that he married at around the age of 23–4, and did little agricultural work while at school. Now, even his spare-time work is valuable, and there has been increasing official concern about peasants withdrawing their children from school altogether.

Daughters were sent to school less in any case. While no detailed sex-breakdown of the 1982 Census figures on literacy has yet been published, a quarter of all women in the population are illiterate or semi-literate compared with a fifth of men. Most illiteracy is in the rural areas. In a Hubei survey, of 707 women of child-bearing age, 42 per cent were illiterate and 45 per cent had a smattering of literacy equivalent to primary school level. Another survey, in Anhui Province in 1982, found that while overall enrolment in primary schools was 83.8 per cent, girls accounted for only 35.8 per cent of the enrolment. Girls are not only less likely to get to school in the first place, but are probably disproportionately represented in the quite high drop-out rates.

The government, in a circular issued by the Central Committee of the Communist Party and the State Council, recently announced intensified measures for rural education, including crash courses for all those below the age of fifteen without a completed primary education, in order to make primary education virtually universal by 1990. It is too early to tell how successful this programme will be. In the meantime, with the extra opportunities for earnings offered by the responsibility systems, the value of girl children, as measured by their contribution to housework and to work in the private plot and so on, may increase, but at the expense of their chances of receiving an education and the job opportunities which go with it.

'In rural areas', the Hubei study noted, 'there is a popular saying "half side family" that means men go to work or become cadres while women stay at home to do agricultural work and rear children. Women are restricted to agricultural labour and seldom have a chance to come into contact with new things; therefore rearing children has become an inevitable trend . . .'[29]

Once the girls are older, their contribution in agriculture and in sideline activities should help to produce the extra profits the peasants are now offered. This could have an effect on the age of marriage: the parents may be reluctant to lose an earning daughter to another family. However, that reluctance, and a recognition by the husband's family that a daughter-in-law is an extra source of income, might increase the bride-payments offered and thus work against the official policy in that area.

The introduction of more flexible economic policies could incidentally have other effects on marriage and on other social relationships. The Guangdong refugee study noted that where inter-village ties had been reduced, because of the increasing prevalence of marriage within a single village and the reduction of opportunities for different villages to meet, for example, at local markets, 'the focus on the interests of one's own team is strengthened, making efforts to broaden the scale of sharing and co-operation more difficult'. Villages with few ties participated less in brigade activities and took longer to get such welfare facilities as co-operative medical insurance and middle schools. The development of private peasant markets may result in strengthening of links between different villages in a brigade, and between different brigades, and offer young people a greater variety of potential marriage partners.

When the responsibility systems were first introduced, there were reports of peasants wanting to dismantle some common facilities at the team and brigade level, such as schools and medical care, on the grounds that they wanted to keep all that they had earned, instead of having some of the surplus allocated to the welfare fund and other collective purposes. This reaction seems to have been as short-lived as it was short-sighted. In fact, additional prosperity in the countryside should help to strengthen collective welfare systems.

Additional prosperity should also, in the long run, lead to greater mechanization and with it less need for agricultural labour and less concern with physical strength as a factor in wages. Government propaganda stresses mechanization as a major reason why sons in particular, and several children in general, will not be all-important in the future. Mechanization is also stressed as a reason for the importance of education: the different kinds of jobs which will be available in the future will need a more qualified work-force. A child, the peasants are told, is not simply a pair of a hands, but somebody who can be educated to become a scientific farmer. The peasants are not entirely convinced. Working as they do mainly with traditional implements, with the possession of a hand-tractor a major source of pride, the prospect of large-scale mechanization frequently seems remote.

In fact, however, in many areas there is already a problem of too much, rather than too little, labour. At peak seasons, every hand may be required, but under-employment in general may be as common in the countryside as in the cities, and merely less visible because more easily absorbed. The responsibility system, by tying earnings to individual or family performance, has increased the amount of surplus labour and 'in some districts more than 30 per cent of the total farm work-force is surplus labour'.[30] Expanding local industries should, in the long term, absorb this surplus labour, but at present in the rural sector 'unemployment is to be seen as a social cost consequent upon efforts to improve economic efficiency'.[31] In due course pressure on jobs may affect family size in the way that land pressure appears to have done. As noted above, however, only a fifth of the Hubei peasants said that to have more hands available was their main reason for having children; most seem more concerned with passing on their own jobs when they grow old and have perhaps not yet realized that those jobs may no longer exist.

The responsibility systems were introduced almost simultaneously with the policy on the one-child family. Policy makers were well aware of the inherent difficulties of persuading the peasants to agree to having a single child, and of some of the reasons why the equally important responsibility system designed to improve China's low productivity and provide the resources for modernization, might militate against reducing fertility. As one policy maker said, 'There are conflicts between the interests of the peasants and those of the country as a whole; the problem is how to balance those interests . . .'

One way of balancing the interests has been to try to persuade the peasants that children are not necessarily economically beneficial. Figures have been published, and widely publicized, on the actual outlay needed to bring up a child (in 1979, it was calculated that it ranged from 6900 *yuan* in cities to around 1600 in rural areas) and on the problems of providing educational facilities on the part of the state for all these children.

The fast growing population also causes serious problems in education. Illiterate or semi-illiterate people make up some 20 per cent of the Chinese population. And every year China has another 20 million babies.

The present universities can hold 1.1 million students, and at most 1.5 million in 1985. By 1985, the number of pupils in elementary schools will have reached 130 million, only a fraction of whom will be enrolled in high schools and universities. This can hardly meet the needs of the development of China's economy.[32]

Different surveys on the relative economic position of families of different sizes have been carried out, with somewhat conflicting results. The Hubei survey found that the larger the family the greater the per capita income tended to be – but it did not distinguish, in the analysis, between working family members and dependants, or give ages of the family members. The Jinan Family Planning Bureau, Shandong, recently surveyed the Xiuhui Commune and found that the income of one-child families was above the average for the commune as a whole and further above the average for families with two children:

The survey shows that one-child families get richer faster. Usually they have more labour force compared with the number of persons to be supported. By the end of 1981, the Xiuhui Commune had 20,509 able-bodied people in 12,413 households supporting 52,804 people (including themselves) — that is one able-bodied person for every 2.57 people (including himself). But in one-child households, one able-bodied person supports an average of 1.85 persons. One-child families averaged 0.72 more able-bodied persons and 0.72 fewer persons to support than families with more children.[33]

The survey leaves unresolved the question of cause and effect: households with an annual per capita income of above 500 *yuan* make up only 1.6 of the commune but 3.8 per cent of the one-child families. Were those with one child richer to start with?

If so, the responsibility systems may provide a further impetus towards the reduction of fertility through the increase in peasant incomes. Observers of the Chinese family-planning programme in the mid-1960s had doubts about whether the Cultural Revolution policies would help persuade parents to have smaller families. The downgrading of consumerism and the lack of individual economic incentives 'have culminated in an across-the-board reduction of such economic incentives for reducing family size . . . however, the social reforms have accompanied the reorganization of channels to mobility. In particular, for women in the villages, there has been an increase in alternative opportunities to childbearing. As the direct costs of children have decreased, opportunity costs have risen . . .'[34] Such observers queried the idea that 'service to the people' could really motivate young parents to reduce the number of children.

In fact, for a variety of reasons, birth rates did go down and family size declined throughout the 1970s. Rural total fertility rates, which had averaged around 6.5 during the 1950s and 1960s, dropped to below 3 during the 1970s. But that is not to say that with more income, greater economic security, and even more incentive for women to work, there might not be still further declines.

One of the ingredients in the success of the family-planning programme has, however, been considerably weakened. The introduction of the one-child family policy has meant that the long discussion sessions in which a team planned its births and provided group pressure to conform to what had been agreed, have become unnecessary. It is no longer the team, but the Birth Planning Leading Group, which makes the straightforward decision to authorize a birth. Members of the group, and other family-planning cadres, like the Women's Federation representatives, are in an unenviable position. They are members of the team or brigade, related to a number of its families and neighbours of the rest. On the one hand they are expected to implement official policies and reach their targets; on the other, they have to live within a small, close-knit community. Many of them, being rather older than the newly-married couples affected by the one-child family policy, have had more children than the current policies allow and so are vulnerable to the accusation that it is all very well for them to recommend a single child when they have three growing offspring. Through their organizations, such as the Women's Federation, they have reported back to the government the difficulties of their position and the reasons that many of the peasants refuse to accept the single-child policy. But, unless and until the policy is changed, they attempt to enforce it within the limits of their own authority, their standing in the community, and a realistic assessment of how far they can go in local circumstances.

This rather flexible approach is not new. The level of unregistered marriages indicates that local cadres, after trying to persuade the two families involved to delay the marriage until the recommended ages, simply accepted the *fait accompli* when they failed. In Chapter 1, it was seen that a survey in Guizhou Province in 1977 revealed that unregistered marriages accounted for 40 per cent of all marriages. Family-planning workers included the unregistered couples in their work, advised them on contraception, and kept statistics on them as on all fertile couples. In some areas they entered the information on 'illegal marriages' separately from that on the other couples but in other parts of the country they made no distinction between those in a registered marriage and those who had set up house together. Sometimes the cadres were in no position to criticize. The 1973-4 Guangdong study found that those who had a fair amount of education, or served as cadres, were more likely to marry early: 'the advantaged are particularly desirable mates and can more easily (and thus earlier) find a spouse'.[35]

In 1982 in Yunnan, a province with a poor record in

reducing birth rates because of its 50 per cent minority populations and the difficulty of implementing an effective programme directed only at the other half of the population, the Han Chinese, cadres were the main focus of the one-child family campaign. It was the cadres who, wanting a second child, would in the rural areas have to pay for its grain ration and have workpoints and some land deducted, and the educational campaign on the single-child policy was addressed to them. Clearly Yunnan believed that without this prior effort to impress upon cadres the importance of the policy, they would do little to spread it to the peasants.

Local-level cadres may turn a blind eye to unauthorized pregnancies, or, faced with pressure from higher levels, may attempt to reach their targets in unauthorized ways. Occasional scandals about coercion, forced abortion and so on (usually given widespread publicity by the government as a warning) reflect the desperation of those caught between the forces of the community and the state. Still more serious have been the scandals about the recurrence of infanticide in some parts of the countryside, because these imply that the team's family-planning cadres knew of the pregnancy and connived at, or at least made no effort to report, the death.

In rural areas where attempts have been made to implement the one-child policy fairly thoroughly, the peasants are appalled if the single pregnancy they have been allowed produces a daughter. The report of the infanticide of 210 baby girls in two counties of Guangdong, in a Guangzhou newspaper, said:

What is even more shocking is that some village officials sympathize with and even support such activities, saying that 'since we're promoting one couple, one child, of course everyone wants a boy and not a girl'.[36]

The government has given enormous publicity to the problem of infanticide, indicating how seriously it is viewed. In his report to the National People's Congress in December 1982, Premier Zhao Ziyang called on the whole of society to 'resolutely condemn the criminal activities of female infanticide and maltreatment of the mothers',[37] and gave his support to the punishment of offenders by the law.

Chinese courts have apparently been somewhat prone to sympathize with, if not to support, such activities: sentences for infanticide have ranged from three to thirteen years' imprisonment. The newspaper *China Youth Daily* had already, in November 1982, commented on the many letters to the editor reporting on cases of abandoned baby girls in some localities: the newspaper insisted that the idea that boys were preferable to girls was 'feudal' and that while it was true that people should be supported in their old age it was not only sons who could perform this function. It claimed that statistics showed that 'serious imbalance characterized by a ratio of 3:2 between male and female babies that have been born and survived in the past two years has occurred in some communes'.

The influential *Beijing Review*, in a leading article in 1983, repeated the same points but did add that the number of people involved was 'a mere handful' although their wrong-doing had caused grave concern.

It is probably true that the number of cases of infanticide is not all that large. Alarmist reports of sex ratios in particular communes or even brigades were probably based on a misunderstanding about the size of the population which has to be studied before valid ratios can be established. The 1982 Census showed an overall sex ratio at all ages for China of 106.3 males for every 100 females, and a ratio at birth in 1981 of 108.5 males for every 100 females (see Table 37).

Table 37 Sex Ratio of Children Aged 0-5 Years in 1982: (Males per 100 females)

Age	Sex ratio
0	107.66
1	107.92
2	107.44
3	106.75
4	106.38
5	106.5

Source: Li Chengrui, Xinhua, 17 April 1983.

These ratios are higher than those in European countries. There is however some evidence that sex ratios do vary a little in different races, and that the Chinese in China and in other South-east Asian countries have higher than average ones. When the figures given here are compared with model life tables — the UN East Asian model and the Coale and Demeny West model — they are quite plausible. This suggests that, as the director of the State Statistical Bureau, Li Chengrui, claimed, infanticide has not been on the kind of scale which affects the national ratios. However, there seem to be some provinces in which the ratios give cause for concern: notably Shandong, Henan and Guangdong (110); Guangxi (111); and Anhui.

Anhui, whose sex ratios for different years as revealed in the 1964 Census show an almost incredible imbalance among surviving 26-year-olds in that year of 131.6 males to 100 females, had a ratio for the new-born in 1966 of 105.4 boys to 100 girls. In 1982 a sample study showed a ratio of 112 to 100 at birth. Anhui was, in the past, as has been discussed earlier, notorious for its baby-ponds; the suspicion must be that infanticide on a substantial scale is occurring there once again.

It was certainly from Anhui that fifteen peasant women wrote to the *People's Daily* to say that as mothers of girls they lacked status and were the subject of mistreatment by husbands, mothers-in-law and even their own parents. 'That is why we will never give up trying to have a boy and why we would rather die than be content with a girl', they wrote. Failure to produce a son in their area of China was a great deal 'worse than death'.[38]

To encourage couples to stop at one child even if it is a girl various measures were introduced by different provinces and units. Rural couples in Shanxi, for example, are offered an extra fifteen days honeymoon leave for late marriage, 100 days maternity leave for deferring the birth of the first child, or four to six months' maternity leave if they sign a single-child pledge. An only child is entitled to five workpoints a month as a health subsidy, is given priority in kindergartens or nurseries and in medical care, is given an adult grain ration and, other things being equal, will have priority in going on for further studies or to become a state worker.

Shanxi's regulations are typical of those adopted around the country, except that Shanxi allowed a second child in rural areas to those couples in which the wife was an only daughter and the husband settled in with her family after marriage, or to two single children who married.

Typical, too, are the disincentives for those who exceed the one-child limit. Commune members would have 10 per cent of their workpoints deducted for seven years, or if not:

... they shall be allotted less responsible plots or assigned higher output quotas, one of their private plots shall be called back, or the proportion of their produce to be retained by the collective shall be increased. In addition, 10% of their total annual income shall be deducted in the two years following the child's birth or adoption or other corresponding economic measures shall be taken to deal with them.[39]

The financial penalties were further increased for children beyond the second. In addition, peasants would not be allowed to extend their houses to accommodate the extra children, nor would they be entitled to a private plot allocation for them.

Such penalties seem to have been less than effective. Peasant houses are a great deal more roomy than city homes in any case so overcrowding is not a major problem. Lack of private plot allocation may be an irritant but is hardly a deciding factor in whether to have another child. The increase in cash income generated by the responsibility schemes reduces the impact of a percentage reduction in workpoints. Accustomed as they are to changes in policy direction, many peasants probably hope that the one-child policy will lapse in due course and that they may not have to suffer penalties for the prescribed number of years, in any case.

A further measure to try and enforce compliance has been the linking of responsibility system contracts to family planning. In some parts of the country 'double production contracts' have been introduced, with the peasant family agreeing not to have a child in the year for which the contract for their agricultural quota is made. If they do have a child, they may be given worse land to work in the next year or have their quota increased. Double production contracts made with a work team or job group may encourage group pressure on individual members to observe the terms; made with an individual family they depend, for their impact, on how severe the penalties for non-compliance are. If large numbers of families within an area ignore the provisions, switching land allocations is probably not sensible or much of a threat; in any event, if the peasants begin to believe that they have only a short-term claim on the land they work they are unlikely to invest much in the way of fertilizer and other resources and its quality and productivity will decrease.

There is so far little evidence that, outside certain model areas, the single-child family has been widely adopted in the country. That being so, it is probable that many of the penalties are being tacitly ignored. The situation is the exact reverse of that in the cities where a high take-up of one-child certificates has meant that some of the promised benefits cannot be provided. If 80 per cent of those eligible have certificates, priority in housing or in kindergartens becomes practically meaningless. In the rural areas, if 80 or 90 per cent of those eligible have not taken out certificates it is equally impossible to give them all worse land, or non-priority in health care and other welfare measures. And when the non-certificated are a large majority, they are unlikely to feel they are under moral pressure to conform to what they perceive to be an unrealistic norm.

Figures for the success or otherwise of the one-child family policy in rural areas are difficult to obtain and such statistics as do exist may be misleading. Three rural counties — Rudong County, Jiangsu; Nangong County, Hubei; and Sifang County, Sichuan — had all achieved 90 per cent certification among eligible couples by the end of 1979, but these are highly atypical counties which have been family planning pace-setters for years. Because of the very high marriage rate in 1981, proportions of first births (percentage of all births) have been much inflated. Of all babies born in that year 46.6 per cent were first births and 25.6 per cent second births. In the rural areas, though, 40 per cent of all births in that year were third or fourth children. The total fertility rate in rural areas was 2.91 children, according to the fertility sample survey, compared with the overall rate of 2.63.

Of those who had only one child in 1981, 31 per cent of the rural mothers signed the one-child certificate; however, as was noted in Chapter 3, these signatories included people of all ages, who might never have wanted a second child, or, in rural areas especially, found themselves unable to produce another. Not more than 5 per cent of the rural women in any educational category, from the illiterate to those (very few) with tertiary education, had signed the certificate. Workers and cadres, making up only 2 per cent of the rural females aged fifteen to forty-nine, were nearly three times as likely to have signed as peasant women. Those who did sign generally had a son as their only child, in a more than two-to-one proportion. Signing was not always an indication of permanent commitment: by 1982 nearly 11 per cent of signatories in the north-west region of China had changed their minds and produced a second child, while only just under 4 per cent of those in the north-east had done so. There is no information available on the rural/urban breakdown of those who reneged but, given that the cities are able to exert more organized pressure for the single child, it is probable that most were rural women.

Over the whole of China 14 million couples, or 42.3 per cent of those with one child, had accepted the one-child certificate; it can be assumed that the vast majority of them do not live in the countryside.

Even in those rural areas with a high take-up of one-child family certificates it is possible that many of the peasants, gambling on a change of policy, were hoping that the certificate would mean no more than the postponement of a second child. In many parts of the country there was a drop in sterilizations performed in 1981, which local officials explicitly linked to the one-child policy. It was not clear whether the couples were choosing to delay being sterilized until the only child was older because of fears of its death or serious illness, or whether they still hoped to be able to reverse their agreement to stop at one. An intensified sterilization campaign launched in 1983 in which sterilization is recommended as the most effective method of birth control for couples with two children suggests a more realistic assessment of an acceptable target for the peasants.

Declining national fertility figures show that not only the urban dwellers but also the peasants have accepted that it is in their interests, as well as in those of the country, to limit their families. They have not been convinced that it is necessary in the interests of the country's future to sacrifice their own future by having a single child. And yet, unless fertility can be reduced below the current national average of 2.63 children, another 300 million people will have been added to China's population by the end of this century.

Notes

1. Myrdal Jan, *Report from a Chinese Village,* Picador, 1975.

2. Luk, Bernard Hung-kay, 'Abortion in Chinese Law', *American Journal of Comparative Law,* vol. 25, no. 2, 1977, pp. 372-90.

3. Luk, B. H., op. cit.

4. Sun Li, *Stormy Years,* Foreign Languages Press, 1982.

5. Chen Da, 'Population in Modern China', *American Journal of Sociology,* vol. 52, no. 1, Part II, University of Chicago Press, 1946, 126 pp.

6. Myrdal, Jan, 1975, op. cit.

7. Smedley, Agnes, *The Great Road,* Monthly Review Press, 1956.

8. Hinton, William, *Fanshen,* Monthly Review Press, 1966.

9. Smedley, Agnes, 'Youth and Women's Committees' in *Portraits of Chinese Women in Revolution,* Feminist Press, 1976.

10. Han Suyin, *Birdless Summer,* part I, Jonathan Cape, 1968.

11. Myrdal, Jan, 1975, op. cit.

12. Davin, Delia, *Women-Work: Women and The Party in Revolutionary China,* Clarendon Press, 1976.

13. Myrdal, Jan, 1975, op. cit.

14. Chen Du et al., 'On Reproduction of Rural Population', *Jingji Yanjiu,* 20 June 1982, *Summary of World Broadcasts,* 24 July 1982. This survey was confined to a few communes only and hence cannot be considered a representative sample of the conditions prevailing in China, but where its findings can be compared with others, such as the one per thousand population fertility sample survey, the discrepancies are minor.

15. Myrdal, Jan and Kessle, Gun, *China: The Revolution Continued,* Pelican Books, 1973.

16. Tien, H. Yuan, 'Sterilization, Oral Contraception and Population Control in China', *Population Studies,* vol. 18, no. 3, 1965.

17. Myrdal, 1975, op. cit.

18. Report of the Guangzhou Second People's Hospital Medical Team: 'Birth Control is an Important Mission', *Guangdong Medical Journal*, June 1966 (English translation in manuscript).

19. Han Suyin, 'Family Planning in China', *Japan Quarterly*, vol. XVII, no. 4, 1970.

20. Chen Pi-Chao, 'China's Birth Control Action Programmes 1956-64', *Population Studies*, vol. 24, no. 2, 1970.

21. Chang Chinwa, 'Why we must reduce urban population', *Daily Worker*, Beijing, 4 January 1958: quoted in Tien, H. Yuan, *China's Population Struggle*, Ohio State University Press, 1973.

22. Yu, Y. C., 'The Population Policy of China', *Population Studies*, vol. 33, no. 1, 1979.

23. Myrdal, J. and Kessle, G., 1973, op. cit.

24. The author's personal observations, 1981.

25. Parish, William L. and Whyte, Martin King, *Village and Family in Contemporary China*, University of Chicago Press, 1978.

26. Croll, Elisabeth J., *The Politics of Marriage in Contemporary China*, Cambridge University Press, 1981.

27. Parish, W. L. and Whyte, M. K., op. cit.

28. Zhong Xiu, 'Tradition and Change', *Women of China*, no. 6, 1979.

29. Chen Du et al., 1982, op. cit.

30. Dernberger, Robert F., 'Economic Consequences and Future Implications of Population Growth in China', Paper no. 76, East-West Population Institute, 1981, 32 pp.

31. Dernberger, R. F., 1981, op. cit.

32. Chen Muhua, 'Controlling Population Growth in a Planned Way', *Beijing Review*, 16 November 1979, pp. 17-24.

33. *China Daily*, undated, approx. March 1983.

34. Salaff, Janet W., 'Institutionalized Motivation for Fertility Limitation in China', *Population Studies*, vol. 26, no. 2, 1972, pp.233-62.

35. Parish, W. L. and Whyte, M. K., 1978, op. cit.

36. *Nanfang*, quoted in *The Times*, 14 February 1983.

37. Zhao Ziyang, 'Report on the 6th Five Year Plan for National Economic and Social Development', *Xinhua*, 13 December 1982.

38. *People's Daily*, 22 February 1983, quoted in the *Irish Times*, 24 February 1983.

39. Regulations of The Shanxi Provincial People's Government on Planned Parenthood, *Shanxi ribao*, 7 November 1982, *Summary of World Broadcasts*, 16 December 1982.

CHAPTER FIVE

MEETING BASIC NEEDS

★★★

In recent years governments around the world have turned increasingly to the concept of meeting basic social and economic needs of the population as a first or further step towards overall development. So far as population policies go, it has been recognized that there is a strong association between 'the level of satisfaction of the basic needs, as reflected in the measures of health, education, levels of poverty, the stage of economic development (as expressed, for instance, in per capita income) and demographic transition'.[1] In other words, people are less likely to want to reduce family size if many of the children they have are liable to die; if they do not have the education either to understand the use of modern contraception or to break out of traditional constraints of belief and behaviour; if their opportunities for jobs are few and children represent their only security; or if they live such a hand-to-mouth existence that planning of any kind is an irrelevance.

Asian countries, in a meeting of the UN's Economic Commission for Asia and the Far East, identified the key sectors in meeting basic needs as health, education, food and nutrition, housing, and the provision of potable water. They also said that a strategy for meeting basic needs should be rural centred, involve the participation of the community in formulating and implementing programmes, command access to resources and the means of production, and create productive employment opportunities.

This chapter looks at some of the ways in which China has attempted to meet these needs and how the various programmes, especially of health and education, have been related to the family-planning programme.

Health

Chinese medicine has a long and reputable history and preventive medicine and public health have always been an important part of that history. Eighteen hundred years ago, the Emperor Huandi was told:

The sages did not treat those who were already ill; they instructed those who were not yet ill. They did not want to rule those who were already rebellious . . . To administer medicines to diseases which have already developed and to suppress revolts which have already developed is comparable to the behavior of those persons who begin to dig a well after they have become thirsty, and of those who begin to cast weapons after they have already engaged in battle. Would these actions not be too late?[2]

Similarly, an old Chinese proverb stated: 'The superior doctor prevents sickness; the mediocre doctor attends to impending sickness; the inferior doctor treats actual sickness.'[3]

There was also a widespread assumption, which is still in operation today, that illness was not simply an affair for the patient and the doctor, but something with which the whole family was involved and about which the whole family should be consulted for decisions on treatment. Nevertheless, such consultation – and most medical care itself – was for those who could afford it. The ordinary peasants turned to local healers with a smattering of knowledge and folklore when they were ill. A study in Yunnan[4] in the 1940s revealed fifteen traditional cures for cholera, 'ranging from a prayer at the Buddhist temple to the drawing of blood from a cock . . .' Lack of resources, knowledge, organizational capacity and will impeded any public health programme which might have prevented the illness occurring.

Death rates were acknowledged to be high, although

statistics were poor. One Chinese demographer estimated that in 1934 the national death rate was around 33 per thousand population; epidemics of cholera, for example, or a famine, could increase the rate for a particular area further in any particular year.

An analysis was made of the causes of death in Chenggong, Yunnan, between 1940 and 1944. There was only one Western doctor in the area and the recorders of deaths were primary school teachers, given a little basic instruction in identifying the likely cause of death, largely from the reported symptoms, and allocating it to one of the twenty-seven categories – groups of diseases or individual diseases. Although their records were checked by the doctor they were not free from error; leprosy, for example, which was common in the area and greatly feared, is never mentioned. Nevertheless the data give some indication of the order of magnitude of particular groups of causes of death.

Table 38 Causes of Death, Chenggong, Yunnan 1940-44

Cause	Number		Rank		Percent	
	Male	Female	Male	Female	Male	Female
Infections	1728	1742	1	1	40.6%	42.1%
Digestive	830	740	2	2	19.5%	17.9%
'Convulsions'	321	288	3	4	7.5%	7.0%
'Senility'	209	306	6	3	4.9%	7.4%
Respiratory	223	190	4	5	5.2%	4.6%
TB	223	185	4	6	5.2%	4.4%
'Cardiac-renal'	115	132	8	7	2.7%	3.2%
External causes	117	68	7	9	2.8%	1.6%
Puerperal fever		93		8		2.2%
Infancy	60	64	9	10	2.4%	1.5%
Cerebro-vascular	14	14			0.3%	0.3%
	3840	3822			90.1%	92.2%
Ill-defined or unknown	414	314			9.7%	7.6%
	4252	4136			99.8%	99.8%

Source: Chen Da, 1946.

Table 38 presents the distribution of the deaths recorded between February 1940 and June 1944 in Chenggong by eleven groups of causes, which were reclassified as far as possible from the twenty-seven categories used by the registrars in the area. The reclassification was done to enable an approximate comparison with the more recent national data for 1973-5 (shown in Table 40).

There were some causes of death, however, which it was impossible to reclassify, such as 'convulsions' which accounted for 609 deaths, all but four of which were of children under the age of fourteen. 'Convulsions' probably covered neonatal tetanus, and the results of a variety of fevers, as well as epilepsy. Thus the deaths listed as being due to infections (including an outbreak of cholera) and to digestive diseases (dysentery, enteritis and diarrhoea) and which make up 60 per cent of all deaths, may have been an underestimate. It can be said that with all its limitations the table shows that the vast majority of deaths were attributable to the lack of basic health care, immunization and sanitation.

Infants were particularly vulnerable. Estimates of infant mortality before 1950 varied from 290 to 500 per thousand live births. A study in Chengdu, Sichuan, carried out in 1942 gave a comparatively low infant mortality rate of 126.5; it noted that nearly 41 per cent of the deaths occurred in the first month and that about 80 per cent of all infant deaths were due to infectious diseases. Tetanus alone accounted for one-third of all infant deaths.

During the Republican period, and perhaps especially during the 1920s and 1930s, efforts were made to provide a network of county hospitals and basic health care; these remained 'largely unrealized under the combined effects of foreign invasion, domestic strife, inflation and corruption'.[5] Women workers organized family service teams to investigate the welfare of women workers, provide women with basic knowledge of hygiene, and teach them how to care for their children. The Chinese Communist Party in Yan'an decided to devote 6 per cent of its budget to health: a not inconsiderable amount, considering that the communists were isolated, beleaguered and fighting the Japanese. After the end of the Sino-Japanese war, as the Nationalists began to fall back, the

Party decided that at least in the already liberated areas, one of the major tasks for women Party workers should be to spread a knowledge of hygiene. The cadres who came to spread that and other messages did not have an easy time:

What made village life a challenge was the dirt and the squalor which surrounded the poorest peasants and the unbearable suffering that was the lot of so many victims of disease. While the itch of lice and the welts left by bedbugs were passed off jokingly as 'the revolutionary heat', the suppurating headsores, malarial fevers, slow deaths from tuberculosis and venereal disease were not joking matters. Land reform workers slept on the same k'angs, ate from the same bowls, and shared lice and fleas with people diseased beyond hope of recovery.[6]

After Liberation the government lost little time in setting out priorities for health care. A National Health Work Conference in 1950 decided that:
1. Health care must serve the people: workers, peasants and soldiers.
2. Priority must be given to the prevention of disease with prophylaxis and treatment combined.
3. Scientific and traditional medicine should work together and eventually be integrated.[7]

Among the most common causes of preventable infant deaths was tetanus. The reason is clear from the description of a childbirth in Longbow Village in 1948. The midwife 'cut the child's cord with a pair of rusty scissors . . . They did not wash the baby for three days. They carefully buried the placenta vertically in the ground outside the door in such a way that the end of the cord protruded as far out of the earth as the matching end of it protruded from the baby's navel. But in spite of these precautions against the "six-day wind" (navel ill) the child fell ill . . .'[8] In another village, the midwife wrapped the end of the cord in earth and white powder and tied it with a cloth; she lived next door to a stables and 'many of the children she delivered died in convulsions'.[9]

In 1950, the Maternal and Health Division of the Health Ministry convened a meeting at which it was decided that the overwhelming priority should be the prevention of tetanus of the new-born and of puerperal sepsis. A massive programme of retraining of traditional midwives to perform normal sterile delivery was undertaken but it took a decade before these complications of childbirth became rare in urban hospitals, and longer still in the countryside. Twenty years later, barefoot doctors were still explaining to rural women that the old Chinese customs of making a newly-delivered mother sit up in bed for three days, and sealing her room to protect her from draughts, were not only unnecessary but could be harmful.

Gradually, routine health checks were introduced for all pregnant women, together with advice on diet and child-care. Pregnant women were given a shorter working day and wherever possible the least unsuitable work. Maternity leave became standard for all state employees, and common in the rural areas. Maternal deaths, however, continued to present a problem even in the mid 1970s, when according to a national survey, the age-specific death rates for women were slightly higher than those for men in the age group 25 to 35 years. As child-bearing in China is heavily concentrated in those years this higher death rate undoubtedly reflects the risk of maternal death.

Table 39 Premature Births, Shanghai, 1936-55

Year	Number	Percentage of live births
1936-40	2,539	6.26
1941-45	2,533	5.49
1946-49	2,648	4.49
1950-55	12,680	3.24

Source: Salaff, Janet W., 1973.

One major contribution to a reduction in maternal deaths has been the family-planning campaign itself. By ensuring a higher age of marriage, and stressing the importance of spacing the children that women have, as well as reducing the overall number of children, the deaths associated with pregnancy under the age of twenty, and over the age of forty, as well as those associated with repeated pregnancies, have declined. The family-planning campaign probably also had an effect on the incidence of low-birthweight babies by reducing, among other things, the incidence of teenage pregnancies. In Shanghai, the percentage of premature births fell steadily during the 1940s and first half of the 1950s (see Table 39).

More recent statistics are not exactly comparable, because they use the more precise measure of low birthweight. In 1957, 10 per cent of all low-birthweight infants in Shanghai weighed 1500 grams or less; by 1964 this proportion had fallen to 4 per cent, 'and this change was reflected in a decreased risk of death among low-weight births taken as a whole'.[10]

The need to give the working mother time and facilities to breast-feed was stressed, as was the importance of breast milk itself. Immunization of children against an increasing number of diseases became widespread, although the difficulties of producing sufficient good quality vaccines and of keeping them from deteriorating before use meant that children in the remoter areas were not always protected. In 1981 the Chinese government conducted an agreement with UNICEF through which the agency will assist in increased vaccine production and the establishment of basic elements of a cold chain. The target number of children to be reached is 50 million in 18,000 communes in remote and mountainous areas.

Generally, however, such infections as measles, diphtheria, polio and encephalitis B have been brought under control as the result of immunization. Other major scourges required a different approach. Mass campaigns, for example to eradicate 'the four pests' – rats, flies, mosquitoes and bedbugs; to limit schistosomiasis by redigging irrigation canals; and to identify and treat venereal diseases, were carried out with nation-wide publicity and with the involvement of a wide range of ministries and official institutions as well as with mass organizations such as the Women's Federation and the Youth League. Some of the campaigns – such as the one to eradicate venereal diseases, which was supplemented by intensive efforts to end prostitution – required only a single major attack. Others, such as the fly-killing campaigns, have to be repeated at regular intervals.

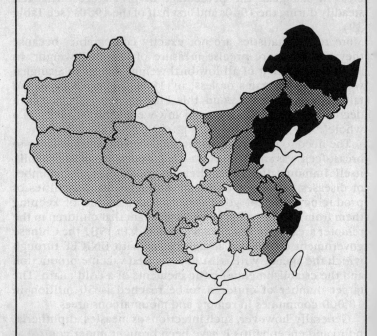

Average Life Expectancy of Chinese Women

- ■ Over 70
- ▨ Above National Average
- ▧ Below National Average
- ░ Below 60
- ☐ Data not available

Life Expectancy of Chinese Men and Women 1973-5:
Provincial Variations
Source: Rong Shoude et al., 1981.

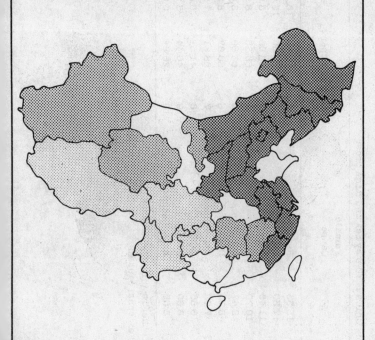

Average Life Expectancy of Chinese Men

Above National Average

Below National Average

Below 60

Data not available

Life Expectancy of Chinese Men and Women 1973-5:
Provincial Variations
Source: Rong Shoude et al., 1981.

Table 40 Ten Most Common Causes of Death, China 1973-5 by Sex and Rank Order

Male				Female			
Cause	Rank	CdR per 100,000	%	Cause	Rank	CdR per 100,000	%
Respiratory+	1	117.52	15.33	Respiratory	1	118.20	16.11
Cardio-vascular	2	94.34	12.30	Cardio-vascular	2	114.55	15.61
Cancers	3	87.77	11.45	Cancers	3	65.96	8.99
Accidents etc.*	4	82.01	10.70	Cerebro-vascular	4	65.55	8.93
Digestive	5	72.60	9.47	Infections	5	63.60	8.64
Infections	6	64.08	8.36	Digestive	6	60.62	8.26
Cerebro-vascular	7	59.73	7.79	Accidents etc.	7	58.61	7.99
Infancy	8	50.98	6.65	Infancy	8	41.51	5.66
TB	9	46.01	6.00	TB	9	40.44	5.51
Arteriosclerosis	10	23.38	3.05	Arteriosclerosis	10	26.54	3.62

+ respiratory includes pneumonia and all other respiratory diseases.

* accidents includes poisons, accidents and external causes.

Source: Rong Shoude et al., 1981.

There were also mass surveys of particular health conditions in which very large numbers of grass-roots medical aides were given a brief training in the detection of the ailment, the use of whatever equipment was necessary, and in how to help persuade the sufferer of the importance of treatment. In many cases the medical aides were instructed in how to carry out the treatment as well. The scale of such training is indicated in the example of leprosy: although the total estimated number of cases in 1949 was only 500,000, over the next thirty years some 10,000 specialized leprosy workers were trained to combat the disease.

A national retrospective study of all causes of death was carried out in twenty-four provinces between 1973 and 1975 through the National Cancer Control Office of the Ministry of Health (see Table 40). It analysed the ten most important causes of death for people of all ages. As would be expected, the major difference between men and women in the rank order of causes of deaths is that men are more likely to die as the result of accidents or other external causes while women are more prone to death due to cerebro-vascular disease.

However, the table masks the extent of the variation around the country in causes of death. Declines in death rates (and therefore increases in life expectancy) largely result from the successful control of infectious and parasitic diseases, maternal mortality, and a large proportion of acute respiratory and gastro-intestinal diseases. Life expectation in China – something under thirty years in the period before 1949 – had increased by 1973-5 to around 63.6 for men and around 66.3 for women which suggests a considerable degree of control of such diseases. But the national average still masks differences between provinces, as the maps on pages 212 and 213 show. The variation between provinces in life expectation at birth – 10.9 years for men and 15.3 for women – can be compared with those of rural India, for example, where the difference between the highest, Kerala (60 years) and the lowest, Uttar Pradesh (35.5 years), was 24 years.

In the parts of China where life expectancy is now high, cardio-vascular diseases, malignancies and cerebro-vascular diseases were the major causes of death. An example of the

Table 41 Ten Leading Causes of Death, Shanghai County, 1960-1962, 1978-1980

		Total		Male		Female	
Rank	Cause of Death	No.	Annual Rate/100,000	No.	Annual Rate/100,000	No.	Annual Rate/100,000
1960-1962							
1	Infectious diseases	1107	78.46	654	94.56	453	69.98
2	Accidents	939	66.56	549	79.38	390	54.22
3	Respiratory disease	689	48.84	424	61.31	265	36.84
4	Digestive disease	568	40.26	313	45.26	255	35.45
5	Neonatal deaths	406	28.78	228	32.97	178	24.75
6	Malignant tumours	331	23.46	171	24.73	160	22.24
7	Cerebro-vascular disease	264	18.71	131	18.94	133	18.49
8	Heart disease	191	13.54	87	12.58	104	14.46
9	Endocrine disease	95	6.73	40	5.78	55	7.65
10	Urinary disease	89	6.31	38	5.49	51	7.09

1978-1980

1	Malignant tumours	2343	142.30	1421	177.70	922	108.87
2	Cerebro-vascular disease	1737	105.49	703	87.91	1034	122.10
3	Heart disease	1697	103.06	806	100.79	891	105.21
4	Respiratory disease	1127	68.45	583	72.90	544	64.24
5	Accidents	813	49.38	479	59.90	334	39.44
6	Infectious diseases	571	34.68	369	46.14	202	23.85
7	Digestive diseases	461	28.00	216	27.01	245	28.93
8	Mental/neurological	214	13.00	95	11.88	119	14.05
9	Urinary disease	170	10.32	82	10.25	88	10.39
10	Neonatal deaths	131	7.96	74	9.25	57	6.73

Source: Gu Xingyuan and Chen Mailing, 1982.

Table 42 Seven Leading Causes of Death Among Children Aged 0-14: Shuangliu County, Chengdu Municipality, Sichuan, 1974-1977

Cause of death	Total		Under 1		Age of death 1-4		5-9		10-14	
	No.	%	No.	%	No.	%	No.	%	No.	%
Accidents	2700	29%	1131	23%	1184	38%	310	36%	75	27%
Diseases of infancy	1724	19%	1724	35%	-	-	-	-	-	-
Respiratory	1641	18%	1009	21%	557	18%	65	8%	10	4%
Contagious	1280	14%	217	4%	756	24%	243	28%	64	23%
Gastro-intestinal	590	6%	232	5%	244	8%	84	10%	30	11%
Malnutrition	321	3%	166	3%	145	5%	9	1%	1	-
Congenital malformation	184	2%	141	3%	26	1%	9	1%	8	3%
Other	762	8%	288	6%	245	8%	144	17%	85	31%
Total	9202	100%	4908	100%	3157	100%	864	100%	273	100%

Source: Tien, H. Yuan, 1983.

changing patterns of cause of death in these more advanced areas is the list of the ten main causes of death in Shanghai County in 1960-62, compared with the ten main causes between 1978 and 1980 (see Table 41). During the eighteen years between 1960-62 and 1978-80, the mortality rate from infectious diseases was reduced by more than a half; that from accidents by about one-third; and that from neonatal deaths by almost three-quarters. In contrast, death rates from chronic disease largely associated with ageing increased.

In the more backward areas, though, the traditional pattern of diseases of the respiratory system, infectious diseases and infant deaths continues to provide the main health problems. In one such area (Sichuan), with a life expectancy at birth for men in 1973-5 of 59.2, and for women of 61.1, survey data provide some indication of the causes of death among children. As part of a national study carried out in 1978, a particular study in Shuangliu County (population 744,000 in 1979) investigated deaths among children aged 0-14 during 1974-7 (see Table 42). Shuangliu, though within the Chengdu municipal boundaries, is largely rural; its conditions would probably be better than those of Sichuan Province as a whole but worse than the national average, to judge from Sichuan's low average life expectancy.

The infant mortality rate was 71.9 (compare this with the rate of 126.5 for Chengdu itself in 1942, given above) and it was reported that tetanus and pneumonia accounted for 39 per cent of all infant deaths. Half of the deaths among children aged one to four were due to diseases of the respiratory and gastro-intestinal tracts and other contagious diseases.

As discussed earlier, infant deaths, and especially deaths of babies in the first month, are generally under-reported. A study of Shifang County in Sichuan suggested that more than half of all infant deaths may go unreported. Shanghai County has been making special efforts to improve the records of infant deaths since 1977, but a 1980 survey revealed that under-reporting continued to exist, and that in that year 21 per cent of infant deaths had not been registered, of which 82 per cent, or more than four-fifths, were deaths in the first four weeks. As a result, perhaps, of these and other studies, the

Chinese appear to have revised their estimates of national infant mortality upwards and now quote a figure of 56 per 1000 live births in 1980. Shanghai County's revised figure, by comparison, was 16 per 1000.

Despite the various limitations, China's record in reducing the national death rate to 6.2 in 1980, and increasing life expectancy to the mid-sixties by 1973-5 is a remarkable one. It has been described as unprecedented among the world's populous developing countries.

Health is more, however, than a matter of just controlling deaths. Some of the illnesses which would often in the past have led to death still occur, even if the outcome is less drastic. Dysentery continues to be a major problem in China: even in Shanghai County the incidence of dysentery has hardly changed in the past twenty-five years, with 686.9 cases per 100,000 population in the period 1956-65, and 657.7 between 1966 and 1980. As a result of the control of other infectious diseases, dysentery now accounts for almost half of the cases of notifiable infections in the county, compared with 14 per cent in the earlier period.

The importance of boiling water, and of developing sources of pure water supplies, are health messages which are constantly stressed. Public supplies may be chlorinated or come at least through a sand filtration plant, but even in cities such supplies are often not piped directly to individual homes, so that education about using clean utensils and boiling water remains necessary.

Human excreta are still the main source of agricultural fertilizers and are carefully collected. Continuing efforts are made to persuade people to store them until they ferment and are largely decontaminated, as well as to emphasize the importance of personal hygiene. This type of education is continuous not only in time but throughout the stages of each individual's life, beginning in nursery school. Nevertheless, as the Shanghai County survey noted, future campaigns will have to stress the prevention of bacillary dysentery.

Another infectious disease has actually increased very considerably during the past 25 years in Shanghai County and perhaps elsewhere, and that is viral hepatitis. From an average annual incidence there of 114.4 per 100,000 in 1956-65, it has risen to 377.3 in the period 1966-80. One possible explanation is the increased number of working women and the consequent greater reliance on canteen and other pre-prepared foods. Unless strict checks are implemented, the presence of a 'carrier' involved in the preparation of food for large numbers can spread the virus very widely.

Tuberculosis is another recurrent problem, especially in the less developed parts of China. Mass X-ray campaigns for its early detection are widespread, between 80 and 90 per cent of newborn children now receive BCG and nonconverters are revaccinated. Poor, and in the cities overcrowded, housing, together with such factors as the Chinese addiction to spitting (which has survived many health campaigns) probably account for the spread of infection.

Accidents are not only a major cause of death but of disability. Children in Shuangliu died particularly as the result of drowning or asphyxiation; drowning was also common among children in Shanghai County. Other not necessarily fatal accidents result from the use of coal briquettes for cooking and heating, the use of oil lamps in unelectrified villages, and the minimal safety precautions in industry. In rural areas anti-tetanus injections may have reduced death rates from accidents with primitive farm implements but that accidents themselves continue to be frequent is indicated by the amount of research and expertise the Chinese have put into the treatment of burns and the reattachment of severed limbs and digits.

Until recently, efforts to ensure environmental cleanliness at the local level were not matched at the level of industrial pollution. Laws on pollution, passed in 1962 and 1973, were largely ignored, although more stringent provisions have now been introduced in a new law passed in September 1979. An estimated 10,000 million tonnes of airborne soot, and 15 million tonnes of carbon dioxide, are discharged into the atmosphere annually. At least 90 per cent of industrial liquid waste is discharged into rivers and streams without treatment. (Over 200 million tonnes of solid waste is produced annually by industry.) Increasing concern is expressed by Chinese medical staff and policy makers about the health impact of such pollution which, although more evident in major cities,

Table 43 Standard Weights of Chinese Boys and Girls Compared with Western Standards

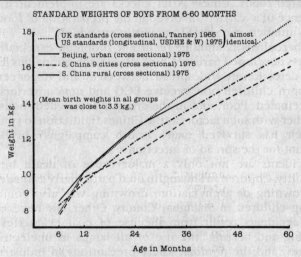

STANDARD WEIGHTS OF BOYS FROM 6-60 MONTHS

UK standards (cross sectional, Tanner) 1965
US standards (longitudinal, USDHE & W) 1975 } almost identical.

Beijing, urban (cross sectional) 1975
S. China 9 cities (cross sectional) 1975
S. China rural (cross sectional) 1975

(Mean birth weights in all groups was close to 3.3 kg.)

Weight in kg. — Age in Months

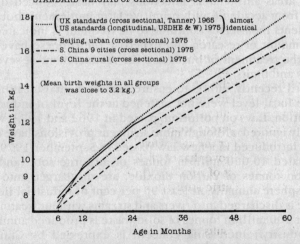

STANDARD WEIGHTS OF GIRLS FROM 6-60 MONTHS

UK standards (cross sectional, Tanner) 1965
US standards (longitudinal, USDHE & W) 1975 } almost identical

Beijing, urban (cross sectional) 1975
S. China 9 cities (cross sectional) 1975
S. China rural (cross sectional) 1975

(Mean birth weights in all groups was close to 3.2 kg.)

Weight in kg. — Age in Months

Source: Cutting, William, 1981.

is not confined to them. Official policies to encourage small-scale industry at the commune level are resulting in an increasing volume of industrial effluent even in rural areas.

Malnutrition may no longer be a major direct killer in China, because the recurrent famines, as well as the absolute poverty, have been largely controlled. Grain production per head has increased very little, if at all, in the past thirty years, the gains having been swallowed by the additional numbers of people. The official emphasis on storing grain, and the government's ability to move grain from one part of the country to another to meet a crisis, have ensured that even quite large-scale natural disasters like the floods and severe drought of 1980-81 did not lead to large numbers of extra deaths.

Nevertheless, the margin is a narrow one. Malnutrition was the sixth most common cause of child death in Shuangliu between 1974 and 1977, although as a percentage of all deaths it was small. A survey in rural Hubei suggested that all the 692 families studied had adequate food; 31.4 per cent had enough clothing and suitable housing but no money to spend; nine per cent had enough clothing but housing problems and no money, while only one family had difficulties with clothes as well as housing. It is not very clear exactly how the adequacy of the facilities, food and clothing was assessed. The report only states: 'With regard to food and clothing, we mean a general standard and not a high standard.' This suggests that for the poorer families nutrition was probably barely adequate. Recently the Chinese have claimed that more than a tenth of the population are not adequately fed.[11]

Again, there is undoubtedly considerable variation in nutrition between different areas of China. The weight of boy and girl children under the age of five years in urban Beijing in the mid-1970s was above that of children in other cities, and still further above that of rural children (see Table 43).

An anthropometric study of children in Shanghai Country reported:

Comparing the results from children living in three different localities (towns, rural areas growing vegetables, and rural areas growing grains and cotton), children residing in towns have higher values for heights and weights than those residing in rural areas; children in the vegetable growing areas (which have higher per capita incomes) are a little taller and heavier than children in the grain and cotton growing areas.

The mean values in the 1981 study in Shanghai County are higher than those from a 1979 study in seven rural counties of Greater Shanghai, but lower than those from urban areas in the 1979 study.[12]

Within the limitations imposed by low levels of national income per head, an increasing number of people to be fed and the difficulties of expanding agricultural production as well as increasing agricultural productivity, real efforts have been made to ensure an equitable distribution of food. In addition, nutrition education programmes were launched. The elements of a balanced diet, and the need for particular foods for vulnerable groups like children or pregnant and nursing mothers, have been promoted for many years through the medical corps and the Women's Federation, as well as by using posters, leaflets and other information channels. The continuing concern at official levels about adequate nutrition is exemplified by the fact that an almost universal bonus for the one-child family is a small cash supplement (usually 5 *yuan* a month) especially allocated for the purchase of supplementary nutritious foods for the child.

As now with declining mortality a larger proportion of the population lives longer, there is an increase in morbidity from the diseases of old age: cardio-vascular diseases, cerebro-vascular diseases and cancers. New campaigns – against smoking, virtually ignored as a health hazard until the mid-1970s; to alter diet; and to further encourage exercise – may have to be launched. Above all, however, more sophisticated techniques of diagnosis and treatment will be needed to meet the new challenges, and this means the reorientation of the training of doctors and, more importantly, of other medical and paramedical workers.

The Chinese approach to the provision of health care has been determined by the extraordinarily high commitment given by the government since 1949 to improving mortality and morbidity, and by the typical developing country's lack of trained doctors and a health infrastructure (see Table 44).

Table 44 Medical Resources in 1949

	Number	Population per health worker/unit
Population	540 million	-
Western doctors	20,000	27,000
Traditional doctors	500,000	1,000
Total health workers	520,000	1,038
No. of beds	90,000	6,000
No. of hospitals	600	900,000

Source: Lisowski, F.P., 1978.

The impossibility of training sufficient numbers of doctors combined with the urgent need to improve health care, especially in the rural areas, led first of all to the training of paramedical workers to recognize and handle specific conditions, and to experiments with different types of alternative health-care structures. Paramedical workers were supplemented by mobile medical teams which toured the rural areas. Development of the basic health-care facilities was intensified and by 1965 it was claimed that all China's 2000 counties had one health centre or hospital with some in-patient facilities which enabled minor or emergency operations to be undertaken and infectious cases isolated. It was clear, however, that much more needed to be done.

A partial substitute for qualified medical practitioners was the barefoot doctor. Especially during and after the Cultural Revolution very large numbers were trained: by 1979 there were 1,575,000 of them. Their initial course was for six months, but from the start further in-service training was an integral feature of their work. This might be achieved by their working with a qualified doctor doing a period of work in the countryside, or by secondments to a hospital, or by courses arranged by teaching hospitals. Many of the original barefoot doctors eventually became fully qualified professionals. In the last few years attempts to up-grade the quality of barefoot doctors have become more stringent and the least effective ones have been weeded out; nevertheless, in 1981 there were 1,393,000, or one barefoot doctor to every 572 rural inhabitants.

The Health Care Referral System in the PRC

	RURAL HEALTH CARE REFERRAL		URBAN HEALTH CARE REFERRAL	
	HEALTH CENTRE	SERVES	HEALTH CENTRE	SERVES
Primary Care	BRIGADE CLINIC	A brigade – composed of approximately 10 villages	WORK UNIT CLINIC or NEIGHBOURHOOD CLINIC	A small work unit or neighbourhood
	COMMUNE HOSPITAL	A commune of about 16 000 people		
Secondary Care	COUNTY HOSPITAL or RURAL DISTRICT HOSPITAL	A county of about 500 000 people or A district of about 4 million people	LARGE WORK UNIT CLINIC or NEIGHBOURHOOD HOSPITAL or URBAN DISTRICT HOSPITAL	A large work unit or urban district
Tertiary Care			MUNICIPAL HOSPITAL or PROVINCIAL HOSPITAL	A city of 3 million people or A province of 35 million people

Barefoot doctors were chosen for training from their own community and returned to work in it. They were paid by that community on the basis of a workpoint allocation, although measures are now being introduced to make them full-time medical workers on a salary provided from public funds. They are expected to have an intimate knowledge and understanding of their community, and to provide preventive and emergency care suited to the local needs. Midwives and other local health workers assist them with the brigade and team. Quite a number of brigades – 61,000 in 1981 – have health stations funded by the brigade itself and from fees paid by its members.

Table 45 Medical Resources 1981

	Number	Population per health worker/unit
Population	996,220,000	-
College-graduated doctors	516,000	1,931
Graduates of secondary medical schools	436,000	2,285
Senior physicians trained in traditional and Western medicine	2,000	498,111
Practitioners of traditional medicine	290,000	3,435
Nurses	525,000	1,897
Pharmacists, anti-epidemic workers	1,242,000	802
Rural barefoot doctors	1,393,000	572
No. Hospital beds	2,000,000*	498
No. County hospitals	2,000	398,485
Commune health centres	55,000	14,490
Brigade health stations	61,000	n/a

*Hospital beds in rural areas were reported as some 1,200,000, giving a rural population per hospital bed of approximately 642.

Source: adapted from Tien, H. Yuan, 1983.

By 1981 about 90 per cent of communes had health centres. Although partially funded by the county or province, such health centres were largely financed by the commune. The county hospitals, on the other hand, are funded from the national budget and act as referral centres and training centres. The levels of health care, and the referral system between them, are set out in the diagram on page 226.

Figures for health-care personnel, and for the various health care facilities in 1981, indicate a quite remarkable improvement over the situation in 1949 (see Table 45).

Given the very different economic conditions in different parts of China, it is not surprising that, below the county hospital level, health care spread more slowly in some provinces than in others. Co-operative medical systems within a commune or brigade, paid for by membership fees and charges for the users, began to be introduced in the mid-1960s, but not only did different areas implement such schemes at a different rate, the schemes themselves were vulnerable to local economic recessions. Reported percentages of brigades with co-operative health schemes fluctuated in different years (see Table 46).

Table 46 Percentage of Production Brigades with Co-operative Health Programmes, by Province, 1969-1975

Province	1969	1970	1971	1972	1973	1974	1975
Anhui			70	68.7	50		
Zhejiang			71				
Fujian				80	74		80
Heilongjiang							94
Henan							75
Hebei			80 (Feb.)	80.6 90			
Hunan		97.4		50			79
Hubei					83		80
Inner Mongolia*					33	50	71

Table 46 cont.

Province	1969	1970	1971	1972	1973	1974	1975
Gansu				85			
Jiangxi				93			
Jiangsu	(June) 80						
	(Sept.) 95						
Jilin*					68	90	90
Guangxi				66.7	70	90	
Guangdong	50	87		100	80		
Guizhou				67.5			
Ningxia							80
Beijing					75		
Shanxi			85				
Shandong			50			53	85
Shaanxi		84					
Xinjiang		70			90		
Sichuan				80			
Tianjin							95
Qinghai				42	70	50	60
Yunnan		90		100		80	

* The 1973 statistics are for model areas only: the provincial rate was presumably lower.

Source: Lampton, David M., 1976.

Welfare funds were usually a fixed percentage of the collective production; when that fell, so too did the amount available for health. Additionally, because each day worked resulted in a certain number of workpoints for which at the end of the accounting period each worker received a share of the collective production, when production fell workers got less for their workpoints. In such circumstances there was a reluctance to pay for medical services. There is some evidence that the growth or shrinkage of collective health schemes was closely linked to provincial grain production in the previous year. In 1980 approximately 30 per cent of the rural Chinese still did not belong to 'a minimally adequate health-insurance programme'.

Even those peasants participating in insurance schemes seldom have all the costs of an illness covered; they generally have to pay at least a proportion of the cost of medicines. For those in need of more sophisticated treatment than is available at the brigade or commune level, costs are high. A recent study carried out in a tertiary care level hospital in Wuhan, Hubei, suggested that an average total charge (including food costs) to patients was 178.3 *yuan,* which might exceed many peasants' annual cash income. It quoted recent interviews of mainland Chinese refugees in Hong Kong who identified hospital bills as a major source of debt in rural areas. However, many infectious and other diseases endemic in the country-side are treated free of charge. In addition, the government is currently attempting to improve the level of care available in rural county and commune hospitals, which should help peasants to avoid the more expensive third-level facilities.

For the foreseeable future, many of China's health personnel, especially in the more backward areas, will have to continue to battle with the prevention of infections and the improvement of hygiene. The 'two controls and five improvements' of the barefoot doctor's task – namely, the control of drinking water and night-soil and the improvement of wells, animal pens, stoves, latrines and the environment – will continue to demand their attention. But the more intensive training now being given to them reflects official recognition that China is progressing, in health terms, beyond the stage where those tactics alone will be sufficient to effect further improvements.

In terms of family planning, barefoot doctors are already being trained to carry out vasectomy and female sterilization. But the one-child family policy has made still more urgent the need to control child mortality, and to make available the techniques of pregnancy monitoring and high-quality ante- and post-natal care. It is probably unrealistic to expect that a shift towards more high-technology medicine can be introduced without greater central funding of local facilities.

Education

Education in traditional China was highly valued both for itself and as the path to preferment, so that any family which could scrape together the funds attempted to set at least one child on the path of learning. Between 1368 and 1911, over a third of those who took the metropolitan examinations (the third stage of qualification) are said to have come from families with little or no educational background.

The numbers involved, however, were tiny. So too was the percentage of children who managed to get to a government or missionary 'modern' school as these were gradually established from the late nineteenth century onwards. Marshall Zhu De was among the lucky ones:

Since tax collectors, officials, and soldiers respected or were afraid of educated men, my family decided to send one or more sons to school. Every peasant longed to educate his children, but in those days there were no public schools, and private schools kept by scholars charged tuition fees that only the well-to-do could afford. Peasants might send a son to school for a year or two, but as soon as the boy was old enough to work in the fields, he was taken out. In my childhood, conditions had become so bad that education was a life necessity for the peasants. A whole clan would pool its resources to educate one son who could talk back to the tax collectors and soldiers, and keep accounts.[13]

The school system was, as one writer observed, 'palpably inadequate'.[14] In 1935 there were 260,000 primary schools serving a population of about 100 million children aged between five and seventeen. Only 13 million, or less than 15 per cent, of these children went to school at all. 'The high schools and colleges served the sons of the landlords and of well-to-do peasants almost exclusively.' Girls, inevitably, fared worse than boys; a survey in the 1930s showed that only 1 per cent of females, as against 30 per cent of males, had attended school long enough to read a common letter. In

1950, a village near Guangzhou with the unusually high literacy rate of 65 per cent for males above the age of ten had a rate for girls above the same age of only 19 per cent.

In the liberated areas, however, the Communist Party was laying great stress on education, and experiments were made with simplified Chinese characters as well as romanized letters to make the process easier. The Party insisted that education was for everybody, that it was a lifelong process, and that it was essential for the success of the struggle for national independence. One visitor described how education was achieved, in the absence of almost all resources (including teachers) and despite the war going on around them:

They combined education with life. Instead of drilling the peasant in school (except in winter) the Communists began teaching him how to read by showing him characters connected with his daily life and occupation. Thus a shepherd would be taught the characters for sheep, dog, stick, grass and so on. A farmer would learn the characters for field, millet, wheat, mule and the like. The methods of teaching were also as ingenious as they were pleasant. A school child would go around at the noon recess to the homes of five or six housewives and paste on the front door, the living-room table, and the kitchen stove the characters for each of these objects. The next day the schoolboy would bring the next characters. Or, as I saw, a farmer ploughing in his field would put up one character on a big board at each end of the field . . . In village after village I have seen these clods of the soil, hitherto barred from any education, poring over lessons, trooping to the winter schools, watching rural character teams perform on the threshing ground, listening to newscasts broadcast through hand megaphones, and studying the slogans painted on the walls, spelling them out in this tortured but practical way.[15]

After 1949, education, both formal and informal, continued to be a major priority. Kindergartens, primary schools, lower and upper middle-schools, technical schools and colleges as well as universities were established; part-time schools and adult literacy classes offered those beyond school age a chance of education too.

What was actually taught in schools varied considerably over time with shifts of political emphasis and educational theory; so too did criteria for admission to the higher levels of educational establishment. Such changes and their effects cannot be discussed here; in the context of the government's attempts to meet the basic needs of the people, this chapter is concerned simply with the achievement of literacy on the one hand, and with the government's broader concept of education for life, on the other.

It should perhaps be noted, though, in the context of family planning, that population education – the relationship between population growth and the use of resources for overall development – was taught increasingly in secondary schools from the early 1970s. So too were the need for female equality, and for late marriage to enable young people to fulfil their potential and to contribute to the country. Until very recently contraception was not discussed in the school syllabus. Experimental courses are now being introduced but they remain somewhat sensitive and controversial.

It should also be noted that among the criteria employed to decide who should go for further training or tertiary education, marital status has been a factor at least since the early 1970s. Only single young people were considered for such training and if they chose to marry during their course, they were seldom allowed to complete it.

According to the Chinese about 20 million children reach primary school age each year and about 95 per cent are said currently to enrol for schooling (see Table 47). The latter figure is probably an over-estimate; a survey in Anhui in 1981 found an enrolment rate of 84 per cent.

Female literacy is much below the national average. The Anhui survey found that girls were only 36 per cent of those enrolled in primary school. The study of mainland Chinese refugees in Hong Kong which 'through sample error or crude reporting' got 100 per cent schooling claims among the youngest generation described in the sample, nevertheless indicated that 80 per cent of the girls had only primary-school education, while 54 per cent of the boys had gone on to middle school or even to further education.

Table 47 Education in the Chinese Population 1982

	Number	%
Population	1,008,882,511	
University graduates	4,414,195	0.44
Undergraduates*	1,602,474	0.16
Senior middle-school*	66,478,028	6.59
Junior middle-school*	178,277,140	17.7
Primary school	355,160,310	35.2
	605,932,140	59.99
Illiterates+	235,820,002	23.5

* includes those currently studying, and those who did not complete
the course, as well as graduates.
+ people 12 years and above who cannot read or can read only a few
words.
Source: 1982 Census.
Note: Presumably the 17.0 per cent unaccounted for in the above table
are children of pre-school age and those of school-age but not enrolled.
Among the latter, girls may be a majority.

Among adult women, the situation is worse. Among 917
women whose pregnancies were studied in two communes in
Shanghai County in 1981, 45 per cent had only primary
school education and 5 per cent had no formal education at
all. The Anhui survey showed that 85.6 per cent of the
mothers in the 8995 households surveyed were illiterate,
compared with 41.5 per cent of the fathers.

The trend, however, is towards increasing education of both
sexes. If the figure of 23.5 per cent illiterates revealed by the
1982 Census is regarded by the government as unacceptably
high, it should be compared with that of 1964, which was
38.1 per cent. The Chinese have not only been able to reduce
illiteracy by more than a third since 1964, but to do so during
a period when the total population increased by 314 million,
or 45 per cent.

Education is far too important in China today to be left to
the schools alone. Sometimes the pupils themselves are
educators, for they too play their part in the mass campaigns,

through, for instance, the Young Pioneers organization, as an account in the 1960s describes:

When there is any social campaign, these young pioneers use their own initiative to plan a working programme. For example, when the campaign for public hygiene was on, the pioneer squads went to the stations, bus stops, and street corners, holding their pioneer flags. There they made speeches and sang songs, repeating slogans asking people not to spit in the streets. They even provided paper for the offenders to wipe up the sputum from the pavement and put it in an antiseptic tank which they carried with them. These are but some examples.[16]

Children also have a part to play in education for family planning. It is family-planning education which will be largely discussed here, as an example of the kinds of social education campaign which have been part of the drive for 'education for life'. In the mid-1970s, the *People's Daily* reported that a middle school in Shuangliao County, Jilin, had organized special peasant classes to teach medical and health courses, as well as planned parenthood.

The kind of approach they may have used is exemplified by a children's play from a kindergarten in Shuangchiao Commune, Beijing, which begins 'Dear uncles and aunts, have you all carried out family planning?' This arresting introduction is followed by two contrasting stories. Hsiao-an has a single older sister:

'Older sister loves me and I love older sister;
The two of us are a pair of good companions.
Father labours in the rice fields;
Mother is busy in the vegetable patch . . .'

The family is politically active and involved in all the current campaigns, but still has time for companionship:

'After we have supper
Father narrates family history to me,
And mother teaches me to sing songs.
Older sister is my counsellor . . .'

Poor Hsiao-kang, on the other hand, has lots of older brothers and sisters as well as a younger sister, Hsiao-fang:

'Father and mother are busy at their work;
Our family affairs are in a complete jumble;
Older brothers and sisters are of no avail.
They bother mother until she is truly frustrated.
I, Hsiao-kang, am like a little sheep;
I run around as I please and bump into everything.
My little friends tattle on me;
So when I get home, I shall surely get slapped.
You who are called Hsiao-an, let me ask you:
Why is your family able to study and to criticize,
While my family from day to night is always in one big mess,
And is always in a meaningless uproar?'[17]

The answer, of course, was obvious. The family was just too big.

This charming sketch was included in a collection of family-planning resource materials collected by the People's Health Press and published, for wider use, in an edition of 330,000. The Press noted that 'in the work of initiating family planning, all localities have greatly stressed propaganda work and compiled large quantities of source materials to propagate the Party's family-planning policies. They have created quite a few vigorous and vibrant themes and forms which . . . have been very popular.'[18]

Among these local initiatives were a number of comedies. In one sly comic dialogue act between two men, it turns out, after long discussion, that the wife of one has gone to propagandize the wife of the other, whose husband, the first explains unwittingly, 'has some ideological problems'. Still trying to keep his identity dark, the second man denies it: 'No, no. Her husband's ideological problems have been solved!'

They have begun by discussing a model leader of a women's brigade. Tell us, says the second man, why she is a model:

'For that I must begin talking about the time she was married.'
'Very interesting. To speak about being considered a model, one has

to begin talking about the time she was married.'
'It was five years ago they were married.'
'How old were they?'
'Over fifty years old.'
'Over fifty years old before she was married?'
'The two together were over fifty years old.'
'Oh.'

A quite different approach is a choral dialogue which chants the various advantages of family planning for the state, rather than the individual:

The significance of family planning is great indeed;
There is no end to speaking of family planning's advantages.
When the national economy has a plan,
Then all enterprises also show development;
If population growth is not planned,
Then the planned economy will be plunged into chaos . . .

The themes of the plays, songs and dialogues cover all the main arguments for family planning in its broad Chinese sense of delayed marriage as well as fewer and better spaced children. They attack the old belief that girls are not as good as boys. In one play, grandmother Li who is opposing her daughter's sterilization (after two girl babies) asks who, if she has no son, will care for her in her old age? The other mother-in-law points out triumphantly that Mother Li herself has no sons. 'Don't we depend on socialism, on collectivism, on our own labours?' Mothers and mothers-in-law are frequently the subjects of the propaganda, being dissuaded from their desire to see a lavish marriage, or to see their children marry young. One mother is not even pacified by the fact that her prospective daughter-in-law is a highly eligible girl, about to join the Party; if the wedding is not fixed up soon, she asks her son, 'Aren't you afraid she'll fly away from you?'

These source materials are designed to be performed by local groups or broadcast over a local radio. By 1955, radio, already widely used in the cities, was being extended to become a means of education throughout the country. In December of that year, the Third National Conference on

Broadcasting Work put forward plans for more than 900 line-broadcasting stations by 1956, with a total of some 500,000 loudspeakers, 80 per cent of which were to be in rural areas. The system was operated by monitors who relayed broadcasts from local or central stations or made their own announcements. 'Careful attention has been given to the training of monitors. They are expected not only to handle the apparatus, select the programmes to be relayed, and handle bulletins of local news and information, but also to mobilize listeners and co-operate in such activities as running local news-sheets, wall newspapers and group meetings.'[19] Each village was to have at least one microphone outlet.

A feature of the past three years has been the rapid increase in television ownership, especially, of course, in the cities; but it was said that by 1982 almost all brigades, at least, would have a communal television set. Like radio, cable TV broadcasts discussions, information and entertainment on family planning; it is also used for training programmes, for example to up-date and improve the barefoot doctors' knowledge.

Films, too, are used both for training – there are excellent technical films on contraception, designed for medical courses – and to spread general educational concepts. One full-length feature film, *Bright Career*, for example, made by one of China's best-known film producers and using top writers, included a song which topped the Chinese 'hit parade'. It introduced a range of themes – the woman who adored small babies and despite the increasing size of her family could not resist having yet another; the man who longed for a daughter with bows and doll, despite his two lively sons; the lovers whose wish to marry was opposed by the girl's parents because they had no son and thus needed her around – handled deftly and amusingly via the story of two pairs of lovers and their families.

The number of messages the film incorporates is not unusual: single slogans are usually reinforced by a number of mutually supportive concepts. One family-planning poster, for instance, shows the village's development (an electricity pylon in the background) and the family's standard of living (a glimpse of a bicycle and sewing machine) with an obviously loved grandmother dispensing hospitality while the only child, a healthy pretty daughter, cuddles her mother who gets pills from the barefoot doctor.

The message may also appeal to a variety of audiences. During the recent 'five emphases and four beauties' campaign to improve standards of morality, public order, cleanliness, politeness and culture, and to stress beauty of the environment, of conduct, of speech and of the soul, a *Collection of Satirical Verses and Pictures for Children* was published.[20] Produced by the Children's Literature Group of the Chongqing Children's Palace, it was designed for children of primary-school age and teases badly-behaved children, like the smug little horror who because of his good school results demands 'a cake from Grandpa, an air-gun from Grandma, new shoes from Dad, new clothes from Mum and still says "It's not enough, not enough!" ' Several of the sketches, however, are addressed to the parents as much as to the child. In the one reproduced below, 'Little Sun' is obviously a long-awaited and only son, and, as a commentator noted, 'his sisters' awareness of their inferior status seems to be reflected in their marked lack of enthusiasm for the services demanded of them'.[21] A criticism of the traditional preference for a son is implied. The verse which accompanies the picture finishes with the ironic:

Nine planets wheel and spin
And revolve around the 'Little Sun'!

The mass media approaches are designed to complement and reinforce the persuasive efforts of an individual family-planning worker talking to a neighbour or fellow worker. 'China's planned-birth persuasion efforts are more of an individual or small group than a mass approach' wrote one specialist, who described the media support as helping to create a favourable, conducive atmosphere for the promotion and adoption of planned-birth methods.[22]

'Family planning communication and motivation', wrote another commentator, 'gradually evolved into a uniquely Chinese procedure which combined a mass-oriented national campaign with the most intimate and personal approach.'[23] Calls for the one-child family and the abandonment, in theory at least, of the need for communal birth-planning discussions as a result, may have lessened the emphasis on individual persuasion, particularly in the cities. Nevertheless, the Chinese are aware that while the outcome of decisions on family size may affect more than the immediate couple concerned, the decision itself is made and adhered to in the privacy of the home.

Thus a North China Planned Parenthood meeting held in September 1981 noted that 'Propaganda cadres and propagandists must make friends with the peasants, use popular peasant forms and language, and use reasoning the peasants can understand to launch planned parenthood propaganda . . .'[24] The belief in 'a key for every lock' described in Chapter 4 means the use of reasoning which is not only understandable in general to the peasants, but which is directly applicable to the particular peasant family being approached.

A peasant in Jiaotian brigade of Zijin county's Shangyi commune was still unprepared to practise birth control although he already had six sons and two daughters. His family had a total of thirteen members and five of his sons were still unmarried. Several cadres reasoned with him patiently, explaining that in a few years his family would have more than 20 members even if each couple gave birth to only one child. They also told him that, by that time, the living standard of his family members would drop drastically because the land available to each family member would be reduced as the number of family members increased. After this explanation, the peasant soon realized that he had had too many children and that he must stop fathering children because his burden was already too heavy. Now he has not only voluntarily undergone birth control surgery, but he has also urged his married children to practise family planning.[25]

As one of the sketches in the *Source Materials for Family Planning* summed it up:

Big Sister Chiang of the Village's east section,
You know, has given birth to three little girls;
But Big Brother Chiang is still hoping for a boy
And the two have been at loggerheads over this question.
Big Sister says:
'If you want to have a boy, then you give birth to one . . .
If you don't change your old concepts, I shall argue with you till doomsday'.[26]

Other Social and Economic Needs

China continues to be an extremely poor, developing country. Total gross national product (GNP) increased 4.5 times between 1953 and 1981, but the increased number of people has reduced the GNP gain per head to a mere doubling. Food supplies have increased, as have textiles, and so too have cultural amenities and major consumer goods (see Table 48).

If diet remains dull, especially in the cities, it is, as has been discussed, generally just adequate. Clothing is seldom fashionable, and in the rural areas will be carefully patched and mended, but people have enough clothes for decency and warmth, and shoes to protect them from water-borne parasites. Heating in public buildings (schools, factories and offices) is almost non-existent, but peasants in North China do seem to be able to afford to heat their homes.

The homes themselves, particularly in the cities, are among the remaining major problems the government has in meeting basic needs. The intensified house-building programme of the post-1978 period has done little as yet to meet the demand for more living space or for homes equipped with basic amenities like running water. None the less, city homes, however crowded, are reasonably clean, near to a pure water supply,

Table 48 Indicators of Improvement in People's Livelihood: China, 1952-1980 (Per capita figures unless otherwise indicated)

Item	1980	1981	1952	Increase 1952-80
Food supplies:				
Grain	427.6 catties[a]		NG[b]	8.2%
Vegetable oils	4.6 catties		NG	9.8%
Pork	22.3 catties		NG	88.6%
Sugar	7.7 catties		NG	320.0%
Textiles (cotton and synthetic):				
Overall	31.1 chi[c]		17.1	76.0%
Urban	49.5 chi		NG	21.9%
Rural	25.8 chi		NG	85.6%
Cultural amenities and major consumer goods:				
Sewing machines	(46,040,000 units)			
Urban	1 per 2 households			
Rural	1 per 5.7 households			
Bicycles	(96,170,000 units)			
Urban	1.2 per household			
Rural	1 per 3 households			
Wrist watches	(128,000,000 pieces)			
Urban	1 per 2 persons			
Rural	1 per 17 persons			

Hospital beds	(1,982,000 units) 2.2 per 1000 persons	(2,017,000 units) 0.3 per 1000	600.0%
Movie units	(125,000 teams) 1 per 10,000 persons	(131,000 teams) 0.2 per 10,000 (1957)	750.0%
Newspapers	(14.0 billion issues) 4 per 100 persons	(14.1 billion issues) NG	500.0%
Books, etc.	(4.6 billion copies) 4.67 per person	(5.6 billion copies) NG	240.0%
Radio stations	160	114	
TV stations	38	42	
TV sets	(9,028,000 units) Urban 1 per 6.8 households Rural 1 per 53 households		

[a] 1 catty = 1.1 lbs.
[b] NG = Not given. However, 1962-80 percentage increases are shown in the original reports.
[c] 1 chi = 13.1 inches.
Source: Tien, H. Yuan, 1983.

transport and a working public telephone, and compare favourably with the slums often seen in other countries in the Third World.

There are continuing inequalities both between the educated élite cadres and the average worker and, more importantly, between the urban and rural areas (as Table 48 shows). But in comparison with the quite recent past, the lives of the majority of the people have improved beyond imagination. As one foreign commentator remarked 'People's wants in any country are relative, and though most Chinese people would be glad of better food supplies and finer consumer goods in the shops, those over forty can remember the bitter years towards the end of the civil war when a cold night might carry off dozens of undernourished street sleepers, and even people who did have a roof over their heads were often bankrupted by inflation, war damage and looting. It is the younger generation – with no recollection of these things – who will become increasingly restive as their growing knowledge of the outside world brings it home to them that their nation still hovers only just above the poverty line.'[27]

Current efforts to modernize China by the end of the century assume annual production growth rates of around 4 per cent; not unreasonable when agricultural output has increased over 5 per cent in 1981 and 1982, and industrial output still faster. Attempting to get a proper balance between the expansion of heavy industry and that of light industry producing, among other things, consumer goods, continues to be something of a problem. The modernization of science and technology, as well as to some extent the modernization of the country's defence forces, faces the handicap of a lack of trained and educated people which has been exacerbated by the educational policies of the Cultural Revolution period and its aftermath. The younger generation, or at least that proportion of it which grew up in the turbulent period between 1966 and 1976 and now finds its skills inadequate and the precepts which were drummed into it scorned, may well be confused or embittered. But to have taken a country as vast as China, with over 1000 million people, 'above the poverty line' – even if only just – is in itself a quite remarkable achievement.

It is an achievement which has created a fundamental level of security for the Chinese. A reasonable degree of confidence can be maintained that one will not starve or die of cold and neglect; that one is unlikely to suffer the old terrifying epidemics; that savings and assistance forthcoming from the government will mitigate natural disasters like floods or crop failures; that one's children have a chance of survival, of education and (though this last is becoming somewhat doubtful) of a job.

Such a climate of basic security has been reinforced by the very strong emphasis on welfare support, however minimal the welfare provision in a poor country may be. As one authority described it, Chinese families have been surrounded:

... by a veritable maze of support services, most of which came from their local community. City dwellers looked to their neighbourhood for services such as child care and home help. Canteens and other services were provided by most work units. In the rural areas peasant families looked to their neighbours for similar services. This pattern of interdependence was fostered by the CCP, which saw it as an expression of class solidarity.

Chinese families accepted counselling by people on a variety of subjects. Marriage guidance counselling was given by neighbourhood mediation committees, team committees, party cadres, trade union activists and cadres, as well as relatives, friends and neighbours ... Budget counselling was provided by trade union cadres and activists or team leaders ... Teachers were expected to provide educational counselling by visiting their students' homes and discussing with parents any problems which might be evident in their children's schoolwork ... Health workers from the local community visited families to discuss such matters as personal and public hygiene.[28]

Within such a network, and given confidence in the present and a hope for the future, parents have been increasingly able to accept that they no longer need large numbers of children, and that it is possible to plan for and to rear those children they do have. They have even come to recognize that their choice of family size has an impact on the community around them.

Demographers and others concerned with population policies have looked to China, with its unusually fast declines in fertility, to provide evidence in the wider debate about how far family-planning programmes affect fertility and how far people's fertility behaviour depends upon social and economic change. One expert[29] drew together the few, and admittedly less than satisfactory, provincial figures for some indicators of change – the percentage of the population which was urbanized; total per capita output; the per capita grain output; and average life expectancy – and tried to correlate them with provincial family-planning performance. He concluded, very tentatively, that social and economic change was related to how well the various provinces had done until 1980, when the intensified family-planning programme linked to the one-child campaign was introduced. The success of that campaign appeared to be independent of the provinces' performance in other fields.

Reanalysis of his data,[30] using only the provinces for which there is directly comparable information for both 1978 and 1980, does not produce the correlations for earlier years between provincial population growth rates and socio-economic change which were postulated. This does not, however, mean that no such link exists; just that those particular indicators, on their own, do not provide one.

It is possible that if and when good statistics become available on a whole range of topics such as girls' education, age of marriage, job opportunities, family incomes and how they are spent and by whose decision, to name but a few, it will become possible to analyse the contribution of any of them to China's declining fertility rates. It could be argued, though, that such an exercise itself would miss the essence of the Chinese family-planning programme.

The family-planning programme has from its inception been a wider one than that of simply providing contraceptives. It has been concerned with late marriage; with the status of women; with health. Since the late 1960s it has also been interwoven with community decision-making and community responsibilities. It has played a part in other campaigns, whether to criticize Confucius and Lin Biao, or to provide safer pregnancy; and it in turn has been reinforced by campaigns as different as those to improve housing or to achieve the 'four modernizations'.

The excellent programme administration is supplemented, on the one hand, by the involvement of top officials with the provincial leading groups, people who have a major overall say in provincial policies, and by a vast corps of local activists chosen from within their own immediate community, on the other. The family-planning messages may be integrated into other political or social themes, or they may be specifically chosen to match the concerns and priorities of one particular family.

Without a good family-planning programme, there would not be the trained personnel, or the contraceptives in the right place at the right time, or the lively local propaganda, or the carefully-kept local statistics. Neither would family planning get the priority which does ensure that its messages are interwoven with other priority topics. At the same time, without certain basic needs having been met to the point where the average Chinese, and above all the average Chinese peasant, does feel some security and hope, even the best family-planning programme would have little to offer beyond respite for women worn out by poverty and constant child-bearing.

Notes

1. Report of the Third Asian and Pacific Population Conference (Colombo, Sri Lanka, 20-29 September 1982), *Asian Population Studies Series no. 55,* UNECOSOC, 1982.

2. Chi Po, quoted in Lampton, David M., 'Health, Conflict and the Chinese Political System', *Michigan Papers in Chinese Studies,* no. 18, 1974.

3. Hume, Edward, *Doctors East, Doctors West,* George Allen and Unwin, 1949.

4. Chen Da, 'Population in Modern China', *American Journal of Sociology,* vol. 52, no. 1, part II, University of Chicago Press, 1946, 126 pp.

5. Lampton, David M., op. cit.

6. Hinton, William, *Fanshen,* Monthly Review Press, 1966.

7. Lisowski, F.P. 'The Evolution of Health Care in China', *Eastern Horizon,* vol. XVII, no. 3, 1978, pp. 5-11.

8. Hinton, William, op. cit.

9. Hume, Edward, op. cit.

10. Chalmers, Iain, 'Better Perinatal Health: Shanghai', *The Lancet,* 19 January 1980, pp. 137-9.

11. 1977 report, quoted in Wren, Christopher S., 'China – New Policies Encourage Wealth', *Asian Post,* 23 April 1983.

12. Yao Yiling and Wang Beijun, 'An Anthropometric Study of Schoolchildren', *American Journal of Public Health,* no. 72 (Supplement), 1982, pp. 41-2.

13. Smedley, Agnes, *The Great Road,* Monthly Review Press, 1956.

14. Lang, Olga, *Chinese Family and Society,* Yale University Press, 1946.

15. Belden, Jack, *China Shakes the World,* Monthly Review Press, 1974.

16. Tsang, Chiusam, *Society, Schools and Progress in China,* Pergamon Press, 1968.

17. The full text, translated by Robert Dunn, appears in Orleans, Leo A., *Chinese Approaches to Family Planning,* Macmillan, 1979.

18. 'Literature and Art Propaganda: Source Materials on Family Planning', in Orleans, Leo A., op. cit.

19. Price, R.F., *Education in Communist China,* Routledge & Kegan Paul, 1970.

20. Collection of Satirical Verses and Pictures for Children, Chongqing Children's Palace Children's Literature Group, discussed by Keating, Pauline, 'Tales for Chinese Children', *China Now,* no. 104, 1982, pp. 11-14.

21. Keating, Pauline, op. cit.

22. Chu, Leonard L., *Planned Birth Campaigns in China 1949-1976,* East-West Communications Institute, East-West Center, 1977.

23. Orleans, Leo A., op. cit.

24. North China Planned Parenthood Meeting, Xi'an, Shaanxi, provincial broadcast report, 26 Sept. 1981, *Summary of World Broadcasts,* 2 October 1981.

25. Achievements of Huiyang prefecture, Guangdong, *Xinhua,* 11 September 1981; *Summary of World Broadcasts,* 2 October 1981.

26. Orleans, Leo A., op. cit.

27. Bonavia, David, *The Chinese,* Allen Lane, 1980.

28. Dixon, John, *The Chinese Welfare System 1949-1979,* Praeger, 1981.

29. Tien, H. Yuan, 'Induced Fertility Transition: Impact of population planning and socioeconomic change in the People's Republic of China', paper prepared for a workshop on the Single Child Family in China, Queen

Elizabeth House, Contemporary China Centre, Oxford, 17-18 March 1983 (manuscript).

30. I am grateful to Dr Lado T. Ruzicka who kindly undertook this reanalysis.

BIBLIOGRAPHY

★★

This Bibliography covers the major sources used in the
preparation of this book. It does not, generally, cover references to ephemeral newspaper or broadcast items. I have tried
to indicate some of the more important sources for those
interested in the subject of population and family planning
through the use of a system of stars: three stars for the most
valuable reports. These 'ratings' are applied only for the
population content, of course: many of the books listed here
have their own, separate significance.

Text of the Marriage Law of the PRC, BBC *Summary of World
Broadcasts*, 23 September 1980.

'The Constitution of the People's Republic of China 1982', *Population
and Development Review*, vol. 9, no. 1, 1983.

The Constitution of the People's Republic of China, Foreign Languages Press, Beijing, 1975 and 1978.

*AIRD, John S., 'Population Studies and Population Policy in China',
Population and Development Review, vol.8, no.2, 1982.

ANDORS, Phyllis, 'The Four Modernizations and Chinese Policy on
Women', *Bulletin of Concerned Asian Scholars*, vol.13, no.2, 1981.

**ANHUI University, 'A Survey of Single-child Families of West-side
Hefei, Anhui Province', *Anhui Population*, 1981.

**ANONYMOUS, 'One-child Family Becoming Norm in Beijing West
District', *Beijing renkou yanjiu* [Beijing population studies], no.1,
January 1981.

ANON., 'China's Position on the Population Problems Expounded', *Peking Review*, vol.17, no.12, 22 March 1974.

BANISTER, Judith, 'The Current Vital Rates and Population Size of the People's Republic of China and its Provinces', Stanford University, unpublished PhD thesis, 1977.

BANISTER, Judith, and PRESTON, Samuel H., 'Mortality in China', *Population and Development Review*, vol.7, no.1, 1981.

BELDEN, Jack, *China Shakes the World*, Monthly Review Press, 1979.

BLENDON, Robert J., 'China's Modernization and Medical Care', *New England Journal of Medicine*, 16 April 1981.

BONAVIA, David, *The Chinese*, Allen Lane, 1980.

BREEZE, Elizabeth, 'Counting People in China', *China Now*, no.103,1982.

BROYELLE, Claudie, *Women's Liberation in China*, Harvester Press, 1977.

BRUGGER, William, 'The Male (and Female) in Chinese Society', *Impact of Science on Society*, vol.21, no.1, 1971

BUCK, J.L., *Land Utilization in China*, Nanking, 1937.

*Central Committee of the Chinese Communist Party, 'Open Letter to All Party and Communist Youth League Members on the Question of Controlling China's Population Growth', BBC *Summary of World Broadcasts*, 25 September 1980.

Central Committee of the Chinese Communist Party, 'Some Questions Concerning the Current Economic Policies', BBC *Summary of World Broadcasts*, 10 April 1983.

CHALMERS, Iain, 'Better Perinatal Health:Shanghai', *The Lancet*, 19 January 1980.

CHANDRASEKHAR,S., *China's Population:Census and Vital Statistics*, Hong Kong University Press, 1960.

CHANG Chingshen (translated by Howard S. Levy), *Sex Histories*, Yokohama, 1967.

CHANG Chiyi, 'China's Population Problem:a Chinese view', *Pacific Affairs*, vol.22, no.4, 1949.

CHEN Da, 'Depopulation and Culture', The Phi Tau Phi Lecture Series, no.11, Lingnan University, Canton, 1934.

***CHEN Da, 'Population in Modern China', Chicago University Press, 1946 (*American Journal of Sociology*, vol.52, supplement).

CHEN Du et al., 'On Reproduction of Rural Population', BBC *Summary of World Broadcasts*, 24 July 1982.

*CHEN Muhua (translated and with notes by Chen Pi-Chao), "To

Realize the Four Modernizations it is Necessary to Control Population Growth in a Planned Way', *International Family Planning Perspectives*, vol.5, no.3, 1979.

CHEN Muhua, 'Controlling Population Growth in a Planned Way', *Beijing Review*, 16 November 1979.

***CHEN Pi-Chao, 'The Politics of Population in Communist China:a case study of birth control policy 1949-1965', Princeton University, unpublished PhD thesis, 1966.

CHEN Pi-Chao, 'China's Birth Control Action Programme 1956-1964', *Population Studies*, vol.24, no.2, 1970.

CHEN Pi-Chao, 'The Political Economics of Population Growth:the case of China', *World Politics*, vol.23, no.2, 1971.

CHEN Pi-Chao, 'Lessons from the Chinese Experience:China's Planned Birth Programme and its Transferability', *Studies in Family Planning*, vol.6, no.10, 1975.

CHEN Pi-Chao, 'Rural Health and Birth Planning in China', International Fertility Research Program, 1981.

**CHEN Pi-Chao and KOLS, Adrienne, 'Population and Birth Planning in the People's Republic of China', *Population Reports*, series J, no.25, 1982.

*CHEN Pi-Chao, *Population and Health Policy in the People's Republic of China*, Smithsonian Institution Occasional Monograph, no.9, 1975.

CHEN Pi-Chao, 'The Chinese Experience', *People*, vol.6, no.2, 1979.

CHENG Meiyu, 'An Investigation of Infant Mortality and its Cause in Chengdu', *Chinese Medical Journal*, vol.62, 1944.

**CHIAO Chiming, 'A Study of the Chinese Population', Milbank Memorial Fund Quarterly Bulletin, vol.11, no.4, 1933, and vol.12, no.1, 1934.

CHU, Leonard L., *Planned Birth Campaigns in China 1949-1976*, East West Communications Center, East West Institute, 1977.

*CHUNG, Arthur W., 'Maternal and Child Health in China 1949-1976', in JELLIFFE, D.B. and Patrice, *Advances in International Maternal and Child Health Care*, vol.1, Oxford University Press, 1981.

*COALE, Ansley J., 'Population Trends, Population Policy and Population Studies in China', *Population and Development Review*, vol.7, no.1, 1981.

COALE, Ansley J. and DEMENY, P., *Regional Model Life Tables and Stable Populations*, Princeton University Press, 1966.

Communist Party of China, *Resolution on CPC History 1949-1981*, Foreign Languages Press, Beijing, 1981.

CROLL, Elisabeth, *The Politics of Marriage in Contemporary China*, Cambridge University Press, 1981.

***CROLL, Elisabeth J., 'The Chinese Household and its Economy:Urban and Rural Survey Data', Queen Elizabeth House, Contemporary China Centre Resource Paper, 1980.

CUTTING, William, 'China's Health Miracle', *World Medicine*, 31 October 1981.

**DAVIN, Delia, *Woman-work:women and the Party in revolutionary China*, Clarendon Press, 1976.

DE HAAS, J. and DE HAAS-POSTHUMA, J.H., 'Sociomedical Achievements in the People's Republic of China', *International Journal of Health Services*, vol.3, no.2, 1973.

DERNBERGER, Robert F., 'Economic Consequences and Future Implications of Population Growth in China', East West Population Institute Paper, no.76, 1981.

*DIXON, John, *The Chinese Welfare System 1949-1979*, Praeger, 1981.

DJERASSI, Carl, 'Fertility Limitation through Contraceptive Steroids in the People's Republic of China', *Studies in Family Planning*, vol.5, no.1, 1974.

*DURAND, John C., 'The Population Statistics of China AD 2-1953', *Population* Studies, vol.13, no.3, 1960.

FENG Zhonghui and CHEN, Charles H.C., 'Induced Abortion in Xian City, China', *International Family Planning Perspectives*, vol.9, no.3, 1983.

FREEBERNE, Michael, 'Birth Control in China', *Population Studies*, vol.18, no.1, 1964.

FREEDMAN, Maurice(ed.), *Family and Kinship in Chinese Society*, Stanford University Press, 1970.

GOODSTADT, Leo F., 'China's One-child Family:Policy and Public Response', *Population and Development Review*, vol.8, no.1, 1982.

GRAY, Madeline, *Margaret Sanger*, Marek Press, 1979.

*GU Xingyuan and CHEN Mailing, 'Vital Statistics', *American Journal of Public Health*, vol.72, 1982(supplement).

GUANGZHOU Second People's Hospital Medical Team, 'Birth Control is an Important Mission', *Guangzhou Medical Journal*, June 1966.

*GULIK, R.H. van, *Sexual Life in Ancient China*, E.J. Brill, Leiden, 1961.

HAN Suyin, *Birdless Summer*, Jonathan Cape, 1968.

HAN Suyin, 'Family Planning in China', *Japan Quarterly*, vol.17, no.4, 1970.

Head of PRC Delegation, Speech to World Population Conference,

Bucharest, 1974(manuscript).

*HENDERSON, Gail E. and COHEN, Myron S., 'Health Care in the People's Republic of China: a view from inside the system', *American Journal of Public Health*, vol.72, no.11(supplement).

**HILLIER, S.M. and JEWELL, J.A., *Health Care and Traditional Medicine in China 1800-1982*, Routledge and Kegan Paul, 1983.

HINES, Noman, *The Medical History of Contraception*, Baltimore Press, 1936.

HINTON, William, *Fanshen*, Monthly Review Press, 1966.

HO Ping-ti, *Studies on the Population of China 1368-1953*, Harvard University Press, 1959.

*HORN, Joshua, *Away With All Pests*, Monthly Review Press, 1974.

HSÜ, Francis L.K., *Under the Ancestors' Shadow:Chinese Culture and Personality*, Columbia University Press, 1948.

HSU, Immanuel C.Y., *The Rise of Modern China*, Oxford University Press, 1975.

HU Huanyong, *A Brief Survey of China's Population Geography*, Shanghai Foreign Language Education Press, 1982.

HUANG Deyu et al., 'Infectious Disease Mortality 1956-1980', *American Journal of Public Health*, vol.72, 1982(supplement).

HUME, Edward, *Doctors East, Doctors West*, George Allen and Unwin, 1949.

JOYCE, Christopher, 'Industrial China's Expensive Dirt', *New Scientist*, 11 September 1980.

KAHN-ACKERMAN, Michael, *Within the Outer Gate*, Marco Polo Press, 1982.

KANE, Penny, 'China's Great Fanfare on Birth Control', *People*, vol.7, no.2, 1980.

KANE, Penny, 'How Women Hold up Half the Sky', *People*, vol.3, no.3, 1976.

KANE, Penny, 'Population Planning in China', in EPSTEIN, T. Scarlett and JACKSON, D., *The Feasibility of Fertility Planning*, Pergamon, 1977.

KANE, Penny, 'Pushing the Only Child', *World Medicine*, 7 March 1981.

KANE, Penny, 'Health Policies in China and Their Effects on Mortality', in *Social Policy, Health Policy and Mortality Prospects*, Institut National D'Études Démographiques and International Union for the Scientific Study of Population, 1985.

KANG Keqing, 'Conscientiously study, actively disseminate and implement the new Marriage Law', BBC *Summary of World Broadcasts*, 23 September 1980.

KEATING, Pauline, 'Tales for Chinese Children', *China Now*, no.104, 1982

LAMPTON, David M., *Health, Conflict and the Chinese Political System*, Michigan Papers in Chinese Studies, no.18, 1974.

LAMPTON, David M., 'Politics and the Determinants of Policy Outcome in China:Post-Cultural Revolution Health Policy', *Australia and New Zealand Journal of Sociology*, vol.12, no.1, 1976.

**LANG, Olga, *Chinese Family and Society*, Yale University Press, 1946.

*LAVELY, William R., 'China's Rural Population Statistics at the Local Level', *Population Index*, vol.48, no.4, 1982.

LEADER, Shelagh Gilbert, 'The Emancipation of Chinese Women', *World Politics*, vol.26, no.1, 1973.

LEYS, Simon, *Chinese Shadows*, Penguin, 1978.

LI Boying et al., 'Outcomes of Pregnancy in Hongqiao and Qiyi Communes', *American Journal of Public Health*, vol.72, 1982(supplement).

LI Shiyi, 'Developmental Trends in Chinese Population Growth', *Beijing Review*, vol.25, no.2, 11 January 1982.

LI Xiuzhen, Statement to the International Conference on Population Planning for National Welfare and Development, Lahore, 1973(manuscript).

LI Xiuzhen, Statement to the International Conference on Family Planning in the 1980s, Jakarta, 1981(manuscript).

LING Ruizhou, 'A Brief Account of 30 Years Mortality of Chinese Population', in 'Mortality in South and East Asia: a review of changing trends and patterns 1950-1975'. Report and selected papers presented at a joint WHO/ESCAP meeting, Manila, 1-5 December 1980, WHO Manila, 1982.

LISOWSKI, F.P., 'The Evolution of Health Care in China', *Eastern Horizon*, vol.17, no.3, 1978.

**LIU Zheng et al.(translated and edited by TIAN, H. Yuan), *Population Theory in China*, Croom Helm, 1980.

LIU Zheng et al., *China's Population:Problems and Prospects*, New World Press, Beijing, 1981.

LUK, Bernard Hung-kay, 'Abortion in Chinese Law', *American Journal of Comparative Law*, vol.25, no.2, 1977.

LYLE, Katherine Ch'iu, 'Planned Birth in Tianjin', *China Quarterly*, no.83, September 1980.

MA Haide, 'China's Fight to End Leprosy', *China Reconstructs*, June 1982.

MACDOUGALL, Colina, 'China's Population:the Missing Millions', *Financial Times*, 15 July 1975.

Mao Zedong, 'Report of an Investigation into the Peasant Movement in Hunan', quoted in SCHRAM, Stuart, *The Political Thought of Mao Tse-tung*, Penguin Books, 1969.

Mao Zedong, 'Be Activists in Promoting the Revolution', *Selected Works of Mao Zedong*, vol.5, Foreign Languages Press, Beijing, 1977.

MAUGER, Peter, 'Chinese Education — Imperial Past to Socialist Present', *Education in China*, Anglo Chinese Educational Institute, 1974.

*MEIJER, M.J., *Marriage Law and Policy in the Chinese People's Republic*, Hong Kong University Press, 1971.

Ministry of Finance, 'Notice Concerning Exemption from Commodity and Business Taxes on the Manufacture and Importation of Contraceptive Devices and Chemicals', PRC State Council Bulletin, no.17, 1957.

MIRSKY, Jonathan, 'Infanticide in the One-child, One-Party State', *Sunday Times*, 18 March 1983.

MYRDAL, Jan, *Report from a Chinese Village*, Heinemann, 1965.

MYRDAL, Jan and KESSLE, G, *China:the Revolution Continued*, Penguin Books, 1973.

ORLEANS, Leo O., 'China's Population Policies and Population Data: Review and Update', US House of Representatives Committee on Foreign Affairs, 1981.

ORLEANS, Leo O., 'Chinese Statistics:The Impossible Dream', *The American Statistician*, vol.28, no.2, 1974.

**ORLEANS, Leo O., *Chinese Approaches to Family Planning*, Macmillan, 1979.

*PAN Yunkang and PAN Naiqu, 'Urban Family Structures and their Changes — a survey of a Tianjin neighbourhood', *Beijing Review*, vol.26, no.9, 28 February 1983.

***PARISH, William L. and WHYTE, Martin King, *Village and Family in Contemporary China*, University of Chicago Press, 1978.

PARSONS, Jack, 'Chinese Must Know Environment is not Infinite', *People*, vol.1, no.5, 1974.

PEIPING Health Committee, First Report on Maternal and Child Health, July 1933.

PENG Kuangshi, *Why China Has No Inflation*, Foreign Languages Press, Beijing, 1976.

PRICE, R.F., *Education in Communist China*, Routledge and Kegan Paul, 1970.

QIAO Xinjian,'Possible Obstacles to the Realization of the One-child Family', extended essay in partial fulfilment of a postgraduate diploma, David Owen Centre for Poulation Growth Studies, Cardiff, 1982.

**RONG Shoude et al., 'Statistical Analysis of the Life Expectancy in the Population of China', from the Symposium of Chinese Population Science, Institute of Population Economics, Beijing College of Economics, China Academic Publishers, 1981.

ROSENTHAL, Marilyn M. and GREINER, Jay R., 'The Barefoot Doctors of China:from Political Creation to Professionalization', *Human Organization*, vol.41, no.4, 1982.

SALAFF, Janet W., 'Mortality Decline in the People's Republic of China and the United States', *Population Studies*, vol.27, no.4, 1973.

SALAFF, Janet W., 'Institutionalised Motivation for Fertility Limitation in China', *Population Studies*, vol.26, no.2, 1972.

SHANGHAI Province, 'Shanghai stipulates a number of planned parenthood regulations', BBC *Summary of World Broadcasts*, 31 August 1981.

SHANXI Province. 'Regulations on Planned Parenthood', BBC *Summary of World Broadcasts*, 16 December 1982.

SIDEL, Victor W. and Ruth, *Serve the People*, Beacon Press, 1973.

SILBERMAN, Leo, 'Hung Liang-Shi:A Chinese Malthus', *Population Studies*, vol.13, no.3, 1960.

SIU, Bobby, *Women of China:Imperialism and Women's Resistance 1900-1949*, Zed Press, 1982.

SMEDLEY, Agnes, *The Great Road*, Monthly Review Press, 1956.

SMEDLEY, Agnes, 'Youth and Women's Committees', *Portraits of Chinese Women in Revolution*, Feminist Press, 1976.

SNOW, Edgar, *Red Star over China*, Gollancz, 1937.

State Family Planning Commission, 'Communiqué on a nationwide fertility sampling survey of 1 in 1000 population', Beijing, 1983(manuscript).

State Family Planning Commission of China, 'An Analysis of a National One per Thousand Population Sample Survey of the Birth Rate', *Population and Economics*,1983(special issue).

State Statistical Bureau, 'Communiqué on Major Figures in the 1982

Population Census', October 1982(manuscript).

SU Chung, 'Facts about China's Population', *Peking Review*, vol.1, no.18, 1958.

SUN Jingzhe, 'A Draft of a Preliminary Analysis of the Distribution of Foreign Workers in the World and the Reasons for their Existence', 1980(manuscript).

SUN Jingzhe and LI Muzhen,'A Discussion of the Ways to Solve Beijing's Population Question', from the Symposium of Chinese Population Science, Institute of Population Economics, Beijing College of Economics, China Academic Publishers, 1981.

SUN Li, *Stormy Years*, Foreign Languages Press, Beijing, 1982.

TAN Manni, 'Why New Marriage Law Was Necessary', *China Reconstructs*, vol.30, no.3, March 1981.

TAUEBER, Irene B. and WANG Naichi, 'Population Reports on the Ching Dynasty', *Journal of Asian Studies*, vol.19, no.4, 1960.

TAYLOR, Richard and KERR, Charles, 'Prevention of Disease and Control of Infection in China', *New Doctor*, no.6, 1977.

THORBURG, Marina, 'Chinese Employment Policy in 1949-1978 with Special Emphasis on Women in Rural Production', *Chinese Economy Post Mao, a compendium of papers submitted to the Joint Economic Committee, Volume 1: Policy and Performance*, Congress of the United States, 1978.

***TIEN, H. Yuan, *China's Population Struggle*, Ohio State University Press, 1973.

TIEN, H. Yuan, 'Sterilization and Contraception and Population Control in China' *Population Studies*, vol.27, no.3, 1965.

TIEN, H. Yuan, 'Wan, Xi, Shao:How China meets its Population Problem', *International Family Planning Perspectives*, vol.6, no.2, 1980.

TIEN, H. Yuan, 'China:Demographic Billionaire', *Population Bulletin*, vol.38, no.2, 1983.

TIEN, H. Yuan, 'Age at Marriage in the People's Republic of China', *China Quarterly*, no.93, March 1983.

*TIEN, H.Yuan, 'Induced Fertility Transition:The Impact of Population Planning and Socioeconomic Change in the People's Republic of China', in CROLL, E., DAVIN, D., and KANE, P., *The Single Child Family in China*, Macmillan, 1985.

TSANG, Chiusam, *Society, Schools and Progress in China*, Pergamon Press, 1968.

TSO Anhua, 'Family Planning in Jutong County', *Peking Review*, vol.21, nos.14 and 15, April 1978.

UNITED Nations, 'Model Life Tables for Developing Countries', *Population Studies*, vol.77, United Nations, 1982.

WANG Gungwu, *China and the World since 1949*, Macmillan, 1977.

WANG Shengquan, 'How the Pressure of Population Hits Chinese Life', *China Daily*, 17 February 1983.

WEISSKOPF, Michael, 'China Begins to Require Couples with Two Children to be Sterilized', *International Herald Tribune*, 28-29 May 1983.

XING Ling, 'Protecting Infant Girls', *Beijing Review*, vol.26, no.5, 31 January 1983.

YAN Jiande, 'China's One-child Policy:Possible Effects after Thirty Years', extended essay in partial fulfilment of a postgraduate diploma, David Owen Centre for Population Growth Studies, Cardiff, 1983.

YAN Keqing, 'Problems and Prospects in Population Planning', *China Reconstructs*, June 1983.

YANG Fan, 'Save the Baby Girls', *China Youth Daily*, 9 November 1982.

YANG, C.K., *Chinese Communist Society:the Family and the Village*, Massachusetts Institute of Technology Press, 1959.

YAO Yiling and WANG Beijun, 'An Anthropometric Study of School-children', *American Journal of Public Health*, vol.72, 1982(supplement).

*YU, Y.C., 'The Demographic Situation in China', *Population Studies*, vol.32, no.3, 1978.

*YU, Y.C., 'The Population Policy of China', *Population Studies*, vol.33, no.1, 1979.

ZHANG Huaiyu et al., *Outline of Population Theory*, Henan Publishing House, 1981.

ZHAO Baoxu, 'Sociology and Population Studies in China', paper delivered at the University of Texas, 1982.

ZHAO Ziyang, 'Report on the 6th Five Year Plan for National Economic and Social Development', New China News Agency, 13 December 1982.

ZHONG Xiu, 'You Should Value Your Marriage', *Women of China*, no.5, 1979.

ZHONG Xiu, 'Tradition and Change', *Women of China*, no.6, 1979.

ZHOU Enlai, *Report on the Proposals for the Second Five Year Plan for Development of the National Economy*, Foreign Languages Press, Beijing, 1966.

INDEX

★★★